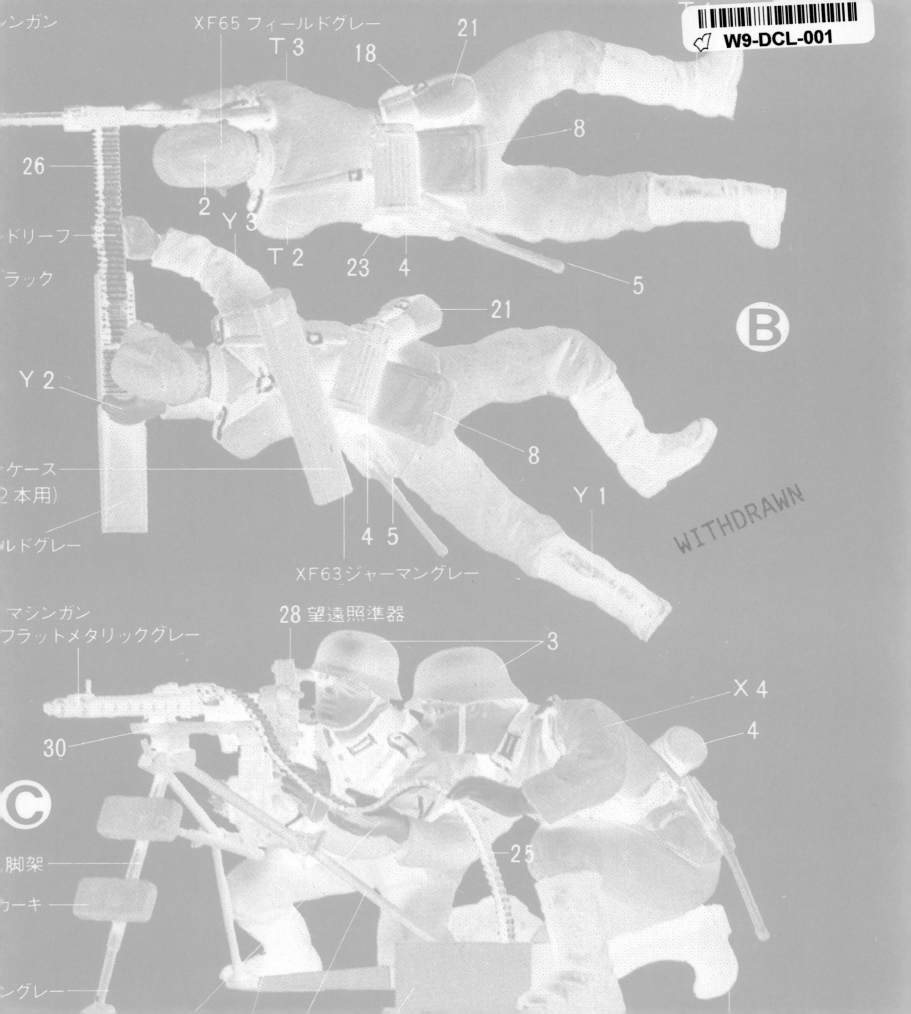

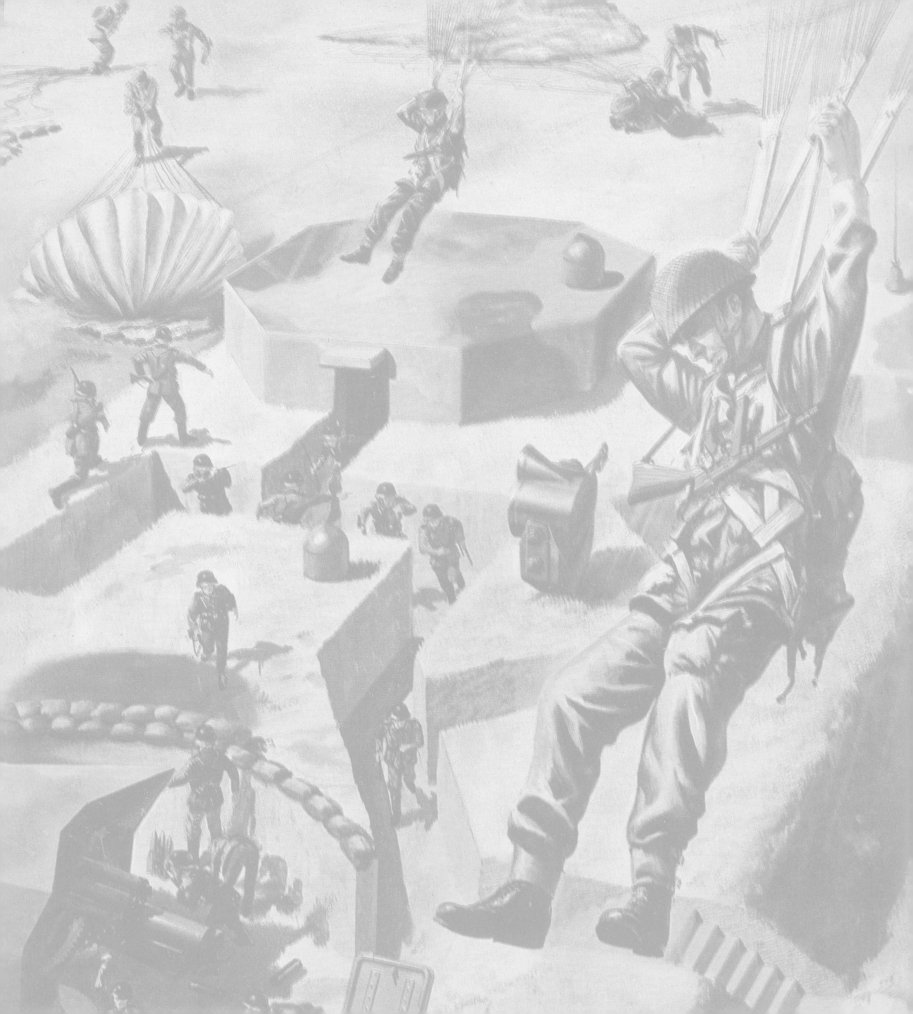

David Levinthal

Work from **1975–1996**

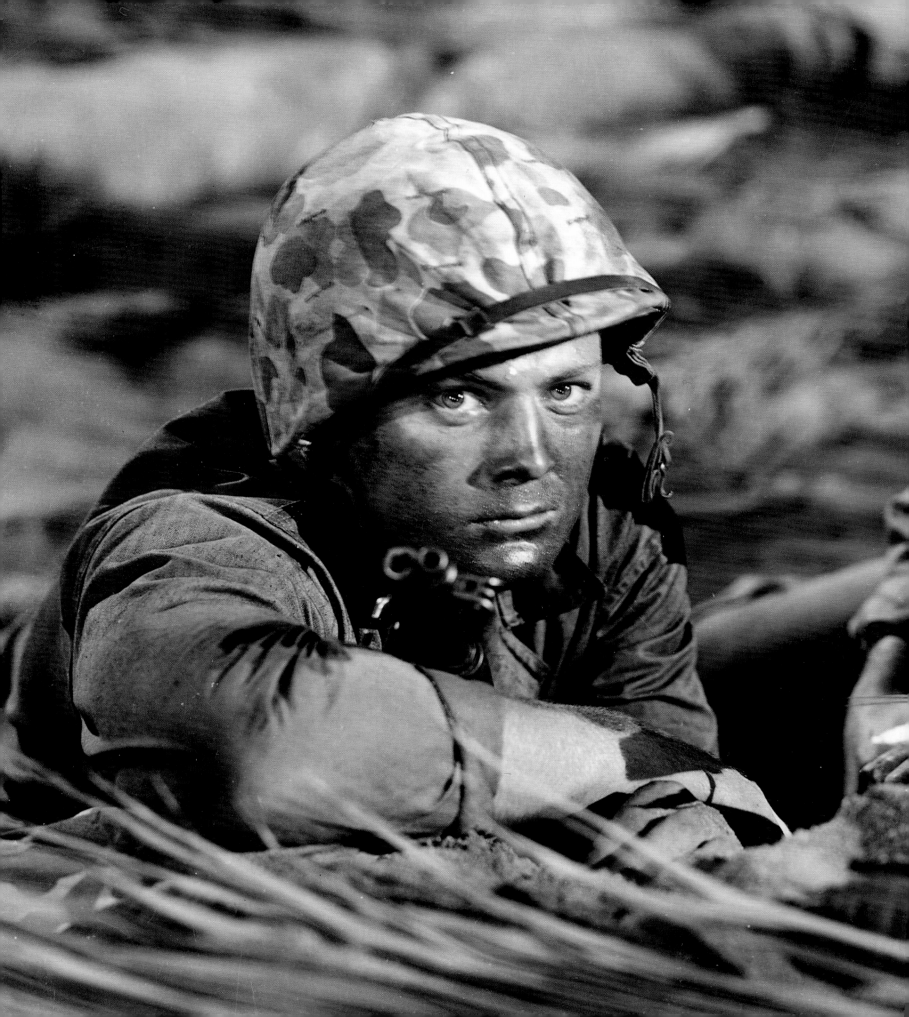

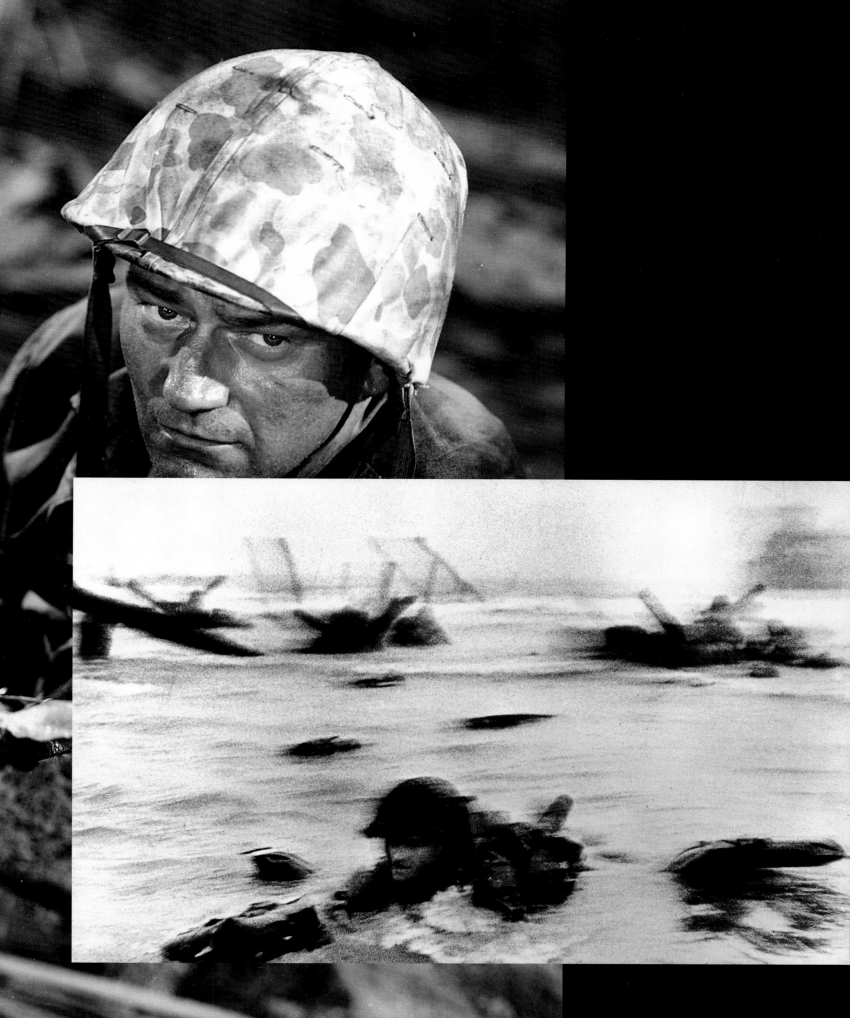

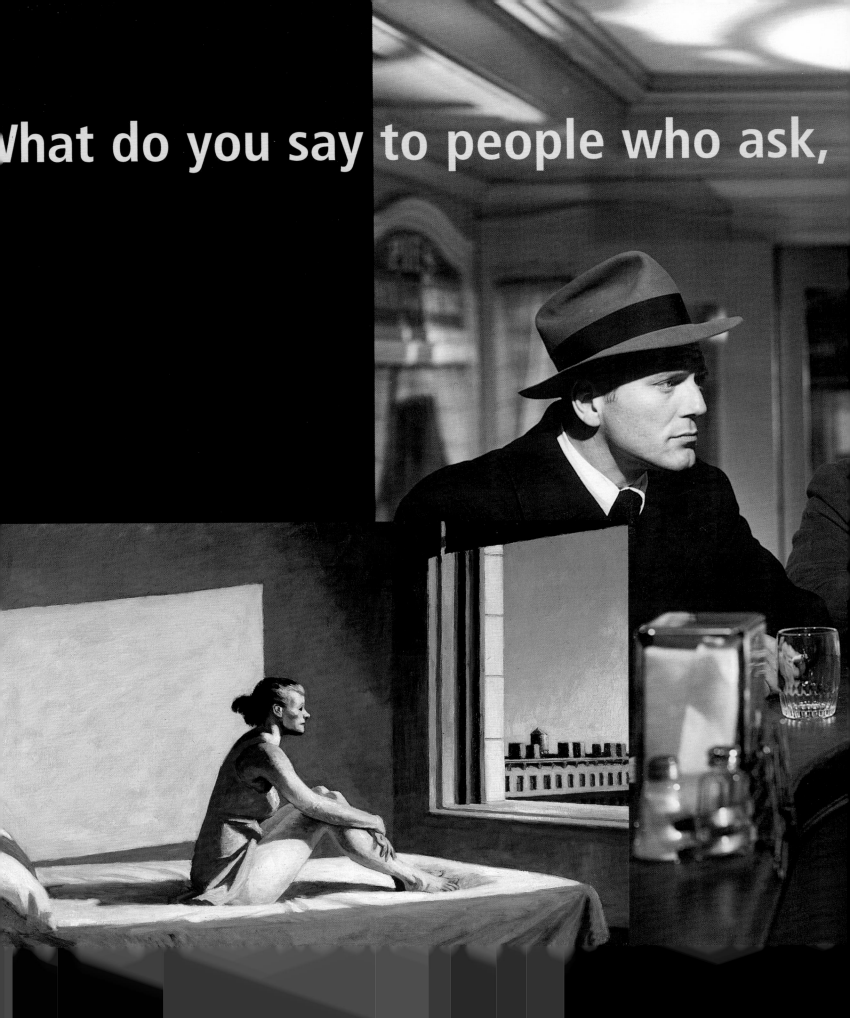

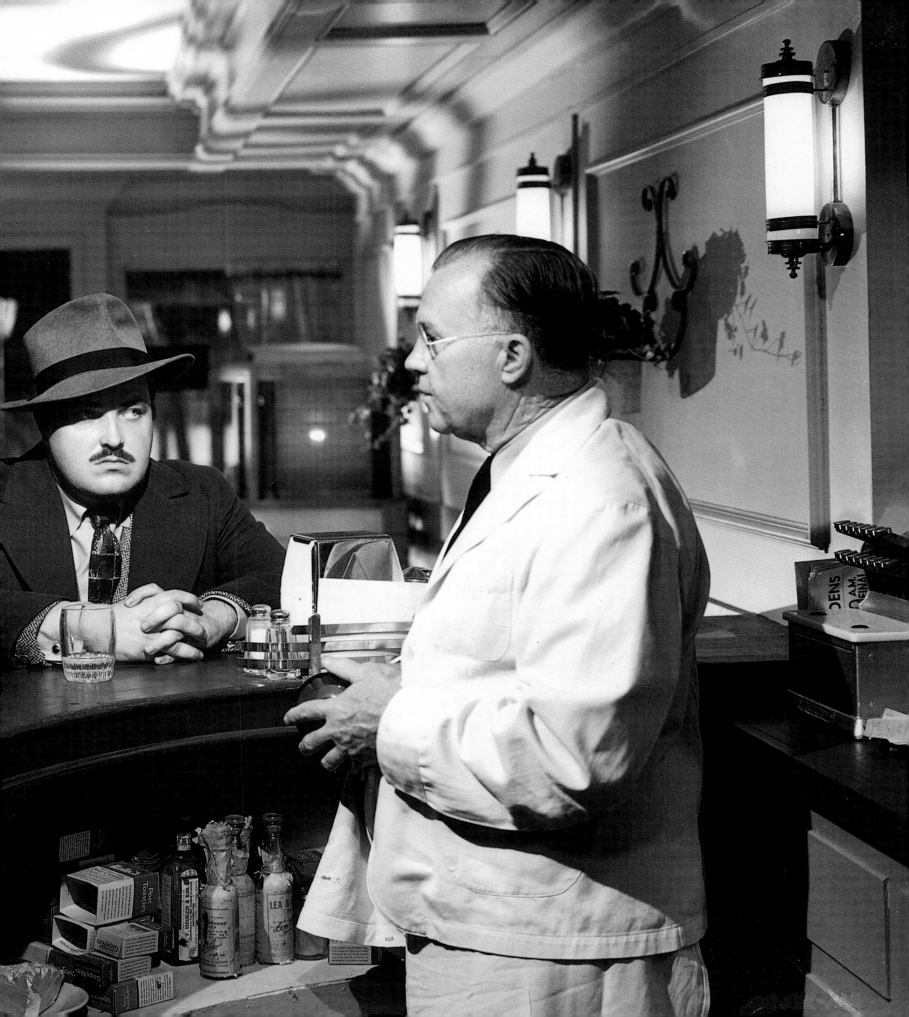

"Why do you play with toys?"

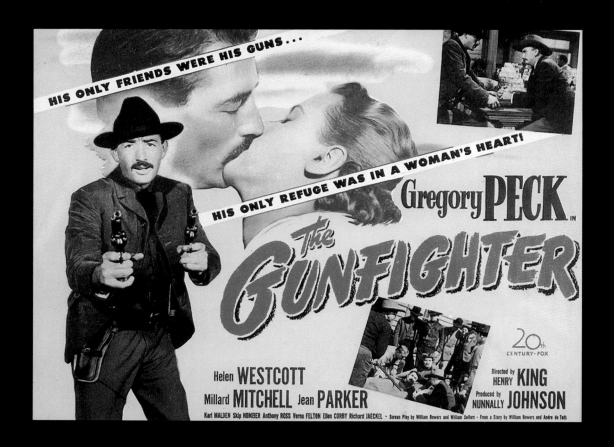

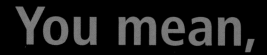
You mean,

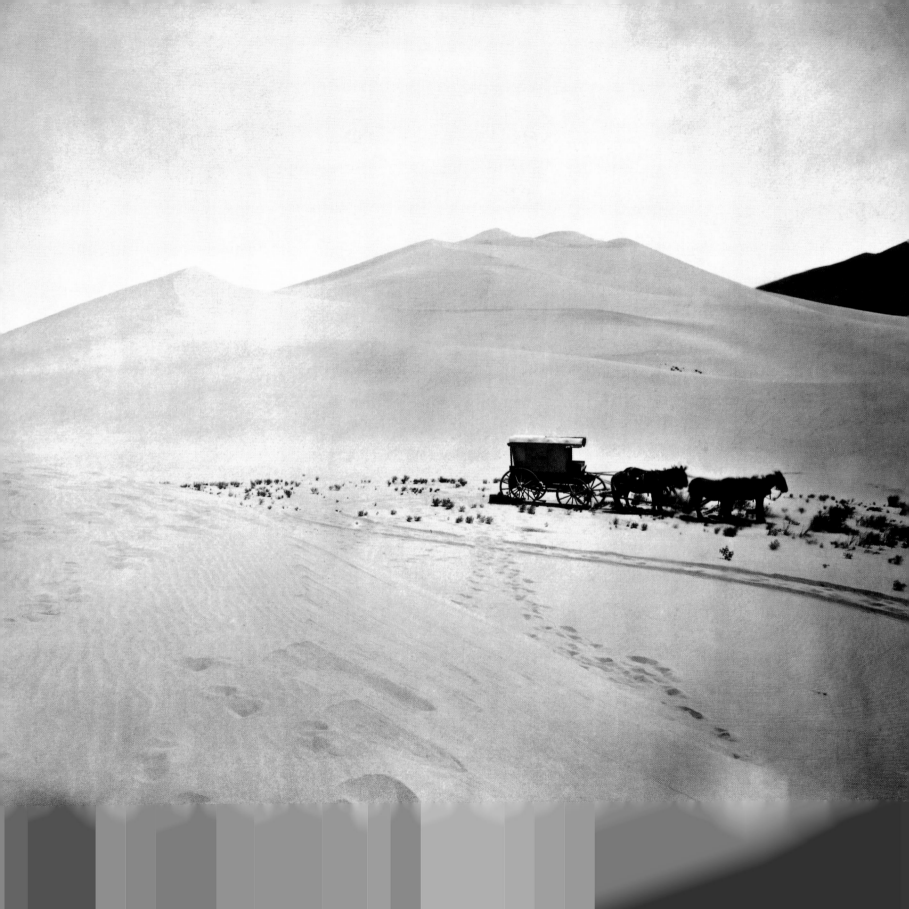

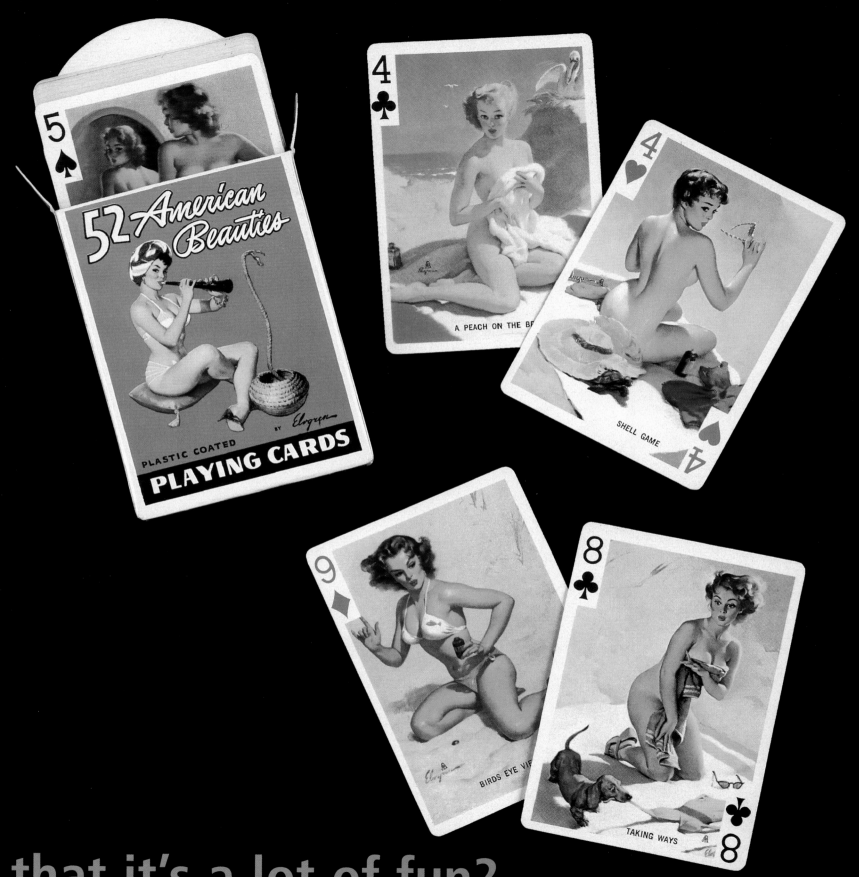

that it's a lot of fun?...

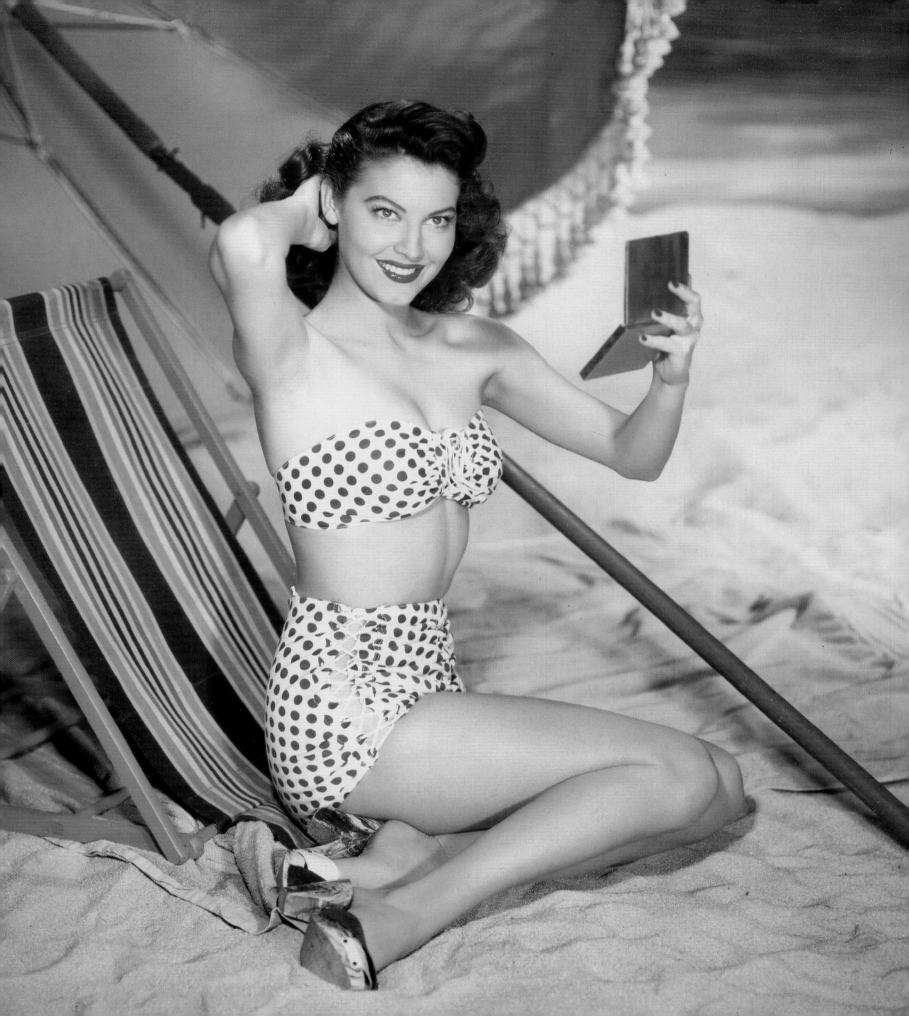

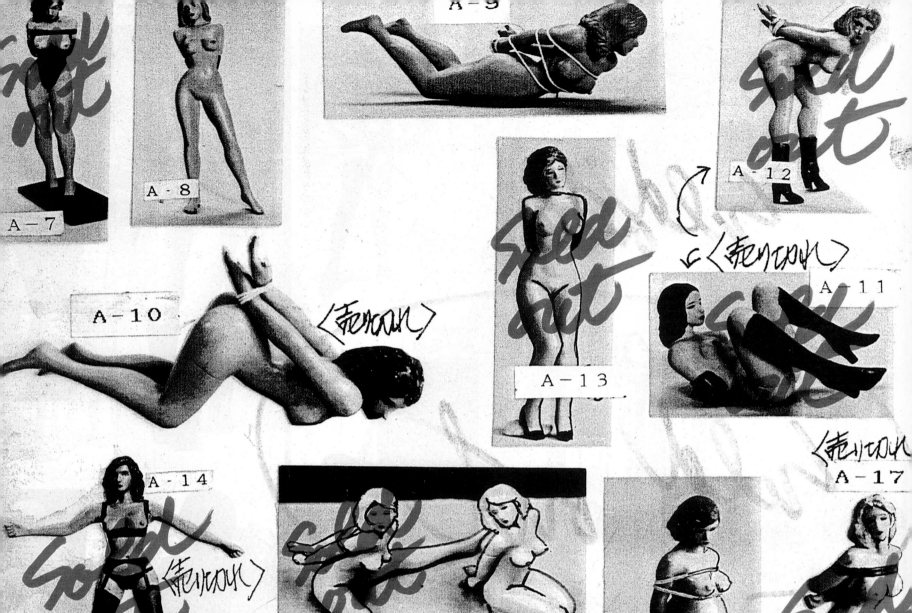

A-7

A-8

A-9

A-10

A-11

A-12

A-13

A-14

A-15

A-16

A-17

A-18

A-19

〈売り切れ〉

〈売り切れ〉

〈売り切れ〉

〈売り切れ〉

Sold out

Sold out

Sold out

Sold out

関東地方のお客様へ
A.S.F.シリーズはポストホビー代々木店
（03-370-0204）にて取り扱い中
お近くの方は御利用下さい。

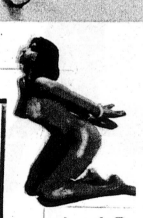
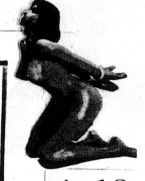

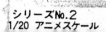
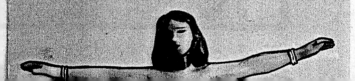

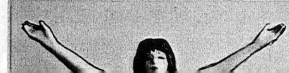

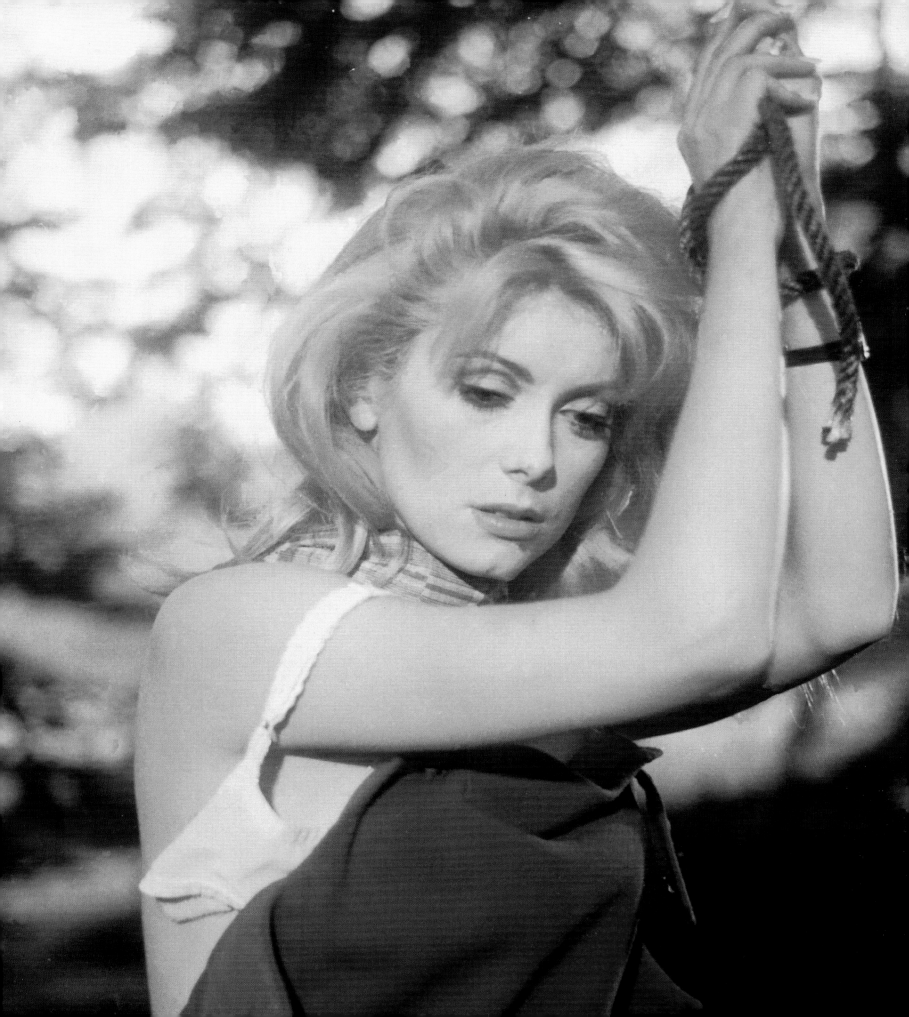

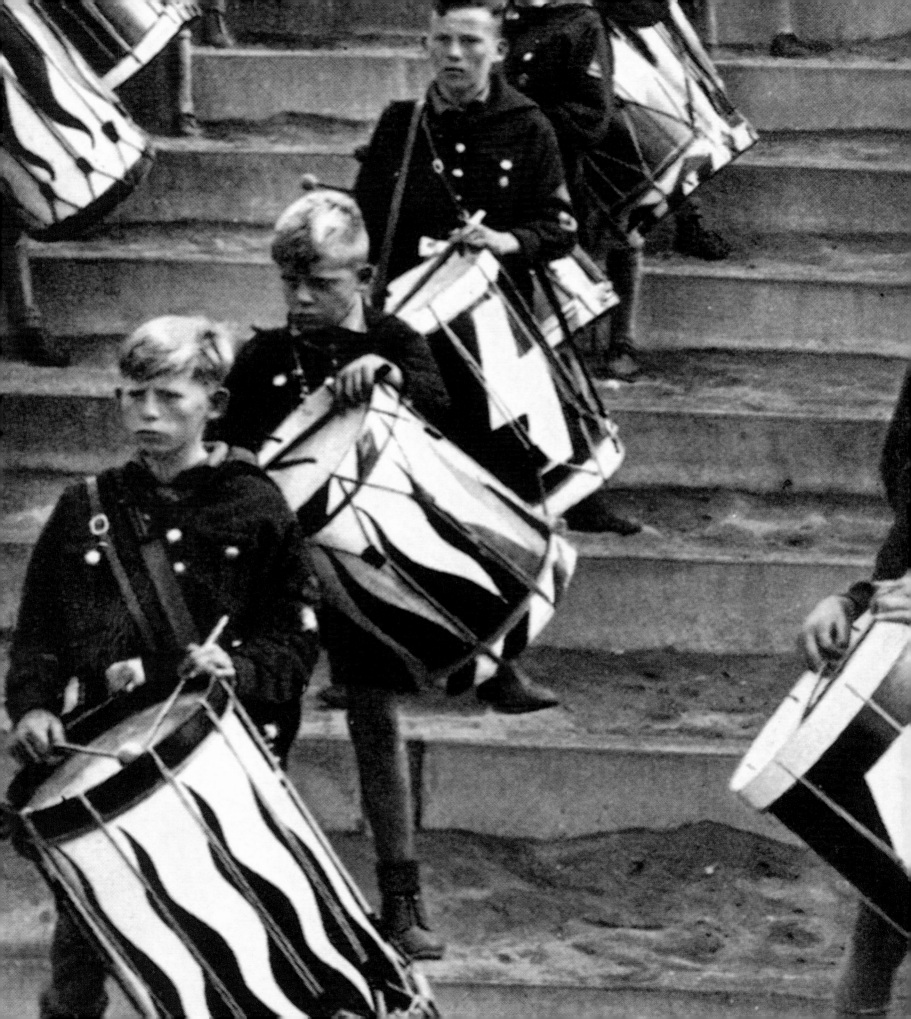

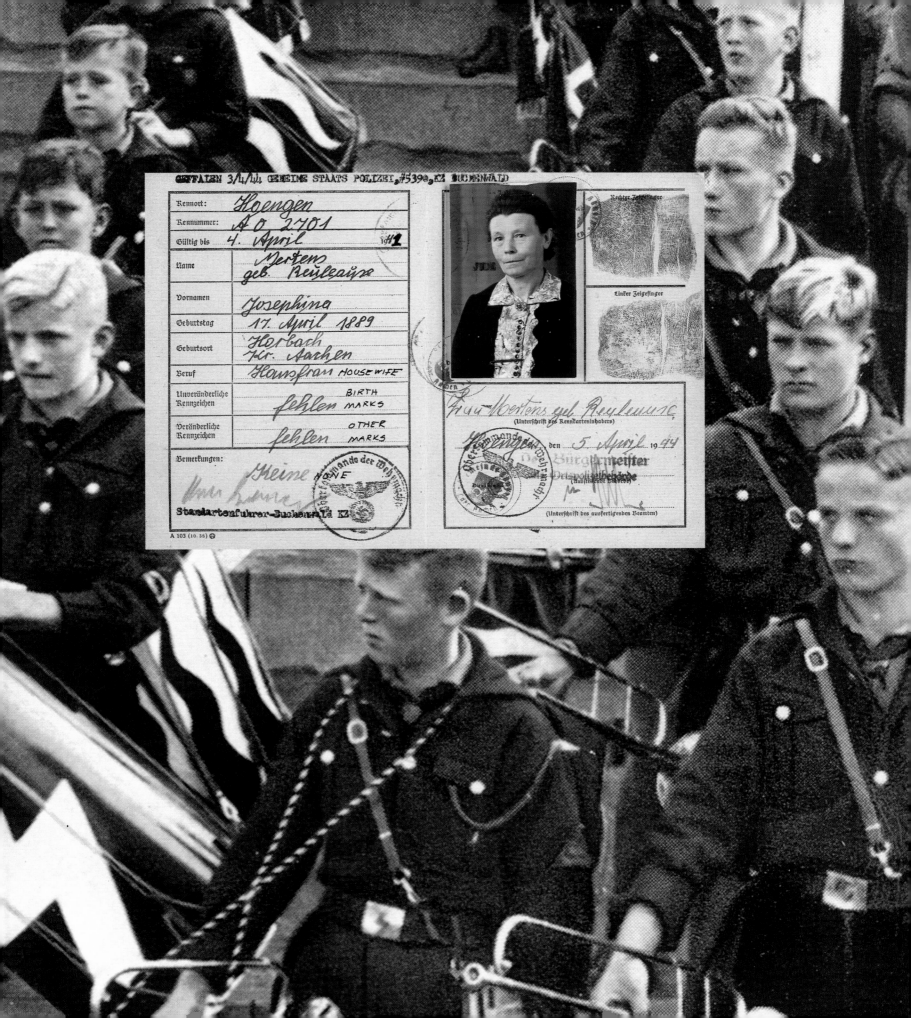

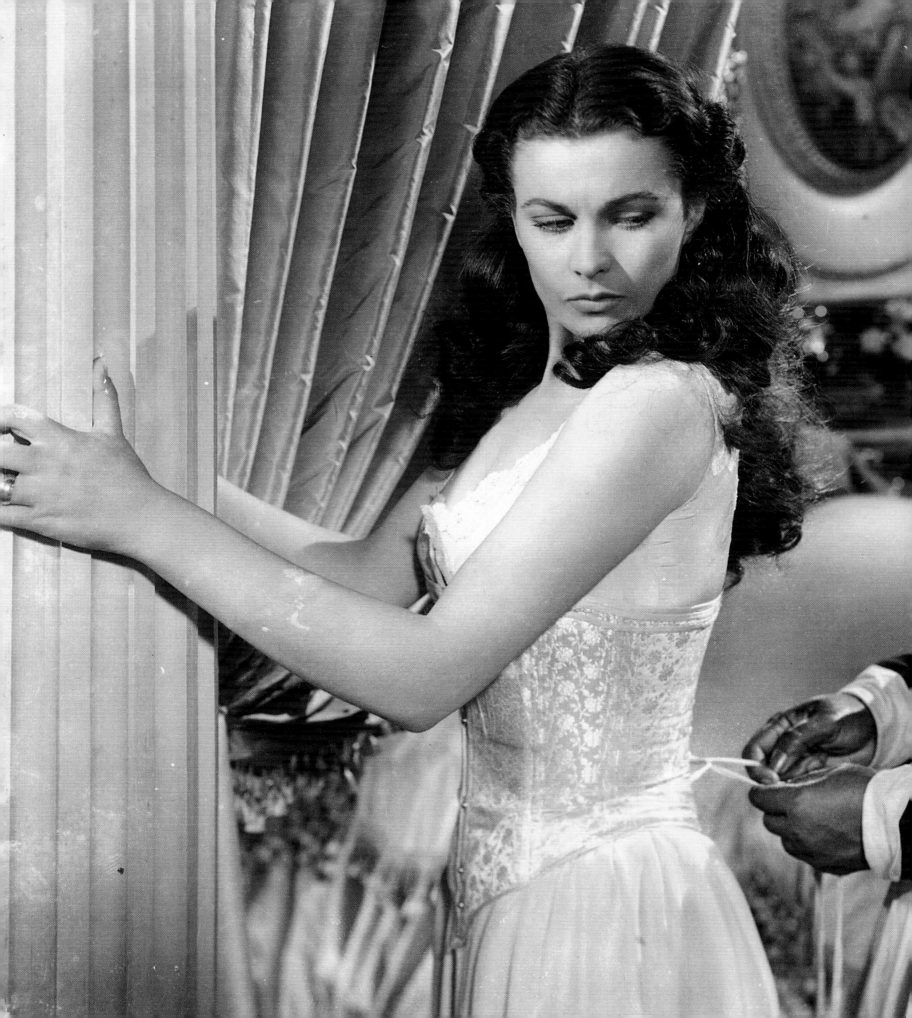

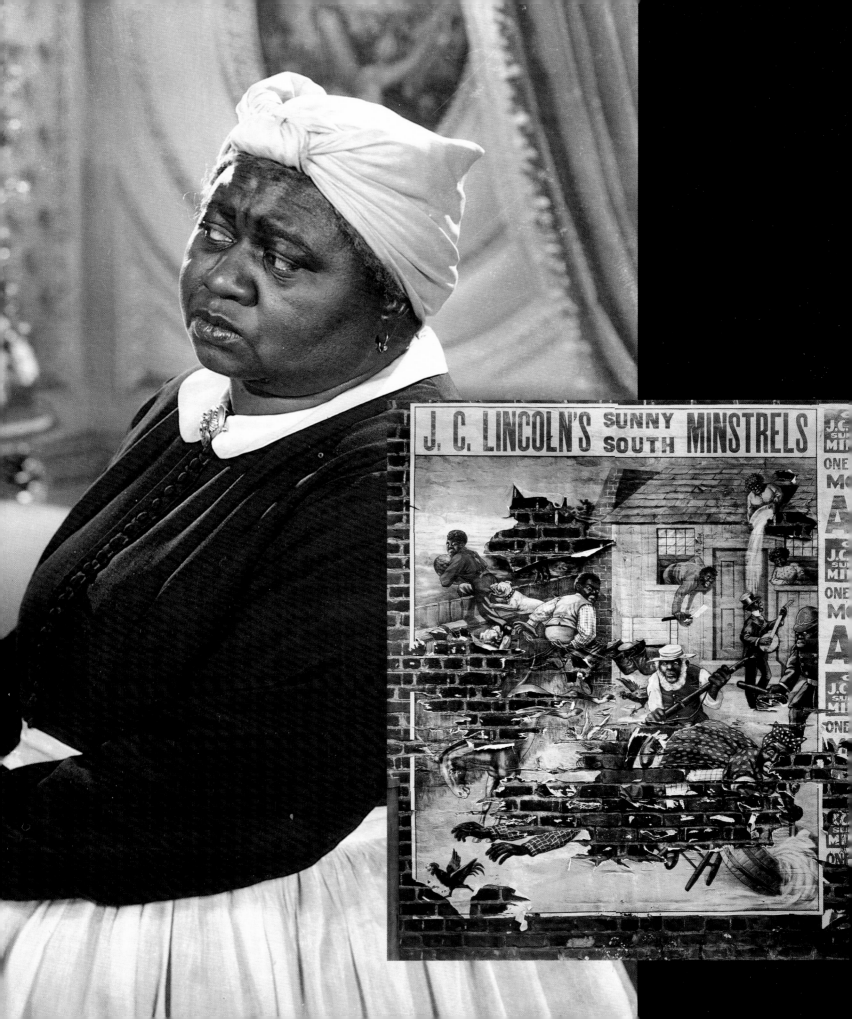

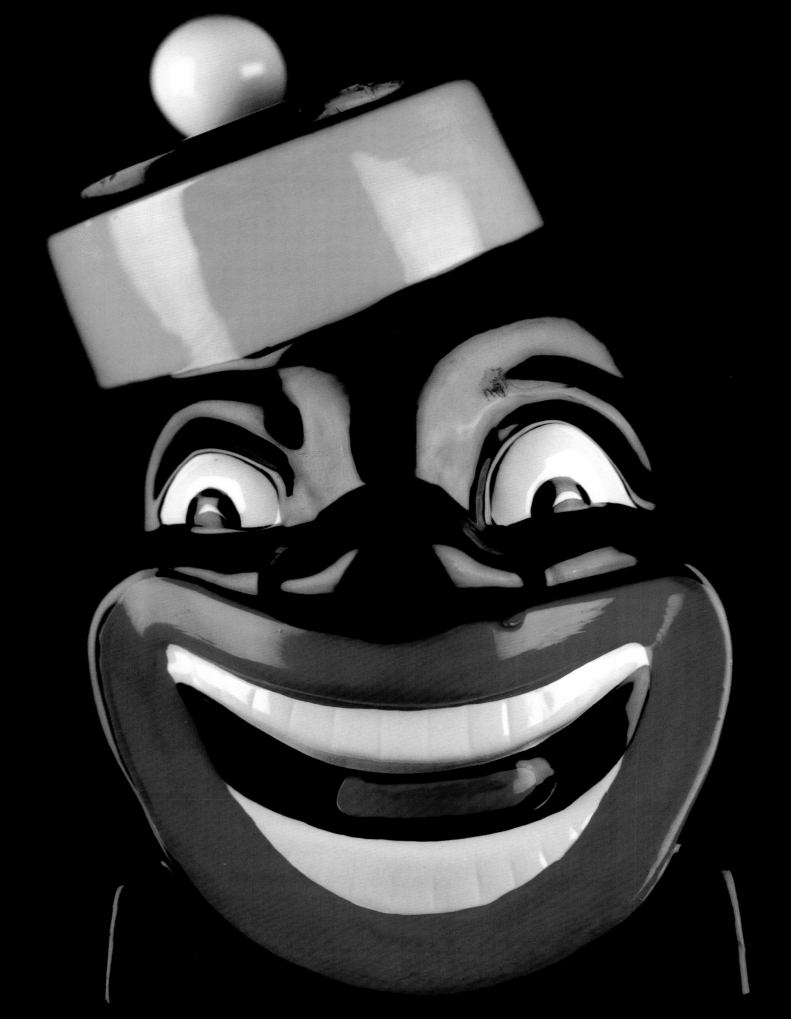

ESSAYS AND INTERVIEW BY

Charles Stainback

AND

Richard B. Woodward

The International Center of Photography, New York

IN ASSOCIATION WITH

D.A.P./Distributed Art Publishers, Inc.

1997

David Levinthal

Work from 1975–1996

David Levinthal: Work from 1975–1996

This publication accompanies the exhibition *David Levinthal 1975–1996*, curated by Charles Stainback and organized by the International Center of Photography, New York, on view January 17 through March 21, 1997. This exhibition is made possible in part with funding from Polaroid Corporation.

Library of Congress Cataloging-In-Publication Data:

Levinthal, David.
　　David Levinthal, work from 1975–1996: with essays and interview by Charles Stainback and Richard B. Woodward.
　　　　p.　　cm.
　　Catalog of exhibition held at International Center of Photography, New York, Jan. 17–Mar. 21, 1997.
　　Includes bibliographical references.
　　ISBN 0-933642-24-5 (hardback)
I. Photography, Artistic—Exhibitions.
2. Levinthal, David—Exhibitions.
　　I. Stainback, Charles, 1952– .
　　II. Woodward, Richard, 1953– .
　　III. International Center of Photography.
　　IV. Title.
TR647.L6495　　　1997
779'.092—dc21

97-5465
CIP

International Center of Photography
1130 Fifth Avenue
New York, NY 10128
Tel. 212–860–1777
Fax. 212–360–6490

Trade edition published by
D.A.P./Distributed Art Publishers, Inc.
155 Sixth Avenue, Second Floor
New York, NY 10013
Tel. 800–338–BOOK
Fax. 212–627–9484

Endpapers:

(front) Detail, *Beachhead*, Airfix-HO-OO Scale Playset Series box cover (photo: David Lubarsky).
pp. 2–3: Film still from *Sands of Iwo Jima* (director: Allan Dwan), 1949. Courtesy Photofest.
p. 3: Robert Capa, *U.S. Troops Landing on D-Day, Omaha Beach, Normandy Coast, June 6, 1944*. Gelatin silver print. © Estate of Robert Capa.
p. 4: Edward Hopper, *Morning Sun*, 1952. Oil on canvas. Courtesy Columbus Museum of Art, Ohio; Museum Purchase: Howald Fund.
pp. 4–5: Film still from *The Killers* (director: Robert Siodmak), 1946. Courtesy Photofest.
p. 6: Poster for *The Gunfighter* (director: Henry King), 1950. Courtesy Jagarts/Photofest.
pp. 6–7: Timothy O'Sullivan, *Sand Dunes Near Sand Spring, Nevada*, 1867. Albumen silver print from glass negative. Courtesy George Eastman House.
p. 8: *52 American Beauties*, plastic-coated playing cards by Elvgren. © Creative Playing Card Co., Inc. (photo: David Lubarsky).
p. 9: Ava Gardner, ca. 1947. Courtesy Photofest.
p. 10: *Adult Sexy Fantasy* figures, Adven catalogue (photo: David Lubarsky).
p. 11: Film still from *Belle de Jour* (director: Luis Bunuel), 1967. Courtesy Photofest.
pp. 12–13: Film still from *Triumph of the Will* (director: Leni Riefenstahl), 1935. Courtesy Photofest.
p. 13: Identification card, Buchenwald, Germany, 1944 (photo: David Lubarsky).
pp. 14–15: Film still from *Gone With the Wind* (director: Victor Fleming), 1939. Courtesy Photofest.
p. 15: Walker Evans, *Minstrel Showbill, Alabama*, 1936. Gelatin silver print. Private collection.
p. 16: David Levinthal, Untitled, from the series *Blackface*, 1996. Polaroid Polacolor ER 20 x 24.
p. 21: Detail, David Levinthal, Untitled, from the series *Hitler Moves East*, 1975. Gelatin silver print.
p. 206: Film still from *Triumph of the Will* (director: Leni Riefenstahl), 1935. Courtesy Photofest.
Inset: David Levinthal, Untitled, from the series *Mein Kampf*, 1993–94. Polaroid Polacolor ER 20 x 24.
p. 207: Instructions for 1/35 scale German military figures, Tamiya Plastic Model Company, ca. 1970 (photo: David Lubarsky).
Inset: David Levinthal, Untitled, from the series *Hitler Moves East*, 1975. Gelatin silver print.
p. 209: Postcard, ca. 1908 (photo: David Lubarsky).
Inset: David Levinthal, Untitled, from the series *Blackface*, 1996. Polaroid Polacolor ER 20 x 24.
p. 210: Detail from cover of *Pick-Up*, by Charles Willeford (New York: Beacon Publication Corporation, 1955) (photo: David Lubarsky).
Inset: David Levinthal, Untitled, from the series *Modern Romance*, 1984–86. Polaroid SX-70.
p. 211: Drawing by John Willie, from *The Art of John Willie: Sophisticated Bondage, 1946–1961* (Firenze: Glittering Images, edizioni d'essai).
Inset: David Levinthal, Untitled, from the series *Desire*, 1990–91. Polaroid Polacolor ER 20 x 24.
p. 213: *52 American Beauties*, plastic-coated playing cards by Elvgren. © Creative Playing Card Co., Inc. (photo: David Lubarsky).
Inset: David Levinthal, Untitled, from the series *American Beauties*, 1989–90. Polaroid Polacolor ER 20 x 24.
p. 214: David Levinthal, Untitled, from the series *The Wild West*, 1987–89. Polaroid Polacolor ER 20 x 24.
p. 215: Film still from *The Good, the Bad and the Ugly* (director: Sergio Leone), 1967. Courtesy Photofest.
(back) *The Lone Ranger*. Published by Western Publishing Company, Inc. © 1956, 1954 The Lone Ranger, Inc. (photo: David Lubarsky).

Cover:
(front) David Levinthal, Untitled, from the series *Modern Romance*, 1984–86. Polaroid SX-70.
(back) David Levinthal, Untitled, from the series *Modern Romance*, 1984–86. Polaroid SX-70.

CONTENTS

. . . Toys are intriguing, and I want to see what I can do with them. On a deeper level, they represent one way that society socializes its young.

Parents bought the Marx Toys dollhouses—father, mother, older sister, brother, and baby of indeterminate sex—by the thousands for their daughters. Boys had Alamos and gas stations. Toys exist for a reason. They allow you to enter a fantasy world. When you're a child with a cap gun, suddenly you're Hopalong Cassidy. German children in the '30s had miniature Hitlers to play with.

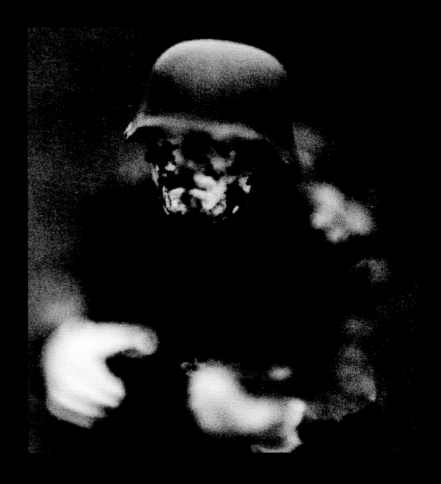

Richard Woodward: I see much of your work as a gleeful perversion of the normal purpose of toys. You take these figures, which are supposedly mementos of innocence and childhood, and put them in situations that are charged with adult threats.

David Levinthal: I don't think childhood is at all innocent, so why should toys be? It's a period of socialization and conformity. Boys are supposed to grow up to be strong and stalwart men, willing to die for their country, and so on. That period of one's life instills certain values. Playing with toys is innocent only in the sense that most people have passed through that stage. I suppose I never have.

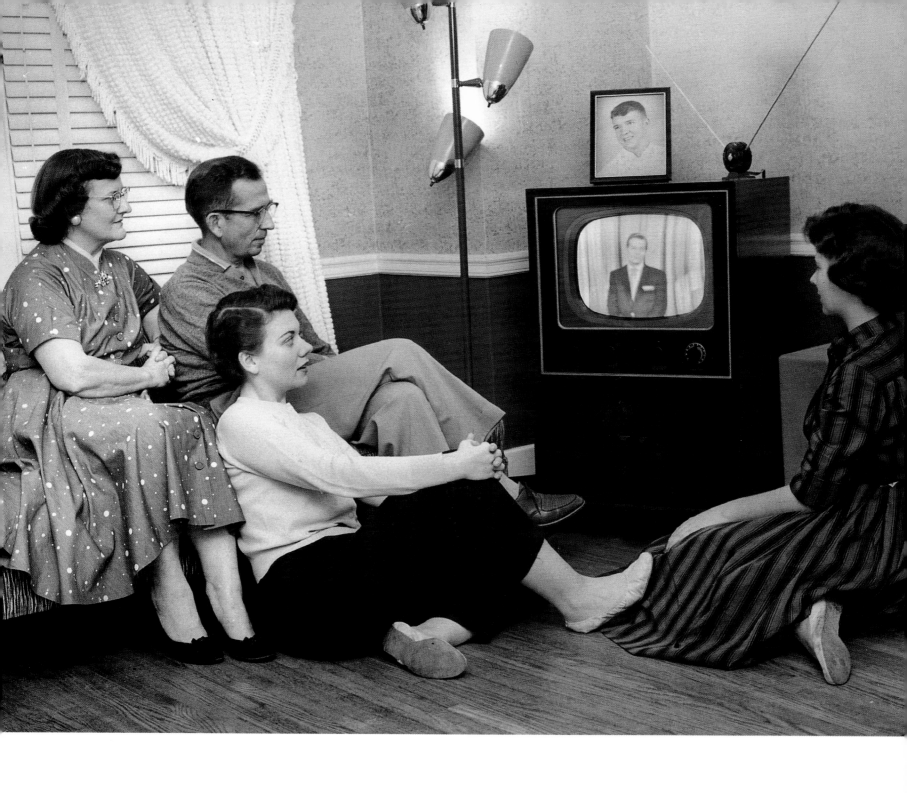

The home of Mr. and Mrs. A. A. Boone, Pat Boone's parents, Nashville, Tenn. The Boone family watch Pat on television, October 4, 1957. Courtesy Photofest.

Charles Stainback

RERUNS FROM HISTORY: COWBOYS, NAZIS, AND BABES IN TOYLAND

Historians are dangerous, and capable of turning everything topsy-turvy. They have to be watched.
—Nikita Khrushchev[1]

*He who controls the past controls the future,
he who controls the present controls the past.*
—George Orwell[2]

Since the invention of photography some hundred and fifty years ago, historically significant events exist for many of us as media images, surrogates of the real thing. David Levinthal understands this fact very well indeed. His photographs, a pastiche of mediated, potentially fleeting memories often based on historical events and news pictures, function as a powerful reminder that much of our knowledge is derived secondhand from visual sources. Part artistic invention, part historical fact, it is no accident that his works look the way they do. Levinthal—like Khrushchev's historians—is "turning everything topsy-turvy," toying with history and, in the process, creating a jolting contradiction between illusion and reality. Unlike the main character in Orwell's 1984, who was employed to rewrite or erase history, Levinthal's intention in recasting history is not to shape the future. His images are more like reruns from history, great episodes seen again and again and again.

The possibilities of electronic forms of reproduction have generated a curious question: how did we experience the world before photography? It is almost impossible to imagine. As Daniel Boorstin observed in 1961, in his book *The Image: The Pseudo Event in America*, "we make, we seek, and finally we enjoy, the contrivance of all experience. We fill our lives not with experience, but with images of experience."[3] In our media-saturated environment, we are constantly tempted with beguiling visual replications that make the natural or real appear virtually contrived. Yet this embrace of the artificial compels a longing for the authentic. Take the image of the "typical" twentieth-century American family watching television in their suburban family room. This is not merely an updated version of the nineteenth-century family viewing exotic lands through a stereopticon. The image of a wholesome entertainer full of family values and the right stuff on a television show, watched raptly by his parents and siblings, is a multilayered fabrication of both the thing itself—Pat Boone—and of celebrity. As in Levinthal's photographs, the line between fact and fiction is blurred. Levinthal's images are not simply illusions mistaken for reality but images produced as pseudo-surrogates of reality—fake fakes.

Levinthal's practice is grounded in a thirst (one could say, almost a longing) for information, and he is not alone among contemporary artists in plundering the visual archives of history to explore myth and memory. Like Barbara Kruger, Gerhard Richter, and Christian Boltanski, for instance, Levinthal's commentaries on history and contemporary culture rely heavily on a reworking of photographic imagery and visual strategies, ultimately recasting the photographic in a distinctly different role. This departure from seemingly "pure" documentation to high-fidelity visual intervention suggests not so much a reinterpretation of the facts but of the basic tenets of photographic representation itself.

For many of his series—for instance, *Hitler Moves East* and *Mein Kampf*—Levinthal has undertaken extensive historical research to ensure that his images contain a semblance of the original event. However, in spite of this vigilant regard for factual detail, Levinthal's notion of photographic veracity skews the final product in such a way that, as he has observed, "we're able to see, simultaneously, the artificiality and the reality" of an event.[4] This liberal approach to "truth" has a long, if uneven, genealogy dating back to noted nineteenth-century photographer Henry Peach Robinson, father (so to speak) of the fabricated photograph, who described his own work as a "mixture of the real and artificial in a picture."[5] Levinthal constructs a strange, often troubling hybrid of adult fantasy and reality with games and props culled from a child's toy box. The end result has the look of film stills promoting a most improbable triple-bill of disparate genres: the spaghetti western, fascist propaganda films of the 1930s, and '50s-style pornography, that is, cowboys, Nazis, and babes in Toyland.

Filmmakers have always understood their medium's capacity for fooling the audience. Movies are essentially a concoction of special effects, visual sleights-of-hand: still images flickering at twenty-four frames per second deceive the eye and brain into believing what is on the screen. Early special effects, crude by today's standards, confirmed the potential to hoodwink the spectator. On December 28, 1895, the Lumière brothers premiered their cinematic invention with ten short selections, primarily mundane subjects of everyday life (men playing cards, a mother feeding her baby). But one moving image, *The Arrival of a Train at Ciotat Station*, shocked spectators into near panic, "when the locomotive appeared about to leave the screen and invade the theatre. Some are said to have even fled from their seats in fear."[6]

Of course, audiences now eagerly await the visual jolt. Close to a century of film watching, combined with over fifty years of television and the new wave of technological breakthroughs made possible by computers, have educated the audience in the tricks of the trade. Today's savvy viewer is so accustomed to three-dimensional illusions that she tends to stay put in her seat.

David Levinthal is of the baby-boom generation bred on television and Saturday matinees. In the suburban

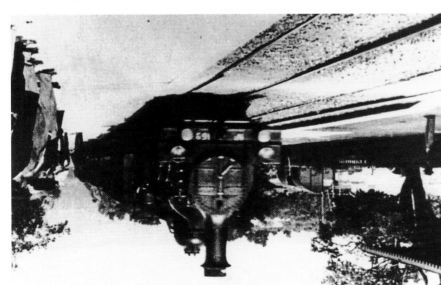

Still from *L'Arrivée d'un Train en Gare de la Ciotat* (director: Lumière brothers), 1895. Courtesy Photofest.

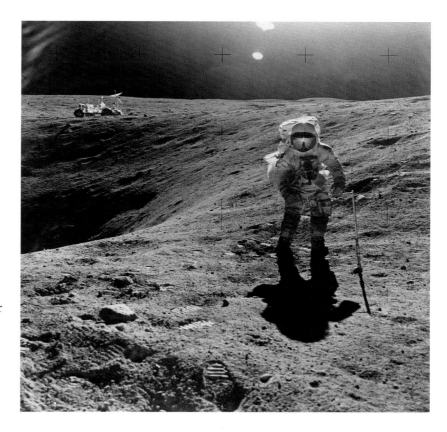

Apollo moon landing, astronaut standing near plum crater, July 20, 1969. Photo courtesy NASA.

pastoral of the fifties, neither anticommunist hysteria nor nuclear terror would puncture the fantasy of an innocent America in which the good guys wore white, the bad guys black, and fathers always knew best. Born in San Francisco in 1949, Levinthal lived through the transition from the seemingly serene 1950s to the social turmoil and transformations of the 1960s. The willful blindness of the Eisenhower decade, in which a perfect lawn signified the attainment of bourgeois status, gave way to the civil rights movement, women's liberation, political assassinations, the Vietnam War, and lunar landings.

Television forced this history-in-the-making into every living room in America, purporting to be an electronic replication of reality. The cathode ray tube offered table-top dioramas of monumental events, downsizing the public cinema's larger-than-life enactments to subcompact illusions projected into the home. Miniatures they might have been, but the impact of images of the 1968 Democratic Convention, the war in Vietnam, and the moon landing galvanized public opinion and action. Previously, the victors had written history. Now, television images were making history for us. For countless individuals, but especially the emerging "TV generation," television became a window onto the world, a vista that shaped perceptions of virtually everything, from the birds and bees to baseball and burglars and beauty pageants and battle scenes.

Here Men From Planet Earth First Set Foot Upon The Moon, July 1969 AD. We Came In Peace For All Mankind.
— Inscription from plaque left behind on the lunar surface

On July 20, 1969, two American astronauts bounded across the moon's surface. The extraordinary event was televised worldwide. But TV's historically significant image of the lunar surface was greeted by many as a fraud perpetrated in the interest of American imperialism. As Harry Hurt explained:

> *Although Project Apollo was one of the most extensively documented undertakings in human history, many of the earth's five billion inhabitants still refuse to believe that twelve astronauts really did set foot on the moon. Exactly how many people cling to this preposterous heresy is unknown because there has never been a worldwide opinion poll on the subject. But just as the Flat Earth Society in London continues to dispute evidence that the world is*

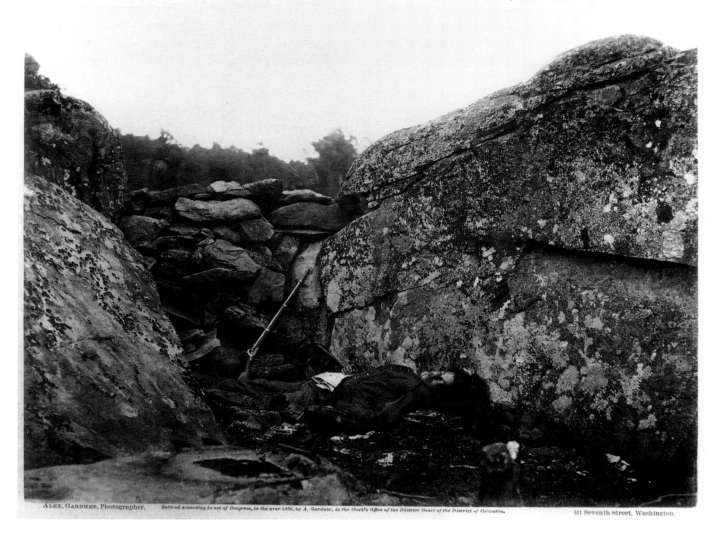

ALEX. GARDNER, Photographer,   Entered according to act of Congress, in the year 1866, by A. Gardner, in the Clerk's Office of the District Court of the District of Columbia.   511 Seventh Street, Washington.

Alexander Gardner, *Home of a Rebel Sharpshooter*, 1863. Albumen print.
Courtesy George Eastman House.

round, untold numbers of serious and not-so-serious disbelievers continue to insist that man's first lunar landings were actually a series of government sponsored Hollywood hoaxes.[7]

By the time Neil Armstrong, Michael Collins, and Edwin "Buzz" Aldrin landed on the moon, the camera's ability to deceive had diminished dramatically from that moment in 1895 when the Lumière brothers' film of the charging locomotive frightened spectators. But the collec-

tive slide from unquestioning acceptance of photographic veracity to suspicions about it—from the Lumière brothers' train to the moon walk—began well before the words "one small step for man, one giant step for mankind" were uttered by Armstrong. One source for this skepticism about the plausibility of images was a developing critique of the media's alliance with corporate and political power, combined with a growing awareness that a picture can be faked.

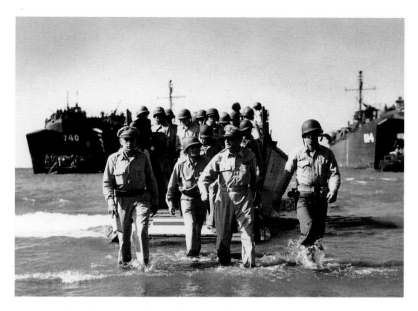

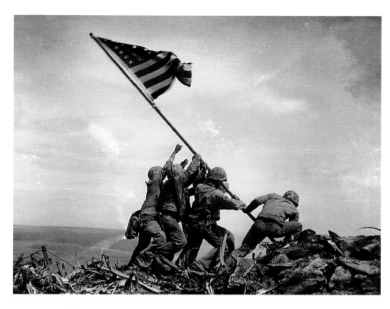

Carl Mydans, *General Douglas MacArthur Wades Ashore at Lingayen Gulf in Luzon, the Philippines*, 1945. Gelatin silver print. Courtesy Time Inc.

Joe Rosenthal, *Old Glory Goes Up on Mt. Suribaci, Iwo Jima*, 1945. Courtesy A/P Wide World Photos.

In journalism, the boundaries between reality and artifice, real life and idealization, are often blurred to such a degree that, in effect, the fake displaces the actual event. Three war photographs, renowned in the history of reportage, serve to illustrate the point. All three come painfully close to crossing the line of propriety.

Alexander Gardner's *Home of a Rebel Sharpshooter* (1863) purports to be an historically accurate account of the aftermath of the Battle of Gettysburg, but is actually a staged tableau. In the interest (we can only assume) of creating a more realistic, more photogenic representation of the destructiveness of war than was actually at hand, Gardner moved a "perfect" corpse from one part of the battlefield to a more "appropriate" site. In Carl Mydans's *MacArthur Wades Ashore at Lingayen Gulf* (1945), the general was given an opportunity to orchestrate for public consumption a heroic return to the Philippines. This return, however, was entirely symbolic, since he had already landed on the Philippines three months earlier. As the boatramp dropped and MacArthur stepped off into knee-deep water, Mydans captured the finessed, more mediagenic, comeback, which quickly became an

iconic image.[8] Finally, Joe Rosenthal's photo of the American flag being raised by Marines on Iwo Jima, *Old Glory Goes Up on Mt. Suribaci* (1945), was initially rejected by his editors at *Life* magazine because the "composition looked too perfect to be true, they suspected that it might be posed. Checking into it, they were told, contrary to Rosenthal, that the photographer was responsible for the larger flag and had in fact re-staged the event."[9] Although *Life* did not initially publish the picture, *Time* magazine did. Rosenthal won the Pulitzer Prize.

From the first issue of *Life*, the exemplar of truth in photography, the magazine's journalists and photoessayists were charged with getting the facts, the who, what, when, where, and how of a story. It was a public trust that, while violated in varying degrees, as in the Mydans and Rosenthal photographs, reveals differing conceptions of the photographer's role in recording history and shaping truth. And the fictitious truths created by countless anonymous photographers have been incorporated unknowingly into Americans' understanding of history.

It is photography's ability to effect such fictitious truths that Levinthal engages in his work. His vision of war, reflected in images from *Hitler Moves East* and *Mein Kampf,* is derived from the manipulation of reality in photographs like those of Rosenthal and Mydans. While many artists of Levinthal's generation who make use of the camera were raised on television, they also share the memory of images of historical events recorded in the pages of *Life* and other picture magazines. Their engagement with these representations is not based in a knowledge of the history of *photography* per se, but on a shared cultural experience of the commonplace photographic image—seen every day, everywhere. The blurred, grainy action shots of D-Day taken by famed photojournalist Robert Capa, which Levinthal saw as a child in old copies of *Life,* were seminal to his series *Hitler Moves East* (1975), in which he simulated the German army's ill-fated invasion of the Soviet Union with toy soldiers. By photographing miniature army figures with a closeup lens positioned no more than a few inches from his subjects, Levinthal seems to have taken Capa's now famous remark—"If your pictures aren't good enough, you're not close enough"—almost too literally.[10]

But unlike *Life*'s photojournalists, Levinthal never intends his pictures to appear exactly like the real thing. His direction of the scene never fully conceals the artifice. When asked once why he didn't photograph reality, Levinthal is said to have responded, "Toys *are* my reality."[11] Reality, like beauty, Levinthal might argue, is in the eye of the beholder. And besides, photographs are themselves mere illusions created from quasi-scientific mechanical and chemical processes, a fact that is often forgotten. By toying with history and treading the line between fantasy and reality, Levinthal acknowledges our culture's endless recycling of imagery and the potential for photographic fakes and hoaxes.

During a break from graduate study at Yale University in winter 1972, Levinthal began photographing toy German soldiers in closeup. Shortly after, he began to work with fellow student Garry Trudeau. Their collaboration eventually led to the publication of *Hitler Moves East* (1977), in which Trudeau's text and graphic design accompany Levinthal's black-and-white newsreel-style images depicting events of World War II unfamiliar to many Americans, despite the loss of 20 to 30 million German and Russian soldiers and civilians.[12] Unwittingly conceiving a methodology that would play out over the next two decades, Levinthal constructed elaborate miniature sets using plastic soldiers and an assortment of model buildings and vehicles. For snow he used liberal amounts of flour, lighter fluid to set dive bombers ablaze, and fire crackers as explosives.

Hitler Moves East was a radical departure from the so-called straight photographic tradition typified by Walker Evans, one of Levinthal's instructors at Yale. This tradition emphasized purely photographic qualities such as framing, detail, and sharp focus as the correct means of picture taking. In retrospect, Levinthal's decision to embark on a methodology so different from that promoted in Yale's photography program was startling. It demonstrated either a strong determination to explore new ideas and methods of utilizing the intrinsic qualities of photography, or a desire to be provocative. Or perhaps he was just a guy in his early twenties who liked to play with plastic soldiers.

Whatever the case, Levinthal was not the first to question (whether intentionally or not) the conventions of the straight, unaltered photograph. The practice of fabricating images for the camera—or the "directorial mode" as A. D. Coleman characterized it in a 1976 essay[13]—became increasingly prevalent in the 1960s and throughout the 1970s. The work of prominent photographers like Les Krims, Robert Cummings, and Ralph Eugene Meatyard, among others, was marked by their rejection of then current assumptions of what

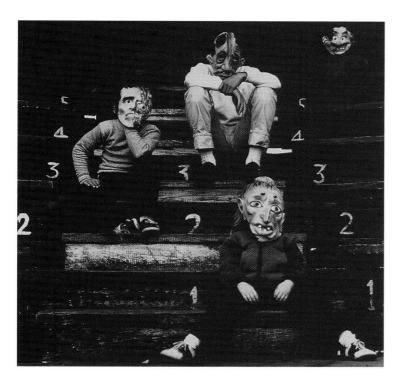

Ralph Eugene Meatyard, *Romance (N.), from Ambrose Bierce #3,* 1962. © The Estate of Ralph Eugene Meatyard/Courtesy Howard Greenberg Gallery.

constituted the photographic. As Krims noted, "I am not a Historian, I create History. These images are anti-decisive moments. It is possible to create any images one thinks of; this possibility, of course, is contingent on being able to think and create. The greatest potential source of photographic history is the mind."[14] Krims, whose work has been neglected in recent surveys of photography, chose to create images rather than seek out that decisive moment, constructing witty and ironic commentaries of contemporary culture that often shock the viewer. For instance, one photograph features a nude woman standing against a bedroom wall as a nude man (her lover, husband, doctor?) aims an aerosol can at her crotch. Another shows a black cat seated next to a nude woman lying face up in a yard covered to her waist with leaves. Krims's unconventional work had an enormous influence on students in the newly emerging photography programs across the United States and, in particular, his

own students at Buffalo State, including Cindy Sherman. His work has also occasionally generated controversy beyond the small and insular photographic community. In 1971, a display of his photographs in Memphis prompted a kidnapping, which was resolved only after Krims's works were removed from the exhibition.[15]

The fabricated photograph has a long history, extending back to the nineteenth century. Levinthal's lineage includes Henry Peach Robinson and O. G. Rejlander, precursors to the directorial mode discussed by Coleman. Both were well known and respected in their day, and their work was quite typical, replicating the manner of painting of the period. Both embraced the artificial not only by contriving photographic scenes but in producing seamless prints made from several negatives. Much later, in the 1920s, their photographs and picture-making style fell into disfavor with a shift in aesthetic values. For decades, Robinson and Rejlander's work was considered a sacrilegious breach of the reigning orthodoxy, namely photographic veracity and purity.

Although Levinthal was among the first postmodern photographers to draw imagery from our culture's storehouse of pictures, objects, myths, and symbols, the precedents extend to artists who were moving their practice off the easel and, at times, out of the studio altogether. The camera became indispensable for documenting earthworks, happenings, and performance, and the photograph (not photography) gained greater acceptance in the art world as artists like Andy Warhol and Robert Rauschenberg increasingly incorporated commercial or found images into their works. Pop, Fluxus, and Conceptual artists of the late 1950s and '60s—Warhol, Wallace Berman, Douglas Huebler, Hannah Höch, Bruce Nauman—paved the way for the dramatic changes to come. But equally significant to the postmodern generation of artists was the work of Marcel Duchamp and the Dadaists almost fifty years earlier.

As with the use of found material by the Dadaists and Duchamp in his readymades, borrowing—or *appropriation* as it came to be characterized in the 1980s—is one of the major strategies of postmodern photography. Levinthal and other postmodern artists and critics rejected photographic conventions endorsed by modernist photographers like Ansel Adams, Edward Weston, and Henri Cartier-Bresson. Instead, they challenged the very notions of tradition, authority, and "high art" by subverting received ideas about originality and authorship. In the work of Cindy Sherman, Bruce Charlesworth, Eileen Cowin, James Casebere, Sandy Skoglund, and JoAnn Callis, to name a few, appropriated images stand in for the everyday or for yesterday, simultaneously coopting and undermining photographic notions of truth and veracity.

Levinthal's knock-offs of experience mimic our culture's endless recycling of imagery, but also introduce a curious twist to our fading confidence in photographic reality. When Levinthal photographs toys in scenes reminiscent of old movies, advertisements, and the icons of our shared visual archive of news images, the "truth" in its original form is mediated. He has discovered and succinctly reveals that toys are not benign objects but metaphors for culture itself, which allow an image to have both "the presence of reality and the illusion of fantasy."[16] Although Levinthal explores familiar turf— the horrors of war, genocide, and icons of American pop culture (the cowboy, soldier, movie starlet)—in his hands, the familiar is simultaneously comforting and unsettling. Our culture's dilemma, as these works make clear, is not that we have lost sight of the authentic. Rather, by blurring the boundaries, the camera's capacity to create illusions has separated us from the primary sources of experience.

In an attempt to come to terms with the complexities, excitement, or alienation of urban life, Levinthal turned away from the bright lights and mean streets of New York and toward studio photography, training his camera on a miniature world constructed on table tops. In Levinthal's *Modern Romance* series, the images of lonely characters sitting in dingy hotels and diners or standing on poorly lit miniature city streets were made shortly after his move to New York in 1983. Sometimes visually reminiscent of Edward Hopper's paintings or evocative of film noir, *Modern Romance* is composed of one-inch toy figures and a melange of pop-cult imagery. The figures are situated in austere setups, bathed in moody colors and harsh lighting, all photographed from a voyeuristic perspective. In varying incarnations, these elements become Levinthal's standard repertoire over the next decade. He would also refine his picture-making strategies by exploring various photographic possibilities, including very small SX-70 Polaroids and reproductions onto large-scale canvas, and the recently introduced Polaroid 20 x 24 camera, which was used in Levinthal's next series, *The Wild West*.

Also reminiscent of media images, specifically from the 1950s, this series evokes children's games in which boys and girls (wearing the obligatory holster set) played cowboys and Indians, emulating their favorite television or movie hero of the moment, both real-life and entertainers in Western guise: Hopalong Cassidy, Roy Rogers, the Lone Ranger, Jesse and Frank James, Wyatt Earp, Calamity Jane, Wild Bill Hickok. Depicting the mythical, glorified lifestyle of the cowboy and a period in U.S. history which has been ingrained in the American psyche through countless television episodes of "Gunsmoke," "Maverick," and "The Rifleman" and even more numerous films, Levinthal probes our fascination with the Wild West by parodying it. Although he does not directly prompt recollections of our forefathers' injustices—cultural expansionism, genocide, racism—the parody itself functions to unmask the innocence of toys, play, and media fictions. In Levinthal's recasting, Hollywood's version of the American frontier *is* the Wild West, or, as he stated, "the West that never was but will always be."[17]

Levinthal continued to mine the pop-culture archive in the *American Beauties* series, this time focusing on the pinup and movie star portrait. These images bear the marked innocence of Hollywood representations of the 1940s or '50s, but in Levinthal's replication the movie starlet has become a faceless, voluptuous girl-next-door. As in earlier series, he intentionally treads the line between presenting the artifice and perpetuating the illusion. Instead of complex sets, however, he now employs minimal props, allowing the viewer to fill in the missing gaps. The women of *American Beauties* are sensual but not erotic. In this way, Levinthal mimes the '50s rejection of overt sexual expression. Sexual liberation was more than a decade away.

Elaborating upon the contested male gaze of *American Beauties*, the photographs of the *Desire* series present eroticized female forms based on six-inch plastic sex dolls purchased from a Japanese mail-order catalogue. Like the title itself, these images are elusive, suggestive, but here the comment on the objectification of women is explicit, evoking porn magazines seen at most newsstands. The inclusion of the body in contemporary cultural production has been a highly contested topic, one that has promoted considerable debate and anxiety as well as testing issues of censorship and artistic freedom. Levinthal's pictures are devoid of explicit detail, yet the suggested sexuality of *Desire* reflects the ongoing stereotyping of women by a masculinist culture. These photographs, which both entice and disturb, are ultimately mirrors of a sexist society, akin to the peepshow window

or the keyhole in their frame of reference. Like much low-rent voyeurism, the images in *Desire* are soft-focus, leaving much to the imagination.

The disturbing images of *Mein Kampf*, Levinthal's next series, developed out of a discovery he made in an Austrian toy shop: a contemporary figure of Adolph Hitler, a name that hovers between nightmare and reality, between our collective understanding of what occurred fifty years ago and Levinthal's synthesis of the documented visual and written history. Depicting Nazi pageantry and the unspeakable violence of concentration camps, Levinthal illustrates with toys (to the dismay of some), and their associated childlike innocence, one of the most horrific events of the twentieth century.

The title of the series is itself loaded. After all, Hitler's manifesto laid the groundwork for his future madness. But it is not the title alone that lends a chilling air to these photographs. The images in the *Mein Kampf* series are haunting in the same way that images of the Holocaust are so unforgettable. For most of us, the word *Holocaust* immediately evokes a somber and menacing darkness in our mind's eye. The atrocities committed upon millions are closer to nightmares than to any reality we have experienced. Most of us *know* the Holocaust through countless images—both news and documentary, seen in motion pictures, on television, in books and magazines—of the coldblooded brutality. Levinthal reinterprets these images, but *Mein Kampf* is not a simplistic resurrection of the terrors wrought by the Third Reich. With his first series, *Hitler Moves East*, the line between childlike playfulness and adult reality was present yet veiled by the omission of any direct reference to the Holocaust. In *Mein Kampf*, Levinthal retells the story of pain and suffering with images of stormtroopers, Nazis, and Hitler, set in stark contrast to the camps and executions.

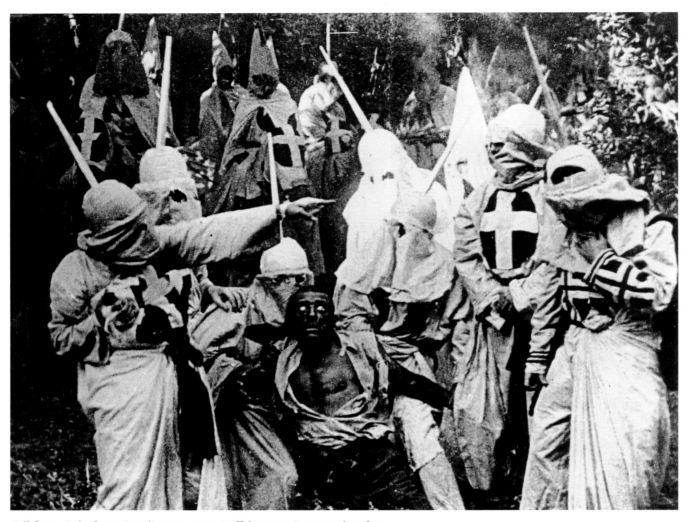

Still from *Birth of a Nation* (director: D. W. Griffith), 1915. Courtesy Photofest.

History written with lightning.
—Woodrow Wilson, after seeing *Birth of a Nation*,
the first film ever shown in the White House, 1915[18]

President Wilson may have been impressed by D. W.
Griffith's homage to the Klan and the return of white
supremacy to the South under Reconstruction. But
African Americans rioted at the film's premiere in 1915
and the NAACP attempted (unsuccessfully) to organize
a boycott. Stunned by the response, Griffith added a
disclaimer to the film: "This is an historical presentation
of the Civil War and Reconstruction period, and is not
intended to reflect upon any race or people of today."

It apparently never occurred to the great director that the
"history" he claimed to be presenting in *Birth of a Nation*
was itself constructed by racists in the interest of perpetuating their own power. Griffith also informed viewers
that many of the sets—Ford's Theater, the Surrender—
were "a historical facsimile in every detail." However, this
penchant for accuracy did not extend to the choice of
actors, most of whom were whites in blackface. (Perhaps
he had trouble recruiting blacks for such a project.)

Levinthal's most recent series began as an attempt to
reinterpret Griffith's historical extravaganza. His original
plan was to construct tableaux, much like his earlier
series, but decided against orchestrating the elements

when he began to locate the objects themselves. Instead, he isolated them, without props or any hint of social context or implied meaning, before a dark background. *Blackface* is composed of objects mass-produced since the late nineteenth century and now commonly referred to as black memorabilia: the Mammy, the Nubian warrior, an Aunt Jemima cookie jar, Amos & Andy, among others. Levinthal found that, as distillations of bogus notions of presumably essential black character traits, the objects alone could convey the oppression of African Americans in our culture.

What began as a response to a landmark film became a full-blown exploration of stereotypical representations of blacks dating back to the country's earliest period. More than antebellum nostalgia, these representations are so pervasive in American society that they are generally accepted as faithful reflections of reality. The objects in *Blackface* embody the hostility of one racial group toward another. As Levinthal has observed, "No ethnic group in history has been so viciously stereotyped in the name of 'fun.'"[19]

Levinthal is well aware that his practice is risky. But he readily accepts the fact that his provocative subjects and his intentions will be misunderstood, even misinterpreted by some viewers. This is unfortunate but unavoidable. An artist who tackles charged subjects—the Holocaust, gender exploitation, racial stereotyping, genocide—cannot expect otherwise. The despicable and demeaning acts depicted in much of Levinthal's work are not his doing. He only asks that we look at and reconsider the world of images that already exist. By making art out of what some consider evil, Levinthal forces the viewer to confront the horrors and human tragedies usually the domain of the photojournalist. However, for Levinthal and many other contemporary artists, artmaking is principally about ideas. Unfortunately, some ideas

are troubling. And like history, which is said to repeat itself, Levinthal's reruns from history reveal our culture's sordid past and the irony that it will always happen again.

Notes

1. Nikita Khrushchev, "All Change on the History Train," *Index on Censorship* 24, no. 3 (May/June 1995): 3.

2. George Orwell, *1984* (1949; reprint, New York: Harcourt Brace Jovanovich, 1983), p. 32.

3. Daniel J. Boorstin, *The Image: The Pseudo Event in America* (1961; reprint, New York: Macmillan Publishing Co., 1987), p. 242.

4. Interview with the artist in his studio, New York, October 1996, with Charles Stainback and Richard Woodward.

5. Henry Peach Robinson, quoted in Shelley Rice, "Parallel Universes," in *Pictorial Effect/Naturalistic Vision: The Photographs and Theories of Henry Peach Robinson and Peter Henry Emerson* (Norfolk, Va.: Chrysler Museum, 1994), p. 69.

6. Christopher Finch, *Cinematography: Special Effects* (New York: Abbeville Press, 1984), p. 16. See also David Shipman, *Cinema: The First Hundred Years* (New York: St. Martin's Press, 1993).

7. Harry Hurt, *For All Mankind* (New York: Atlantic Monthly Press, 1988), p. 323.

8. Carl Mydans and Philip B. Kunhardt, Jr., *Carl Mydans: Photojournalist* (New York: Harry N. Abrams, 1995), p. 13.

9. Marianne Fulton, *Eyes of Time: Photojournalism in America* (Boston: New York Graphic Society, 1988), p. 161.

10. Judith Friedberg and Robert Sagalyn, "Robert Capa," in *The Concerned Photographer*, ed. Cornell Capa (New York: Grossman Publishers, 1968), n.p.

11. Myriad Horn, "Dark Stirrings in Toyland," *U.S. News & World Report* (February 3, 1997), p. 51.

12. Len Deighton, *Blood, Tears, and Folly* (New York: Harper Collins, 1993), p. 496.

13. A. D. Coleman, "The Directorial Mode: Notes Toward a Definition," *Artforum* (September 1976), reprinted in *Light Readings: A Photography Critic's Writings, 1968–1978* (New York: Oxford University Press, 1979).

14. Les Krims, *The Incredible Case of the Stack O'Wheats Murder*, a limited edition folio published by the artist (Buffalo, N.Y., 1972), n.p.

15. "Boy Freed After Art Academy Bows," *Memphis Press-Scimitar* (March 29, 1971), p. 1.

16. Vik Muniz, *Making It Real* (New York: Independent Curators, Inc., 1996), p. 50.

17. Interview with the artist.

18. Fred Silva, *Focus on "Birth of a Nation"* (Englewood Cliffs, N.J.: Prentice-Hall, 1971), p. 108.

19. Interview with the artist.

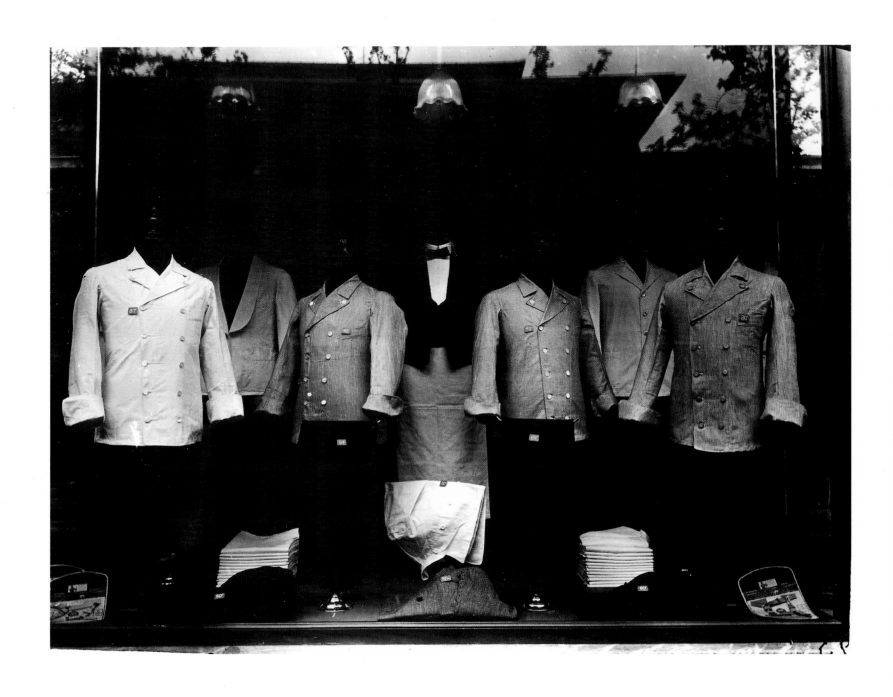

Eugène Atget, *Boutique aux Halles*, 1925. Albumen silver print. The Museum of Modern Art. Abbott-Levy Collection. Partial gift of Shirley C. Burden. © 1996 The Museum of Modern Art, New York.

Richard B. Woodward

TOY STORIES: DAVID LEVINTHAL AND THE UNCERTAINTY PRINCIPLE

It had been believed that when battle scenes were brought into the living room the reality of war would at last be brought home to a civilian audience. But Michael Arlen was quick to point out, in "The New Yorker," that by the same process battle scenes are made less real, "diminished in part by the physical size of the television screen, which, for all the industry's advances, still shows one a picture of men three inches tall shooting at other men three inches tall."
—Philip Knightley[1]

In his short and bittersweet essay, "The Lesson of Toys,"[2] published in 1853, Baudelaire plays around in the sandbox of his own childhood. A confessional piece of writing— what he offers is less an interlocking set of arguments than personal reflections on the relationship of toys to the imagination and to art—it is also an early variation on *les paradis artificiels*. To the celebrant of *volupté*, the moments of pleasure enjoyed by children playing and talking with their manufactured or handmade toys invoke a state of bliss that adult life, with its sinful consciousness of reality, can never deliver.

His memories of boyhood hurt and deprivation date from a visit with his mother to a Madame Panckoucke. A saloniste who impressed the young sensualist by dressing in velvet and fur, she asked at the end of one visit if he would like to select and take home a toy. He was shocked and delighted not only by the kindness of the gesture but by the sparkling variety she offered in a room stocked with special gifts for children. Greedily, he chose the strangest, newest, most expensive and beautiful toy within sight. He was heading for the door with his prize

when his mother intervened and forbade him from accepting it. "She wanted me to be contented with an infinitely ordinary object," he sniffs.

The burning regret of this episode, he claims, explains why he cannot stand in front of a toy store window without thinking of Madame Panckoucke. To him she will always be the "toy fairy." The critic of modern life would have us believe that he likes nothing better than to linger and look back at childhood from the vantage point of these places. No plush or fashionable apartment can ever compare to a good toy store. "All of life can be found there in miniature—and far more brightly colored, glittery and polished than in the real world," he declares.

The memory also accounts for his "lasting affection and rational admiration for that strange statuary art which, with its lustrous exactitude, its blinding flashes of color, its violent gestures and logical contours, best represents childhood's ideas of beauty." A toy is "a child's earliest introduction to art, or rather for him it is the first concrete example of art, and even after maturity, perfect examples will not bring the same feelings of warmth and enthusiasm, nor carry with them the same sense of conviction."

The childless writer also advises parents not to forget the frivolous joys their children can have from toys. He defends their right to manhandle, even maul, dolls without adult interference; and he warns against the "man-child"—toy collectors who never touch their investments for fear of lowering their resale value. The destruction of toys, thinks Baudelaire, teaches a crucial metaphysical lesson. Once a child has dismembered or torn apart a beloved thing, asserting dominance but finding only a hollow core without a soul, he or she has taken a bite out of philosophy and religion. "This is the beginning of despair and gloom."

The idler sketches scenes from his off hours. Strolling the boulevards, his pockets stuffed with cheap toys as giveaways, he observes that poor children at first refuse his gifts and then seize them hungrily. "They will scamper off like cats running away to eat the morsel you have given them." Most memorably, in a scene that could have been written by Dickens or Orwell or Buñuel, he describes watching a runny-nosed urchin on the road entrance a pampered contemporary inside a chateau garden. The poor child tantalizes the rich one by rattling the bars of the fence with a macabre homemade toy: a live rat in a box. Baudelaire's pointed summation of this encounter is that "to cut costs the child's parents had made a toy out of real life."

The essay has the highborn tone of a flaneur who has been out slumming, but it also reveals Baudelaire's populist knack for finding treasure where others would never deign to look. Like C. Auguste Dupin in "The Purloined Letter," he could spot clues to a deeper mystery hidden in plain sight. By arguing that toy figures might have the significance of any other statuary, the art critic advanced the cause of the lowly and overlooked,

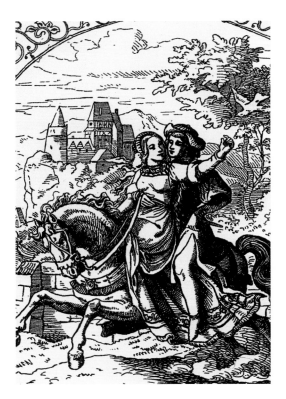

Moritz von Schwind, illustration for Grimm's "Sleeping Beauty," ca. 1800s.

gleefully chipping away at brittle hierarchies of thought, as he did in lauding Daumier's caricatures over state-sponsored salon painting. The shocking unsentimentalist in him also liked purging childhood of its innocence in the eyes of patronizing adults. He didn't overlook the class distinctions of toys and their owners, or ignore the darker meanings that cling to mementos—how they may begin as vehicles for open-ended fantasy but end up as relics of one's own buried past.

"The Lesson of Toys" is a melancholy footnote to Romantic thought which gave new prominence to the role of inanimate figures in the mental lives and rituals of adults and children alike. The theme runs throughout Romantic literature of the supernatural. The tales of E.T.A. Hoffmann and the Brothers Grimm are populated with automata, exquisite varnished dolls, and gallant toy soldiers. Similarly, the observation by folklorists that totemic figures exercised enormous power in "primitive" cultures was also a theme in early anthropological studies on the origins of myth and religion. Baudelaire's musings on the importance of toys are those of an urban explorer who, instead of finding animism among aboriginals or gypsies, notes the endurance of these same beliefs in the homes of the Parisian bourgeoisie.

In Hoffmann and Grimm, toys and dolls come alive of their own will, when their human masters are unaware or asleep; or they may owe their existence to human tinkering and the jump-start of an inventor's love, malice, or curiosity. The hand of creation can determine if a figure is demonic or chivalrous, a cute miniature or a monster. The Jewish myth of the golem, a clay figure that in Rabbi Loew's stories can move but not speak, acts as a sort of medieval Superman, saving Jews from murderous anti-Semites. But Mary Shelley's pitiful brute is forever cursed by science's unholy yearning to match the Christian miracle of reanimating dead flesh.

Hoffmann's influential story, "The Sand-Man"—about an agitated young student who falls in love with a glass-eyed mechanical doll named Olympia—was sanitized when it became the basis of the first act for Offenbach's opera, *Tales of Hoffmann*, and for Delibes's comic ballet, *Coppélia*. But Freud's psychoanalytic reading of the tale in "The Uncanny," his essay on the aesthetics of horror, doesn't omit the original gore.[3]

He dwells on the fearful meaning of the Sand-Man, a nighttime monster that the student first heard about as a boy from his nurse. The Sand-Man attacks children who won't go to bed, throwing sand in their eyes until they pop out, bleeding, from their heads. Each night he collects the eyes of disobedient children in a sack and carries them off to the moon where his own children, who have hooked beaks like owls', eat the eyes in their nest. Hoffmann gradually lets the reader know the student is insane in suspecting that a repulsive lawyer, Coppelius, and an optician, Coppola, are conflated into

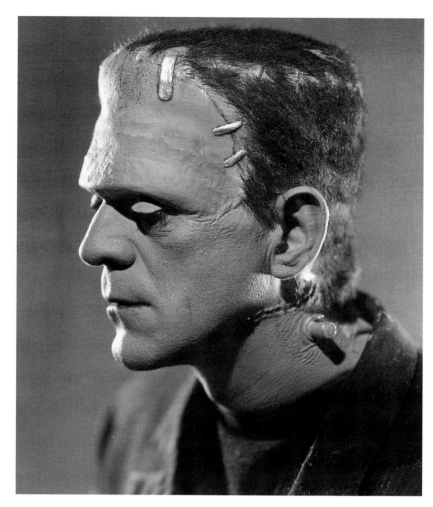

Boris Karloff in *The Bride of Frankenstein* (director: James Whale), 1935. Courtesy Photofest.

the dreaded Sand-Man. Freud asserts confidently that the main source of fear in the story, which also has scenes of voyeuristic spying with a telescope, is located in Oedipal castration fantasies, specifically "the idea of being robbed of one's eyes." He admits that the reading downplays the ambiguous role of the mechanical doll (and the dollmaker) in unhinging the student, who is no longer certain if he loves a real woman or her lifelike double.

The connection between artifice and terror, even if not first drawn by the German Romantics, certainly was strengthened by them. Serving to remind readers of the irrational dangers still afoot from ancient times, these stories also dramatized the new forces then being discovered and harnessed in factories and cities during the

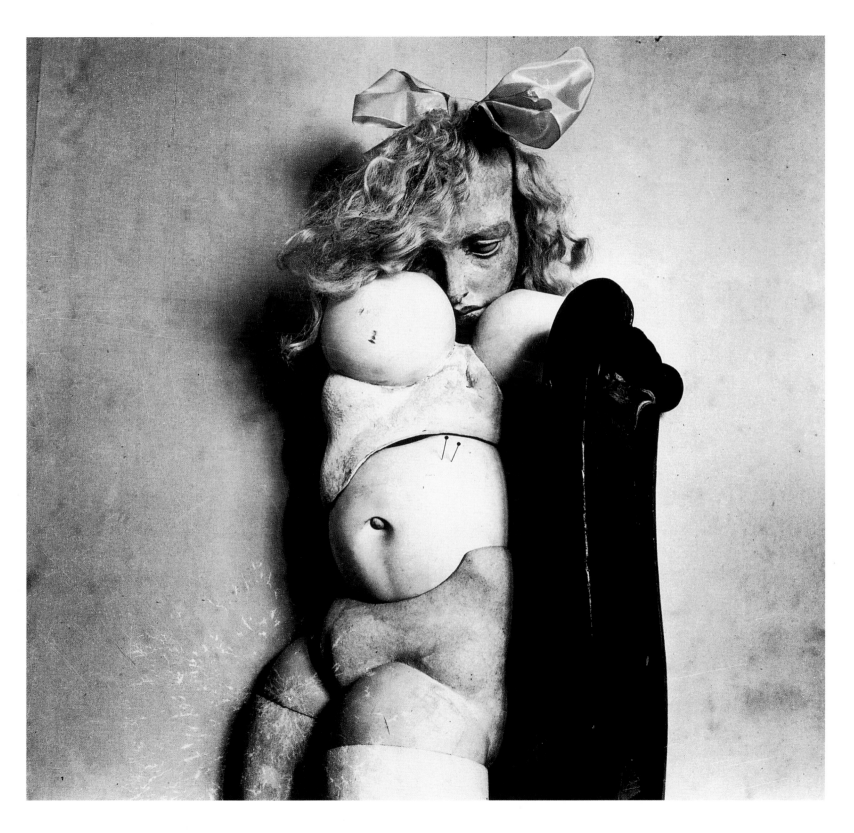

Hans Bellmer, *Morning Sun*, 1952. © ICP Permanent Collection,
Gift of Herbert Lust.

early industrial age. The doll as toy was itself a product of this period. According to historian Carl Fox, "not until the commercial floodgates were opened for the mass-production and distribution of the doll did it become accepted as a child's toy and plaything. But that did not begin until the eighteenth century, when the efficiently organized German craftsmen merchandised their production throughout Europe and America at prices almost everyone could afford."[4]

When David Levinthal decided to stage battles with toy Nazi soldiers as a Yale graduate student in photography during the early 1970s, he was in a sense telling a gothic horror story for the late industrial age. Fifty years later, World War II is still the nightmare from which we are trying to awaken, the most devastating civilian catastrophe of the twentieth century. In reanimating scenes of the German invasion of the Soviet Union, Levinthal was necessarily invoking Hitler—historic embodiment of evil and Teutonic bogeyman, a monster of the twentieth century more savage and frightening than any Sand-Man. For a Jewish photographer to consort with Nazis, even in plastic miniature, was to dance with the devil.

Levinthal's experiments were unknowing, however, and begun without any high-art purpose in mind. The book finally published in 1977 as *Hitler Moves East: A Graphic Chronicle, 1941–43* (in collaboration with his classmate, the cartoonist Garry Trudeau) bears no trace of cathartic or expressionistic intent. It puzzles rather than alarms the reader. What kind of pictures are these anyway, documents or tableaux? Why would anyone go to the trouble to "fake" pictures from World War II? It is a boys' book and an American book, specifically an American art-school book of the '70s. One sign of the confusion provoked by Levinthal's pictures is that his teachers, when they saw he was playing with toy figures,

suggested he look at Hans Bellmer's mutilated dolls from the '30s and '40s. As Levinthal has said, "that proved to me they had no idea what I was doing."[5]

Had his teachers understood (or had anyone else, for that matter), they might have seen that he was interested not in delivering a surrealist shock to the body but in following the dictum handed out to every young writer or artist: describe what you know. By arranging two-inch helmeted German soldiers with toy motorcycles on a field of Gold Medal flour to simulate the snows of the Russian steppe, meanwhile pushing his film for a blurred, high-grain resolution and then printing on paper, which gives the look of images bathed in sepia, Levinthal was violating some fundamental rules of straight photography. But at the same time he was sincerely seeking to document images that had been playing in his head since he was a boy.

Born in 1949 and raised in the suburbs of Northern California, Levinthal belongs to the first generation of Americans to receive much of their entertainment and information from television. His family was among the first in his neighborhood to have a color set. He knew little and cared less about German Romantic writers or their offspring. Any familiarity he had with the story of Pinocchio came not by reading Carlo Gollodi's 1883 children's story but from seeing Disney's 1940 cartoon on screen. Frankenstein meant the 1931 black-and-white movie directed by James Whale and featuring Boris Karloff, or the creature in the Abbott and Costello farce, neither of which bore much, if any, semblance to the original novel.

Likewise, his knowledge of World War II was in large part determined by television and the movies. The conflict was refought every week on dramatic series ("Twelve O'Clock High," "The Gallant Years," and "Combat!"), as well as on historical news shows (Walter Cronkite's "The

Twentieth Century") and in feature films from the '60s (*The Longest Day* and *The Great Escape*). World War II has saturated the airwaves of America for the last fifty years unlike any event in history. However distorting and distancing these images absorbed by a California teenager may have been—and it is questionable that they were any more so than documentary shots of the war from issues of *Life*—they offered the vicarious thrill and terror of war. The actual events were far away in place and time. Levinthal had no immediate relatives who had perished in battle or in the Holocaust.

But even if *Hitler Moves East* began as a Dada-like joke and a vaguely rebellious gesture toward the Yale art-school faculty, Levinthal felt himself slowly being transformed by his material. The despair of soldiers on the Eastern Front found a repressed eloquence in the helplessness of toys. As the work evolved, with the "action" becoming more "realistic" and the figures less toylike, the bloody consequence of war seeped into the plastic figures.

The puppet-master's zaniness is still apparent in the finished product. The book's title suggests a chapter heading from a vast chronicle of the war, or a weekly installment in a comprehensive documentary TV series, the kind that opens with the sound of Stukas strafing the countryside and a somber narration by Laurence Olivier. Still, along with the trumpery is an anxiety about history, an uncertainty about true suffering and one's own removal from it. Cindy Sherman's series of *Film Stills*, begun the year the Levinthal/Trudeau book appeared, is similarly heartfelt, mocking, and strange, an elaborate ruse that also serves as a tribute to the emotive currency of the photographic image.

The lesson of toys and the '70s zeitgeist conspired to lend an unexpected pathos to a book about Nazis. The authors did not think they were taking cues from news headlines. "Had it been conscious, it probably would have been too *self*-conscious," says Levinthal. But the plight of young men killing and being killed far from home, in a futile, barbaric war, could not but affect any North American male in the early '70s. The Vietnam War seemed interminable; pictures of firefights and body bags were unavoidable in magazines and on television. Not that the photographer ever saw action. He was no closer to Saigon and Hue than he had been to Stalingrad or Moscow. Levinthal's medical deferment and his status as a student kept him out of the service. Like most white, middle-class American male artists his age, he has been a spectator of the sweeping headline events of his time. He proudly diagnoses himself as a voyeur.

It is his twice-removed distance from highly wrought experience—his quixotic attempts to recreate with only toy figures the heightened "reality of an image"—that accounts for the cool, melancholy air surrounding Levinthal's pictures. The frozen quality of any photograph, its mortifying, temporal touch, is deepened by his choice of themes. The images and objects that trigger a response in him are rarely contemporary. The New York that he loves best can be found in Hopper's paintings and in film noir. The myth of the American West, as much a staple for Hollywood movies and television as World War II when he was growing up, has never died for Levinthal. A brooding, if skeptical, nostalgia separates his work (as well as that of Sherman and Laurie Simmons) from that of pop-cult trendsetters like Warhol and Rosenquist. When Levinthal brings his toys to life, they never act in the present. Like the characters in one of his favorite movies, they are always haunted by being "out of the past."

He has systematically tested his own reactions to some of the most disturbing pictures or objects that he finds; and the warning light on the hot-button issues he has pushed has flashed steadily in recent years. Over the last decade he has staged and photographed series on the isolation of urban life (*Modern Romance*), S&M photography (*Desire*), the ideology of the Third Reich and the Holocaust (*Mein Kampf*), and totems of white racism (*Blackface*). Lately, the horror stories he likes to tell are about toys: their producers, consumers, and latent power to entice or wound.

The bondage dolls of Western women from *Desire* (1990–91) were manufactured by a Japanese mail-order house; the most popular pose in its catalogue shows a voluptuous nude held hostage by an unseen master. This "Story of O" debasement carries a peculiar erotic charge in Levinthal's photographs, as though he wanted to send up the stylized routines of soft-focus porn but still couldn't deny its manacled hold on the imagination. The *Blackface* series also dramatizes his fascination with the monstrous and his own risky complicity as a photographer in perpetuating an ugly historical reality. Mass-produced by white companies for a white audience that found racial caricatures amusing, many of these toys were done with malicious intent; others are only cutely demeaning. (The tin figures of Amos & Andy even bear traces of empathetic craftsmanship.) Some date back to the start of the century; others to last year. The act of lavishing attention on these figures with a camera automatically strengthens their fetish status. The photographs, which record the unprecedented fear, hatred, and diminishment of one racial group by another, echo with a kind of psychotic laughter that every American has heard. As Levinthal says, "no ethnic group in history has been so viciously stereotyped in the name of 'fun.'"

Whatever ominous overtones they sound, however, Levinthal's photographs never stop being "fun" themselves. Unlike Bellmer's (and Sherman's) scenarios for dismembered dolls, Levinthal's unthreatening setups don't ask you to squirm. The quality of innocent play is never sacrificed for an effect of repelling the viewer with the gross-out or the grotesque. The most disconcerting fact about the *Blackface* material may be that for decades, these figures were not considered offensive. Children talked to their golliwogs and pickaninnies without malice. Families placed the servile black butler figurine on the mantelpiece, or the black "cannibal corkscrew" above the bar next to the hula dancer. The movement afoot to decontaminate Little Black Sambo and display him and his kin again in public requires an advanced degree in irony. But Amos & Andy and Mr. Bojangles dolls could be found in many black homes, as well as white, during the '30s and '40s.

Since *Hitler Moves East*, Levinthal has observed how the cinematic image translates into the commercial toy (and vice versa). The rise of the American toy industry as the largest in the world coincides with the domination of American film in international markets during the '30s. Toy companies seem to have understood immediately that a desire existed—or could be manufactured—to hold in your hand what you saw on the screen. Toys and movies enhance fantasies at the same time, of course, that they exploit them.

The Walt Disney Company, which has pioneered the synergy between image and merchandise, was built on the back of an animated rodent. Mickey Mouse first appeared on November 18, 1928, as a sound short, "Steamboat Willie." But it wasn't long before a stuffed doll appeared. By 1931, he had been spun off into fifteen different manifestations. "Mickey Mouse bailed out a lot of toy companies during the Depression," notes Richard O'Brien in his book *The Story of American Toys*.[6] Fans of Charlie Chaplin in 1929 could buy him as the bell toy, the windup, the composition doll, or the tin puppet. Shirley Temple was not only the biggest box-office star of

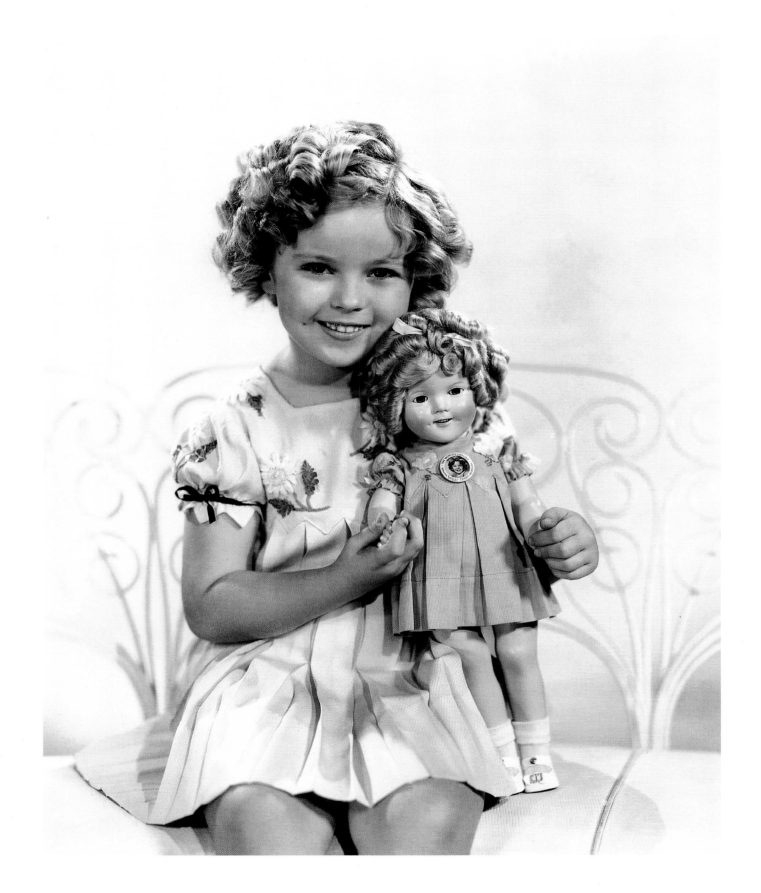

Shirley Temple holding a doll of herself. Courtesy Photofest.

the '30s but one of the most popular dolls, the Ideal toy company selling some $1.5 million worth. As a child star, she was ideal material to be repackaged as a plaything for little girls.

Levinthal is a Marxist photographer, albeit in the sense that many of his pictures were made with toys produced during the '50s and '60s in the factories of Louis Marx. It was not enough for customers of this colorful American merchant to buy a single figure. There was a milieu and—before the word was coined—a lifestyle in which a toy was born and without which it was impoverished or incomplete. Levinthal's New York loft is stacked with playsets and dioramas from the Marx Toy Co., which went bankrupt in 1980. He collects as much as he photographs, for—unlike Cindy Sherman, who acts in as well as directs her productions—he requires toymakers to prompt and reify his imagination.

Marilyn Monroe inspired Levinthal's *American Beauties*, a series completed in 1990 that looks back with wistfulness and foreboding on sex and death during the Cold War. The curvaceous movie stars of the '50s and early '60s were eidetic objects, inflated daydreams of male lust as well as fertility figures for baby-boomer women. The perfect commercial incarnation of this mythmaking can be found in the most successful doll of the era, Barbie, whose best-selling feature will always be her gigantic breasts.

Levinthal's spare, eloquent settings for his buxom females evoke this distorted sexual innocence along with the dark threat from above that could not be ignored during the time. Lone figures in the sand look away from the viewer and toward the horizon. Posed nude or in swimsuits, they could be sunbathers without a thought in their heads were it not for a black, sunless sky that contradicts the burst of golden warmth. The lighting is irrational, hot and cold, brightest day with impending

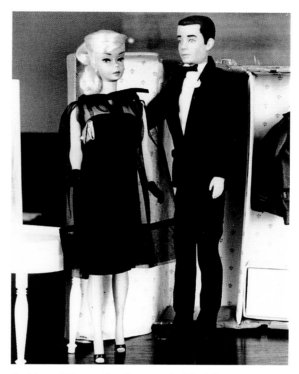

Barbie and Ken, 1964. Courtesy Archive Photos.

night. This is less a picnic on the beach than a remake of the movie *On the Beach*. Deliberate or not, it is hard not to read the series both as an Oedipal son gazing back at his idealized '50s mom, and as a meditation on nuclear winter, a topic much in the air when these photographs were made.

The challenge of realizing his attraction/repulsion to an image or an object is discovering how the Polaroid 20 x 24 camera will sort out his often unresolved feelings once he enters the studio. All of Levinthal's work depends on solutions to theatrical and photographic problems on a tiny scale, and he relies less and less on sketches or pre-visualization. He can't expect—nor does he hope—that adjustments in lighting, focus, and depth-of-field will entirely conceal his behind-the-scenes fakery. Yet he wants the viewer to be uncertain, on edge, about the result, as though the toys could be stand-ins for the "real thing" if needed.

Improvisation and accident account for some of these effects, such as the black skies over *American Beauties*. He also can reach into a small bag of tricks. The persistent blur in his color is a standard technique of sports photographers who want to insinuate speed into their frames. But even a blur is contextual. In *The Wild West* it implies that we behold decisive men of action, myths filtered through the mists of time; while the hazy smears of *Desire* and *Mein Kampf* are furtive, rushed, as though these were illicitly obtained surveillance shots. Except for the *Blackface* series, we almost never see the faces of Levinthal's figures. The reason is mainly technical—he doesn't want to shatter the illusion of uncertainty. As Alan McCollum and Laurie Simmons showed in their untitled closeups of toy faces from 1987, the modeling on these figures is typically crude and, when magnified into portraits, deformed and monstrous.

Levinthal prefers to suggest horror rather than to state it. Like the mannequins in Parisian store windows that caught Atget's eye, his dolls are worldly documents of their time and disquieting reminders of otherworldly terrors. His anthropologic artifacts of American paganism are as telltale of the worshippers' wishes as a Hopi kachina, a Dogon power figure, or the Virgin Mary.

Playing with toys not as a "man-child" but with an obsessive respect that Baudelaire would admire, he has let them talk. And what his German soldiers, cowboys and Indians, naked corpses, and grinning black men and women have to say—about the persistence of the past and its mutating ability to inflict pleasure and pain, even by constructed means—is worth attending to.

If the sobering lesson of toys, for Baudelaire, is that they don't have souls, the sadder lesson, with Levinthal, is that the soul has dissolved into images. His portraits in miniature of artificial, evacuated desire nonetheless are uneasy, to-scale likenesses of a world taking shape on screen and on-line, one with limitless options for trans-formation and a shrunken sense that reality and its virtual doppelgangers are any longer so frighteningly far apart.

Notes

1. Philip Knightley, *The First Casualty: From Crimea to Vietnam: The War Correspondent as Hero, Propagandist, and Myth Maker* (New York: Harcourt Brace Jovanovich, 1982), p. 361.

2. Originally published in French as "Morale du Joujou" in *Monde Littéraire* on April 17, 1853, it was translated into English by Jonathan Mayne for his book of selected criticism by Baudelaire, *The Painter of Modern Life and Other Essays* (London: Phaidon, 1964). I have amended Mayne's translation in places, including in the title, which he renders as "A Philosophy of Toys."

3. Originally published in German as "Das Unheimliche" in *Imago* (1919). Translated into English by Joan Riviere for the *Standard Edition* (London: Hogarth Press, 1959), pp. 368–407.

4. Carl Fox, *The Doll* (New York: Harry N. Abrams, 1981), p. 26.

5. All quotations by David Levinthal are from conversations with the author during 1996.

6. Richard O'Brien, *The Story of American Toys* (New York: Knopf, 1990), pp. 137–142.

Work from **1975–1996**

HITLER MOVES EAST, 1975–77

RW: Don't you find it interesting that as children we didn't act out the Cold War with toy soldiers?

DL: We had "James Bond" and "The Man from Uncle," S.M.E.R.S.H. and T.H.R.U.S.H. But the Cold War lacked the sweep of cinematic battlefronts.

RW: It went on for 44 years, during our entire lives until a few years ago, but it was so disguised and coded. The fighting involved surveillance, secret agents and surrogate states. Toy manufacturers must have thought they were protecting us from something. Maybe it just wasn't visual enough for kids.

DL: Marx had a "Guerrilla Warfare" miniature play-set produced in the '60s. But by and large when you bought play-sets in the '50s and '60s, they were American GIs and Germans. There are a couple of play-sets about the War in the Pacific. Considering that we played a far greater role there than in Europe, it's surprising toy manufacturers didn't grant equal time to the war with Japan. I don't know why.

RW: Maybe because of the way that war ended. If you play that game out, it ends with a couple of atomic blasts. I don't think it has been appreciated how much the images of World War II shaped our generation.

DL: There was a romanticism about World War II. It was a moral war. We were fighting an evil enemy. It was the ultimate fantasy for kids. Television heightened the fantasy.

Charles Stainback: I first saw "Hitler Moves East" at the George Eastman House in 1978. It was at a point when the notion of fabricating photographs was quite prevalent. At that time, the art world was inundated with it—Cindy Sherman's film stills and cut-outs come immediately to mind. Were you trying to be provocative? Was there a philosophical motive behind it?

DL: No to both questions. By the time I came to Yale from California in 1971 I had moved from a traditional landscape phase in the style of Weston and Adams to the small camera, social document style of Lee Friedlander and Bruce Davidson. The work with toys grew, quite simply, out of a desire to explore photography in a studio. My first attempt was with a Marx dollhouse that I had bought in a department store; it was far more complex than I had imagined. The interior spaces were especially difficult to work with.

I went back to the department store and bought toy soldiers—ones that were reminiscent of the ones I had played with as a child. It must have been

Christmas time, because I had them wrapped, and I photographed them coming out of their boxes.

The whole process was a combination of challenge and youthful enthusiasm. Later that year I arranged small plastic soldiers on my linoleum floor and photographed them. Before I knew it I was going to the hobby shop and buying a little bridge and photographing that. Then I lit the bridge on fire. Then I made a river out of blue crêpe paper. I was simply caught up in the child-like workings of toys. Something just happened, emotionally as well as aesthetically. I didn't have an articulated philosophy. I didn't even consciously mimic documentary photography. That came much later.

CS: You mentioned once that Robert Capa's blurred action pictures struck your imagination. Capa surely didn't intend for them to come out like that....

DL: That doesn't matter. People also bring lots of interpretations to my work that I might not agree with, or may not have intended. In Capa's photos the viewer gets the ambiance of what he was going through. It doesn't matter, finally, that they took rolls of film of the flag raising at Iwo Jima, or of General MacArthur coming ashore in the Philippines. Look at all those Civil War photographs that were staged. Bodies were moved around to heighten the effect. We are a generation that has embraced those images. We can't let go of it; it's part of who we are.

CS: Most people, on the other hand, know that photographs aren't real and shouldn't be trusted. You are setting up realities and historical events much like documentary photographers. Your work is certainly not journalistic, it's not news, yet it could be thought of in the same way as those historical photographs that aren't, we later learn, historical fact.

DL: You've hit on the central point of my work. All my work involves artifice— whether it's the cowboy images of the West, fabricated images of the Eastern Front, or the iconography of sexuality. I set things up in an artificial context and arrange them in such a way that we're able to see, simultaneously, the artificiality and the reality of it at the same time.

RW: Your series "Hitler Moves East," which was published as a book in collaboration with Garry Trudeau in 1977, has the look of documentary photography. But doesn't it also play into the romantic fantasy of war?

DL: Only on a superficial level. If one reads the text, almost all of which is drawn from letters and other original source material, the opposite conclusion could be drawn. We pushed the toy imagery beyond fantasy into a Twilight Zone, where plastic soldiers become horribly maimed and killed.

RW: Did anyone criticize you for being Jewish and making art that, in a sense, empathizes with the Nazis?

DL: The book was not about exonerating or condemning the Nazis. It was much more about military imagery and the personal horror of war. It was a coincidence, really, that the toy soldiers I photographed were German. Sixty percent of the toy soldier models in model stores were German. There were hardly any Russians. Naturally, the story was easier to tell from a German perspective. I didn't intend for it to become descriptive in an historical sense.

CS: So you chose the subject because there were more miniature play-sets of Nazis than anything else?

DL: Well, picking the Eastern Front was also a way of giving the project structure, and it left me with visual freedom. Everyone has an image of D-Day; we've all seen John Wayne in *The Longest Day*. But the Eastern Front was terra incognita, at least to many Americans. We really knew so little about the enormity of the casualties.

RW: How did Garry Trudeau get involved in the project?

DL: Coincidentally, Garry and I were looking at similar images at the same time. He was researching his thesis project, which was a fictional biography of a Luftwaffe pilot named Erich Becker. His publisher saw my photos over at his house and immediately suggested that the two of us do a book together. We were both twenty-four years old and said, "cool," or the equivalent.

RW: You started working with toy figures during the Vietnam War. Do you see any connection?

DL: I don't think Garry and I consciously thought of Vietnam vis-à-vis *Hitler Moves East*, although the diary entries we quoted do have a sense of fatalism, even nihilism; people stranded thousands of miles from home, fighting a war they knew they weren't winning. The book does have a powerful anti-war sentiment.

CS: How long did the two of you work on the book together?

DL: Three and a half years. During that time my style changed radically, and the final pictures were really the result of only six to nine months work. Initially my pictures weren't realistic; I was painting the trees and making rivers out of crêpe paper. By the time we finished I was making detailed scale figures and painting them delicately. It changed the whole tone of the project.

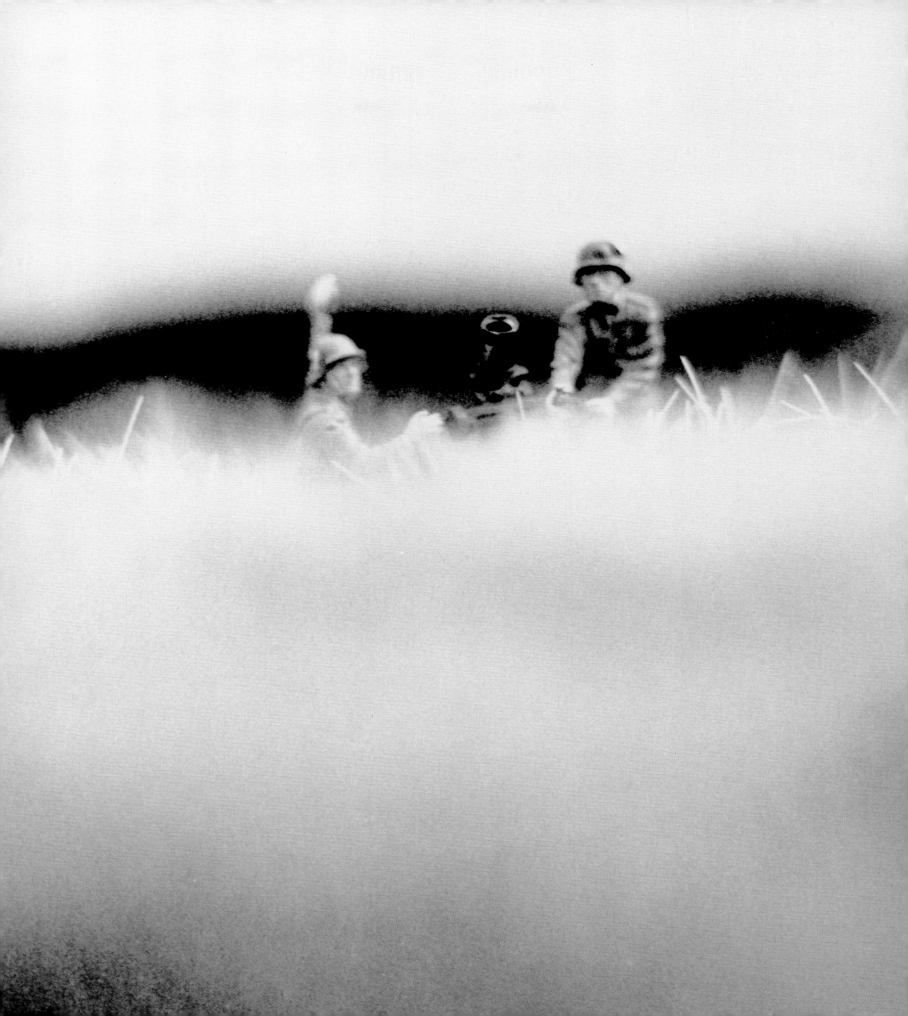

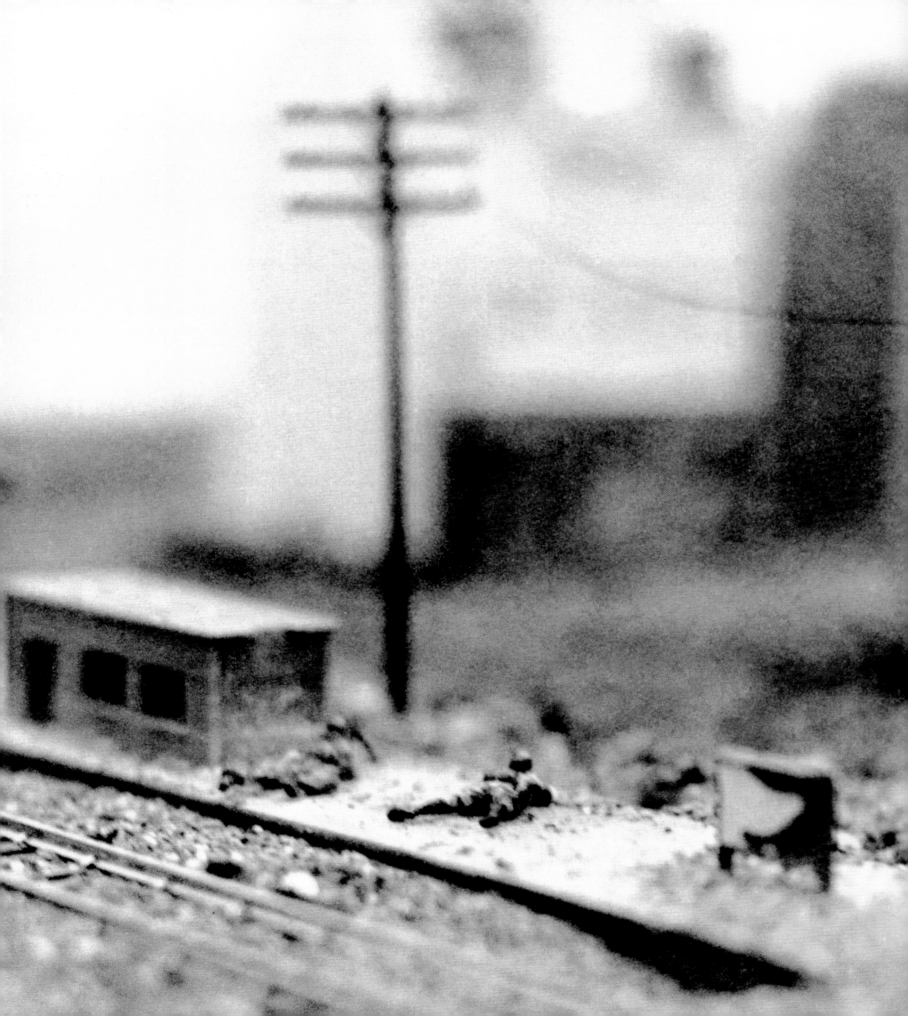

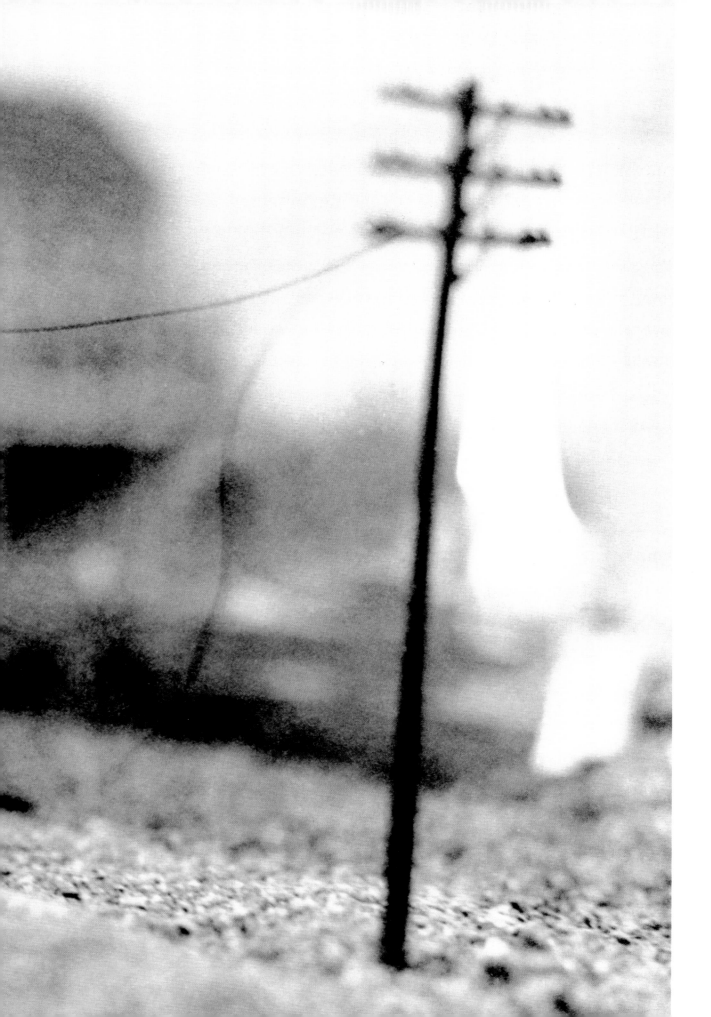

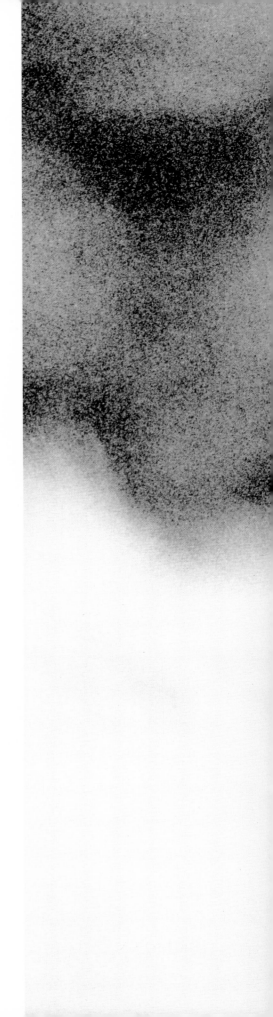

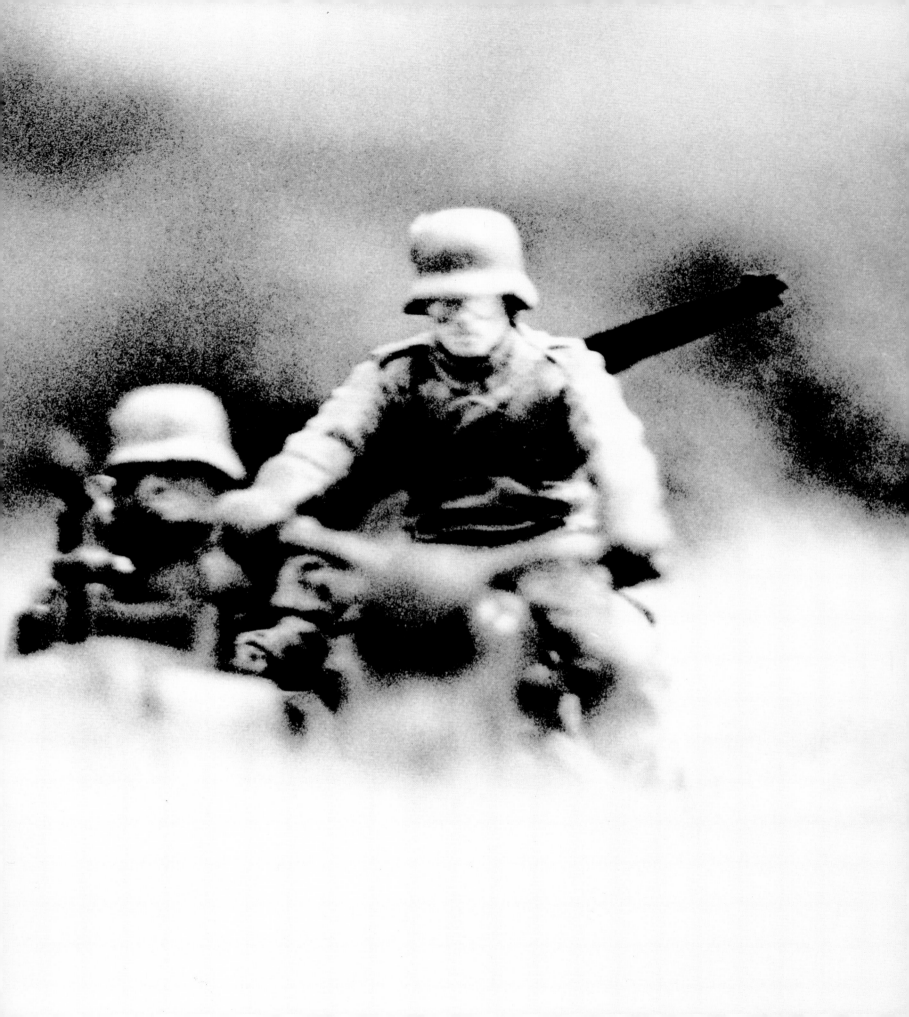

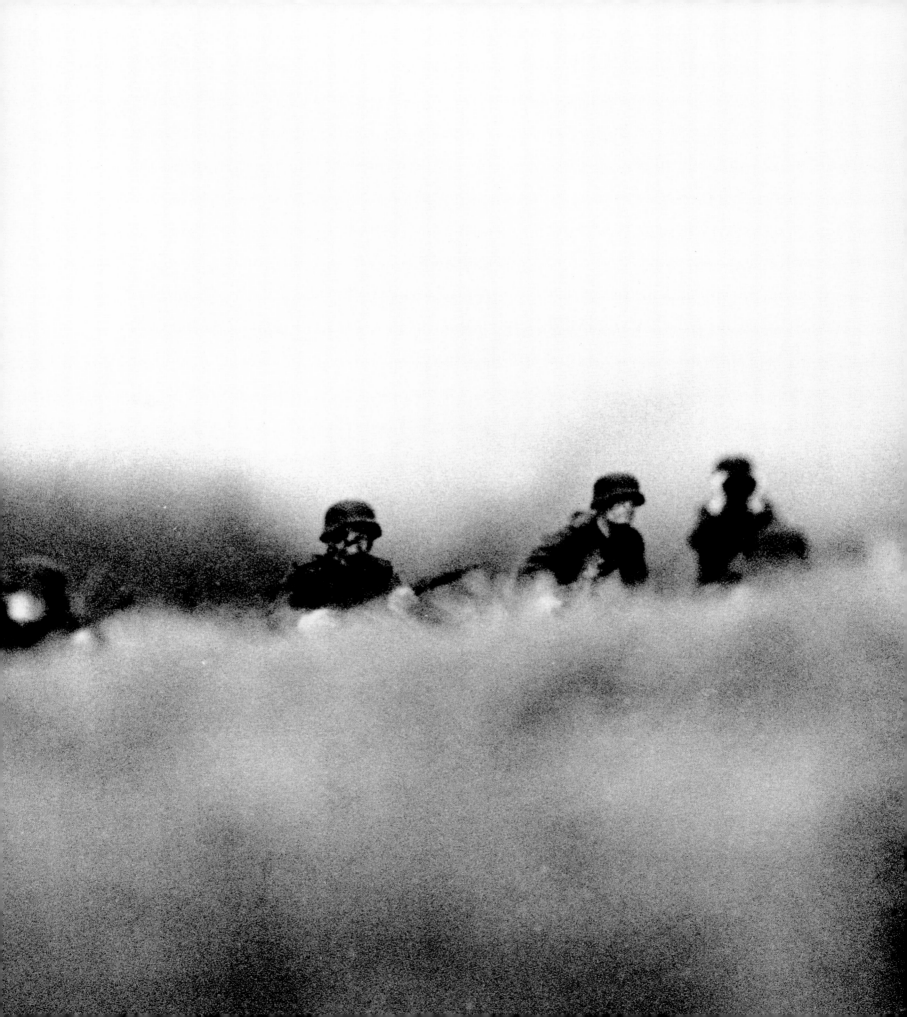

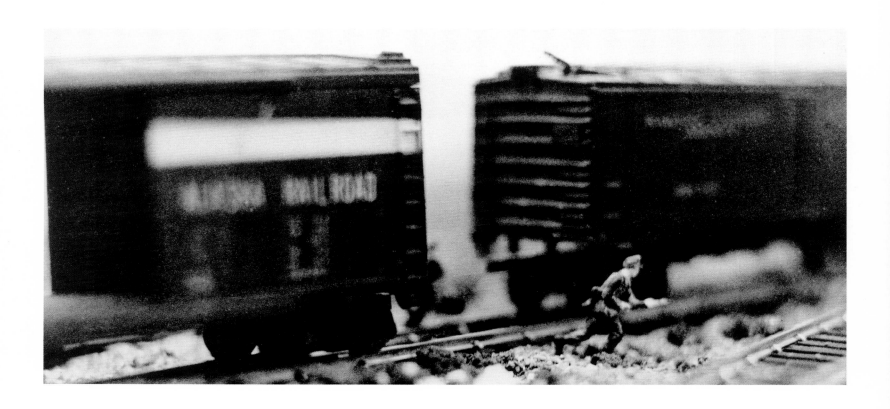

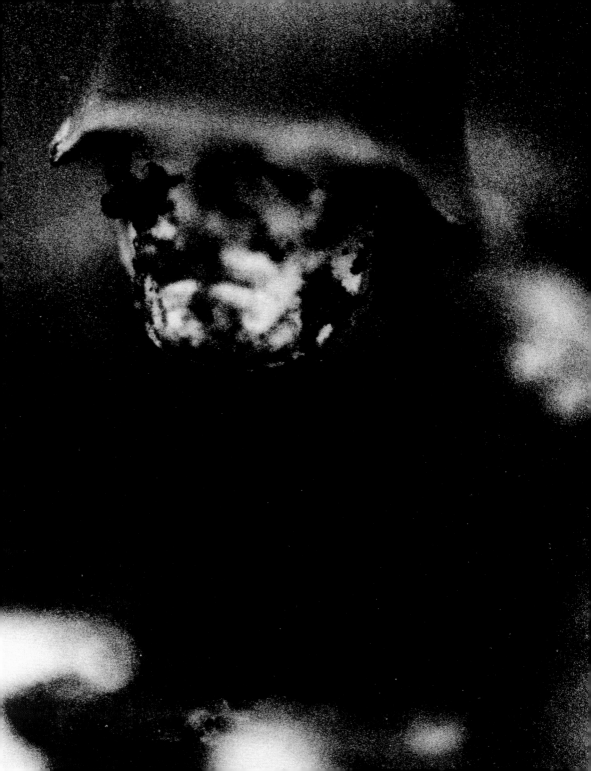

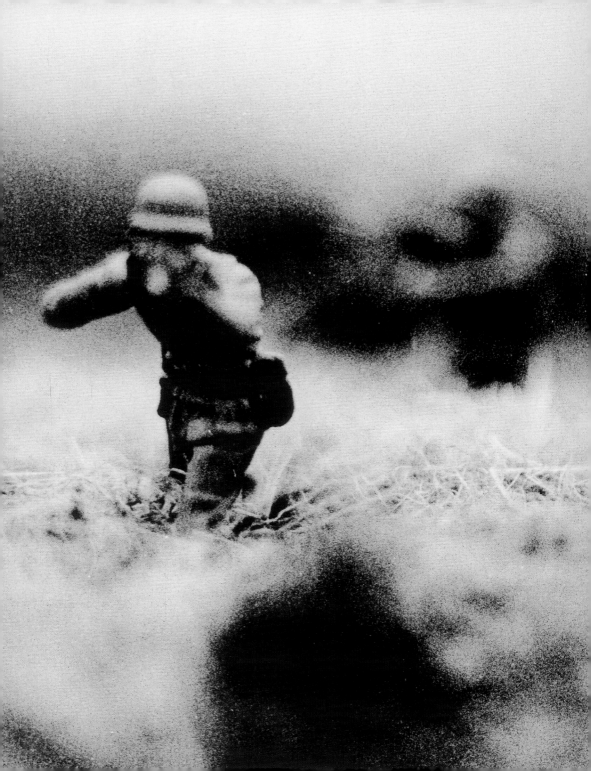

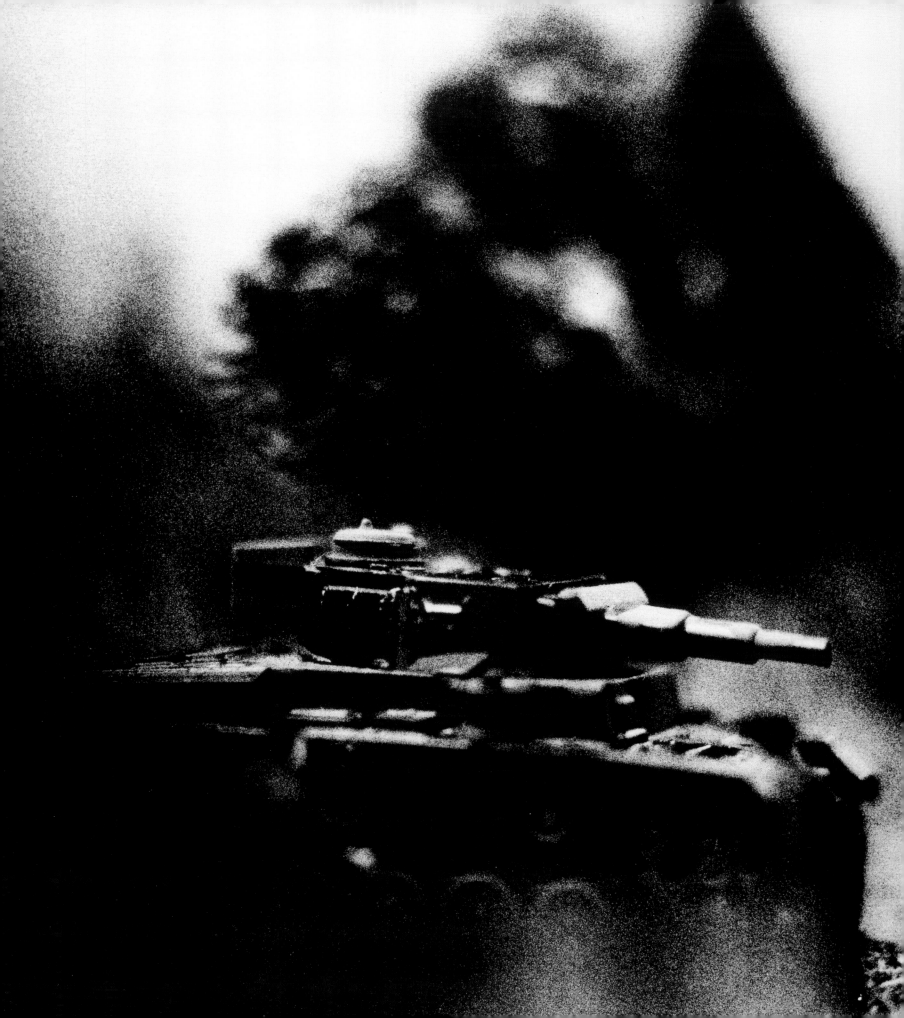

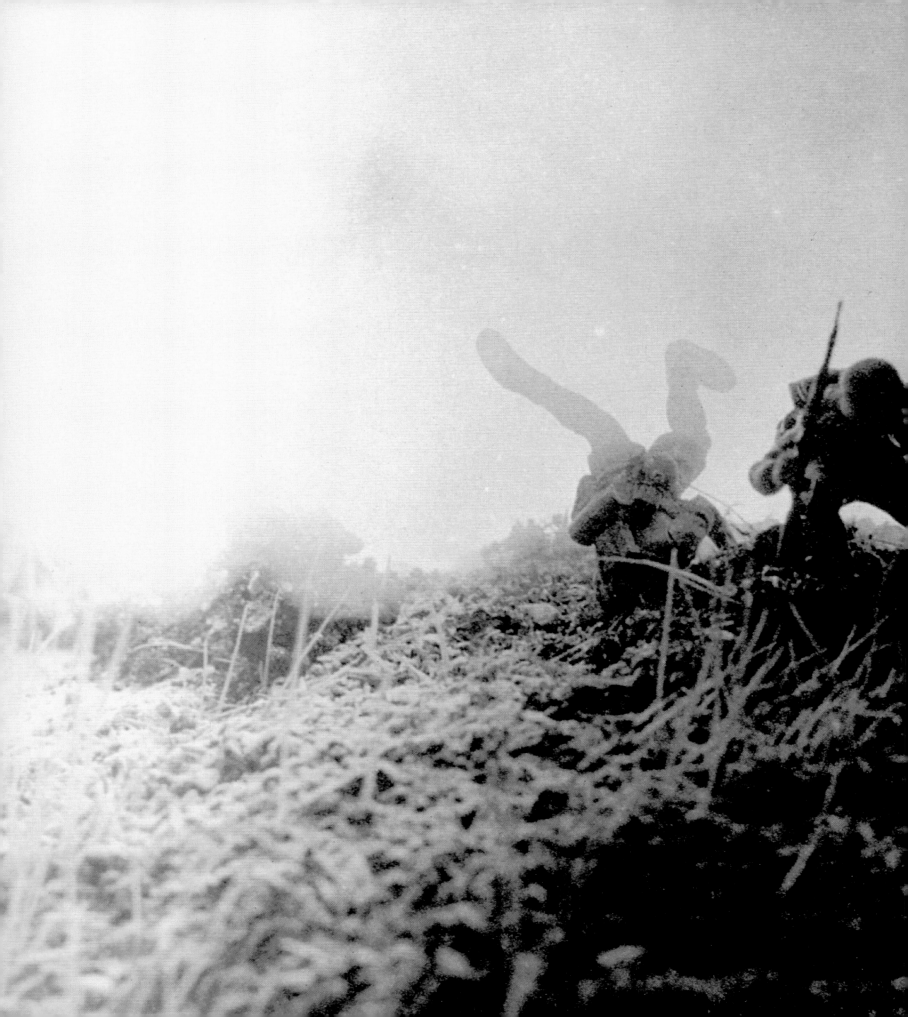

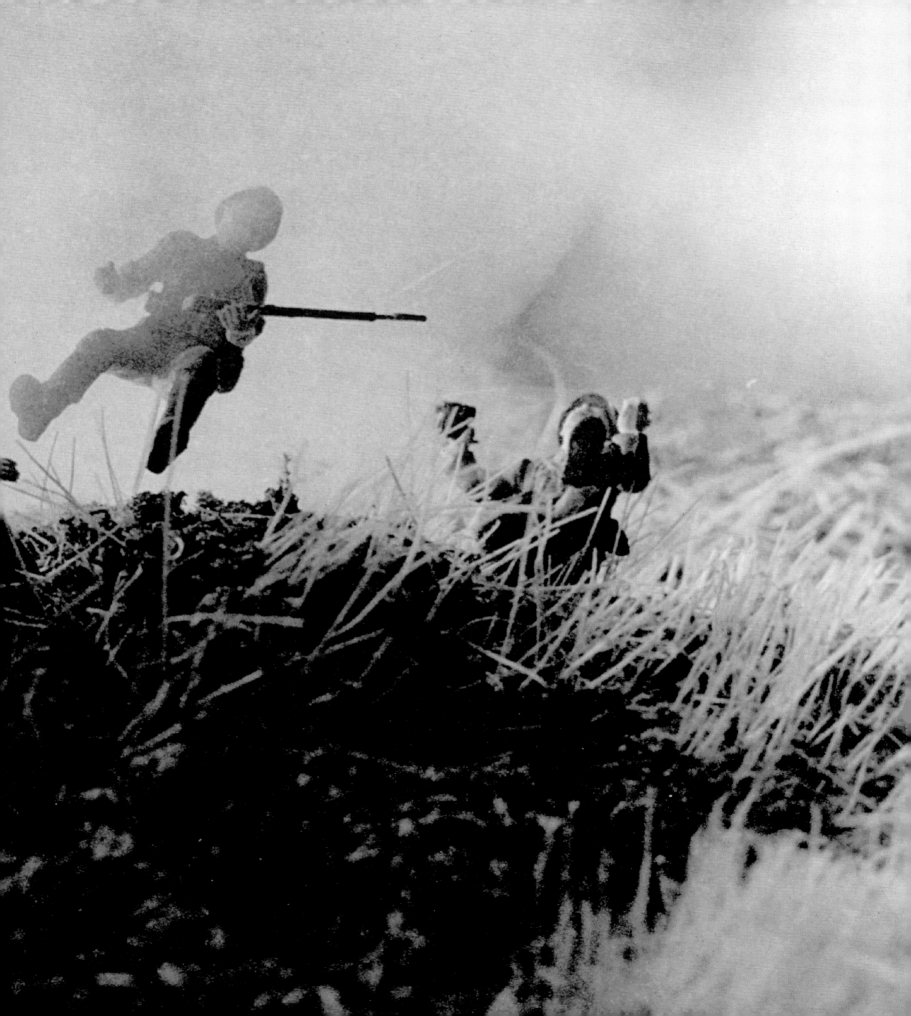

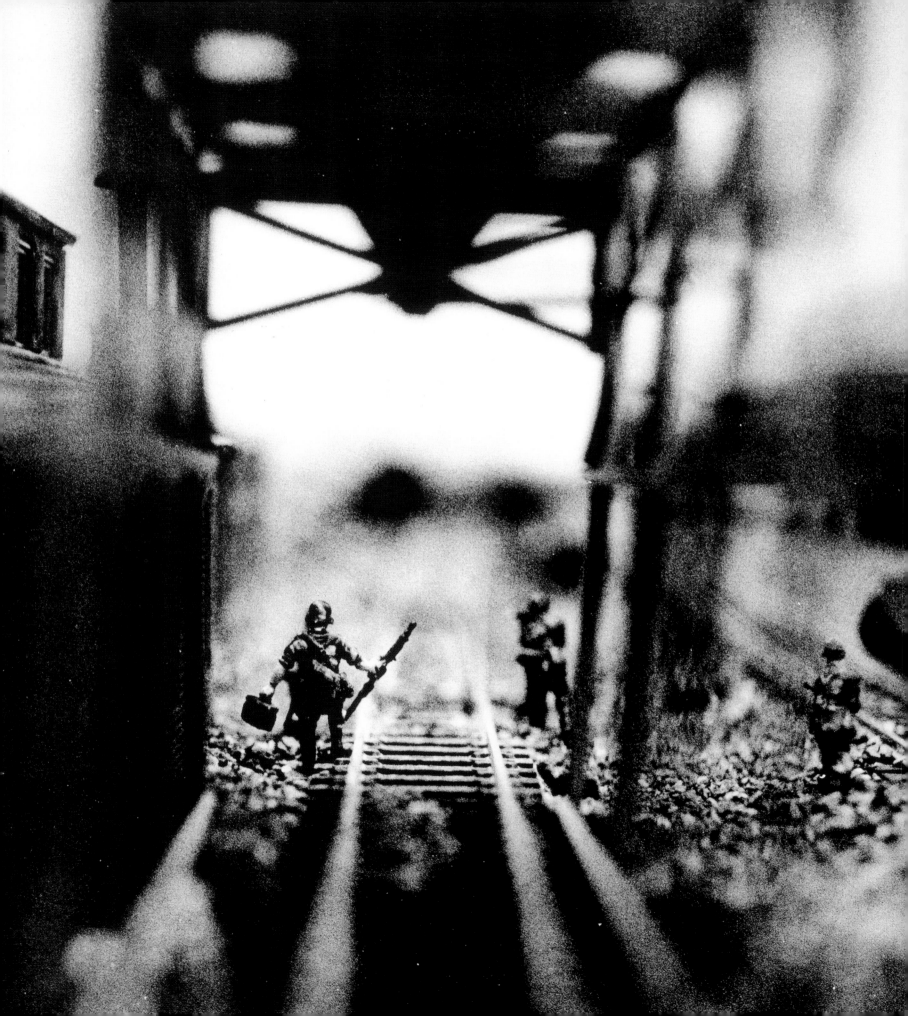

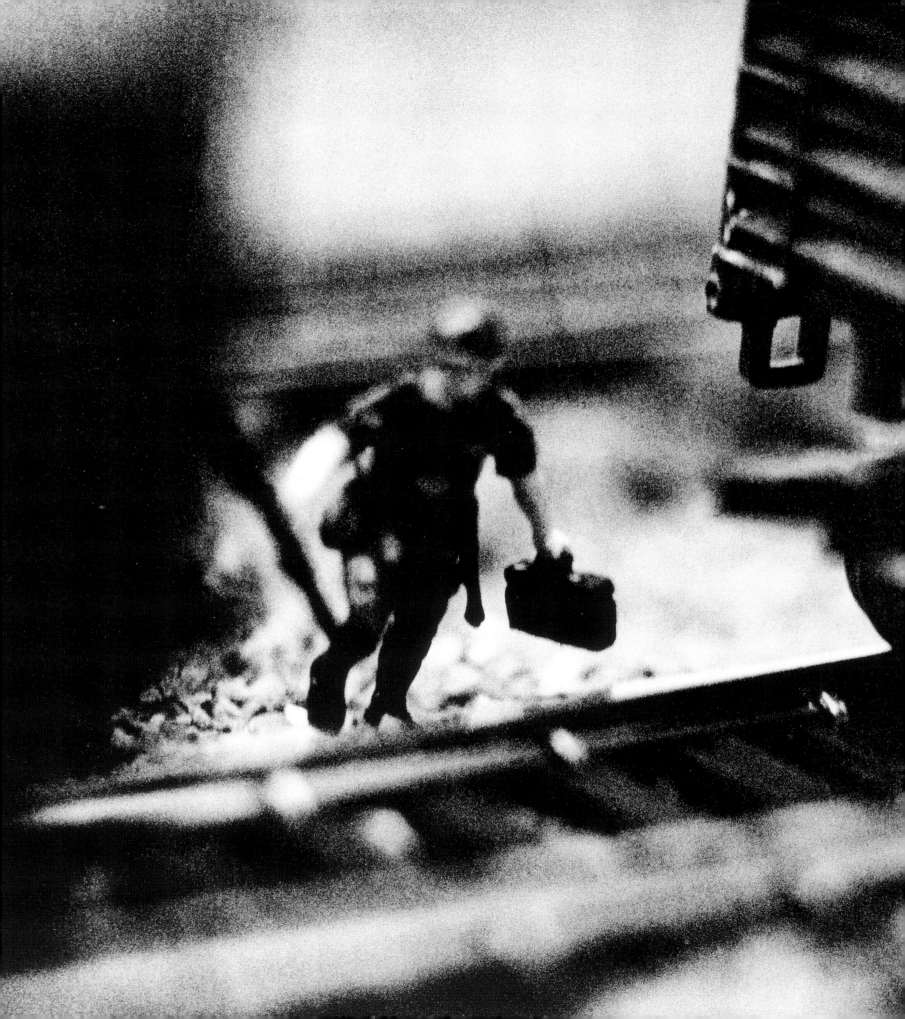

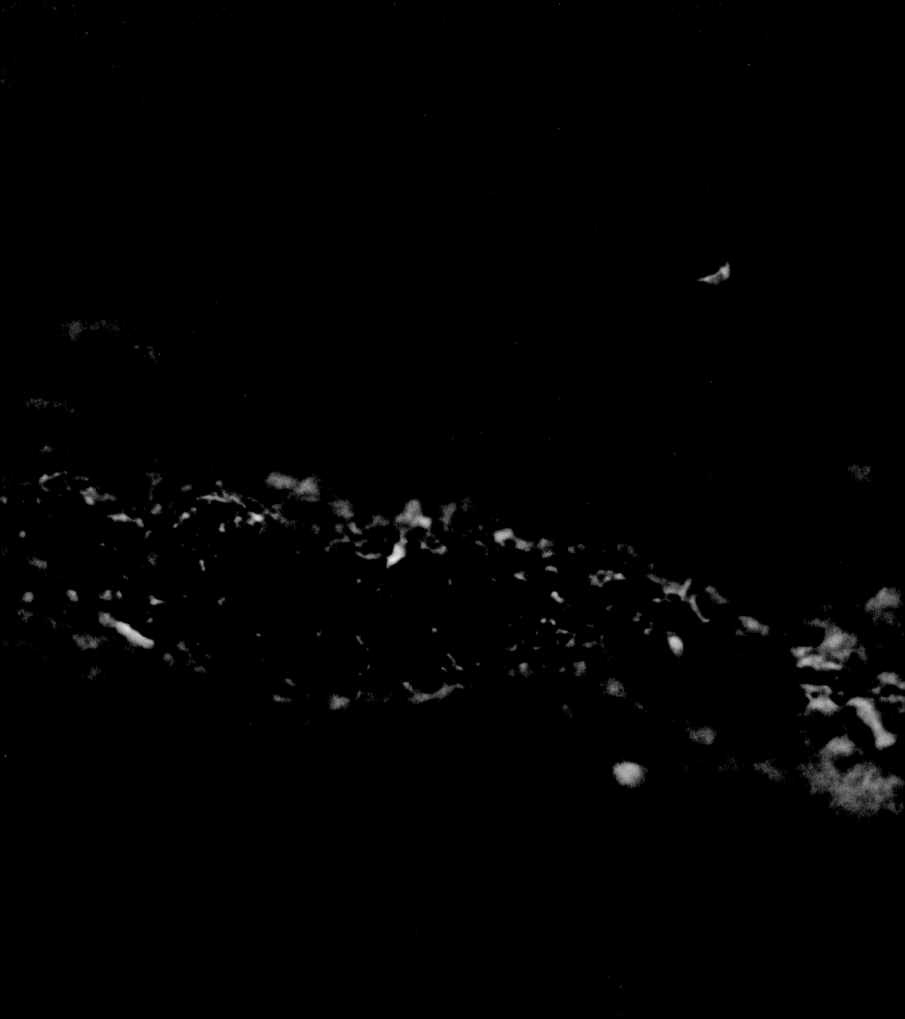

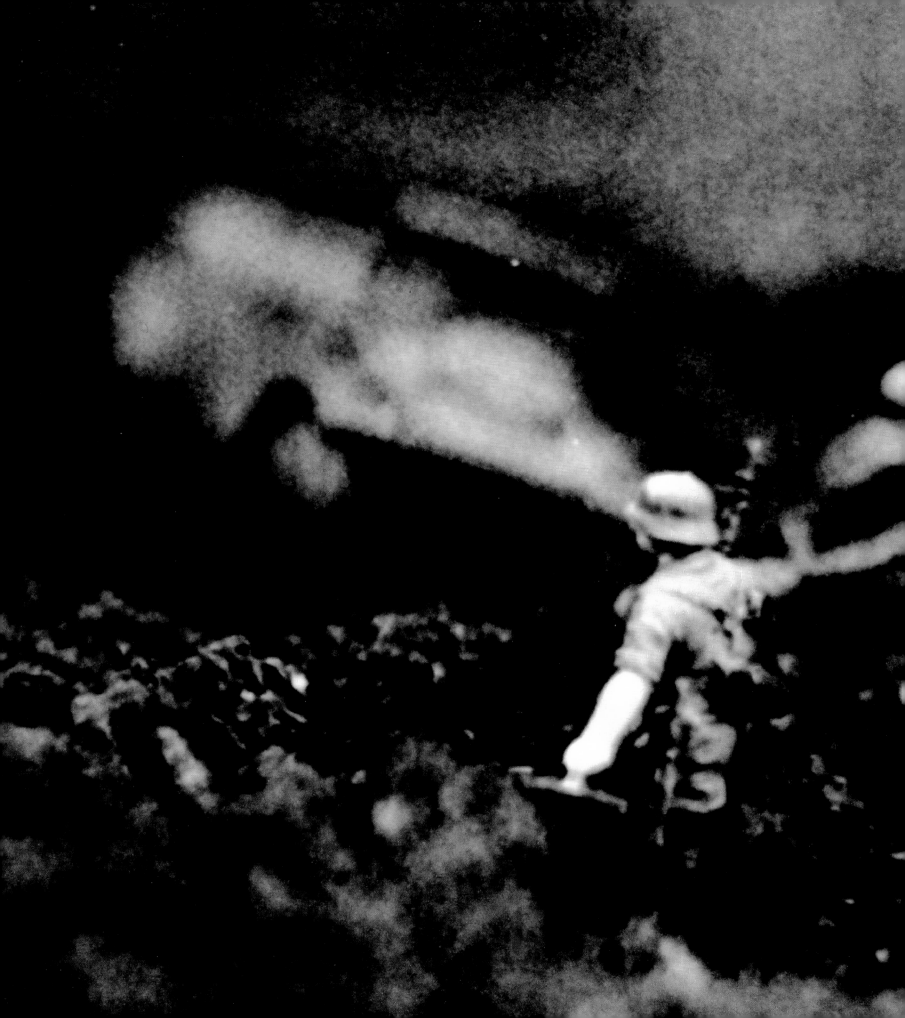

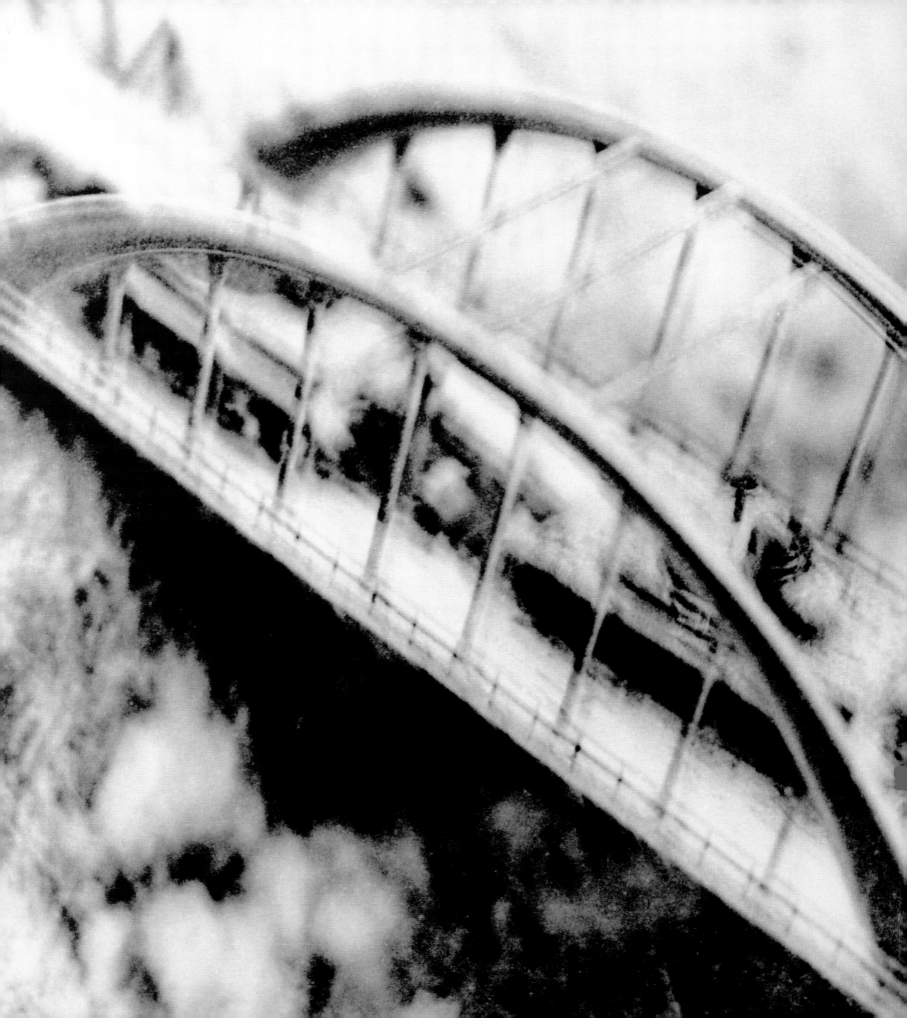

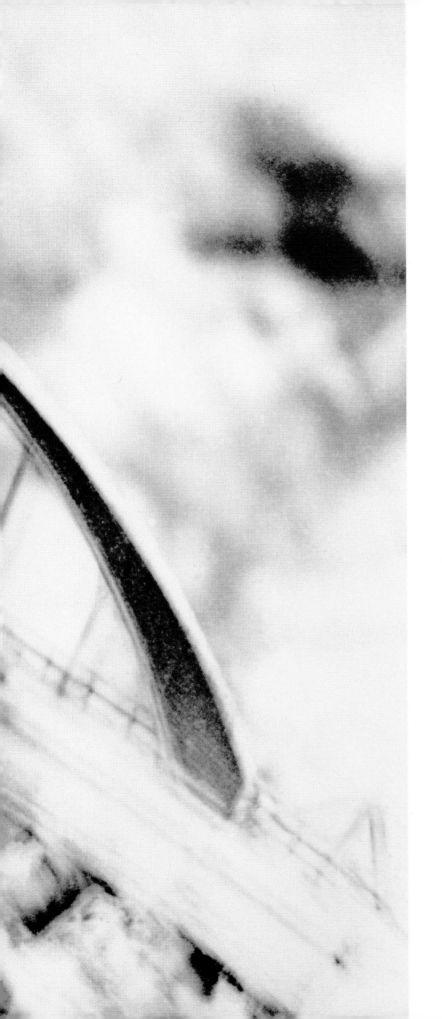

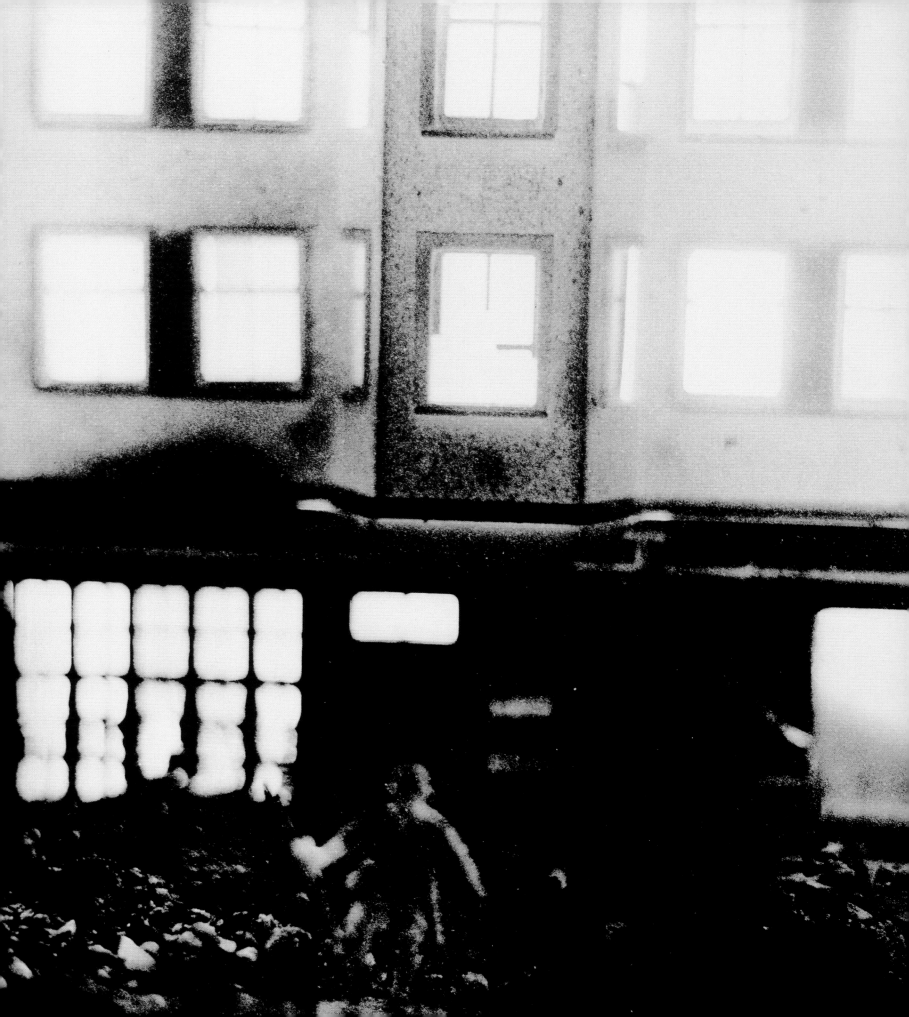

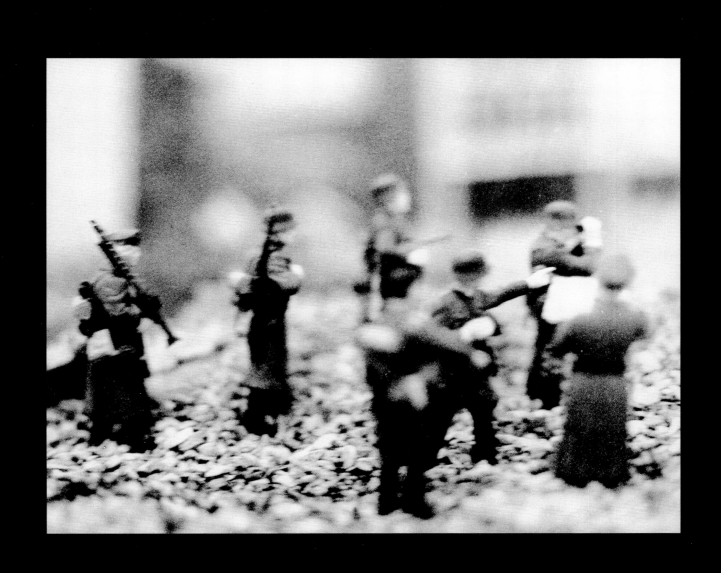

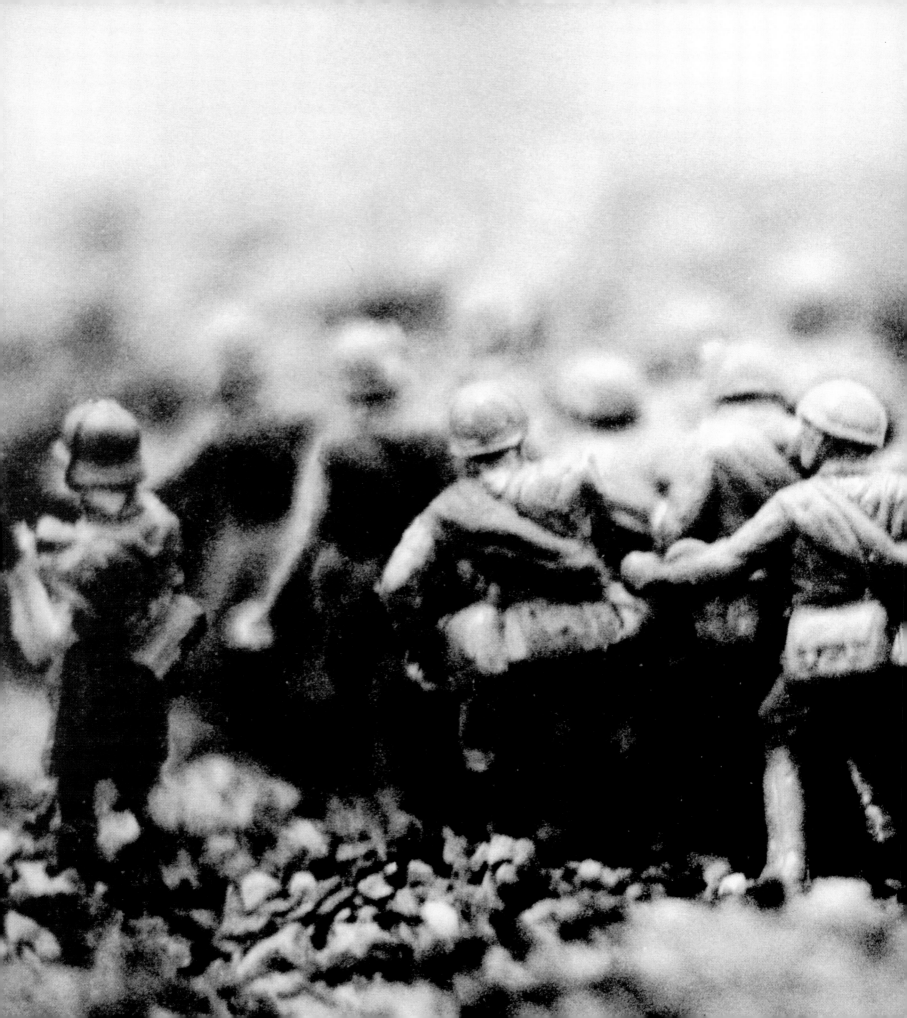

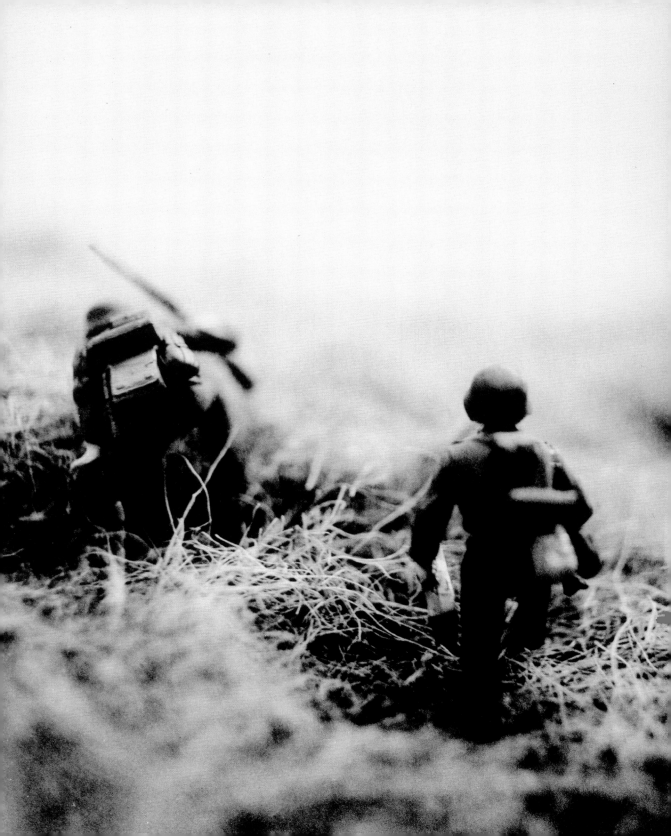

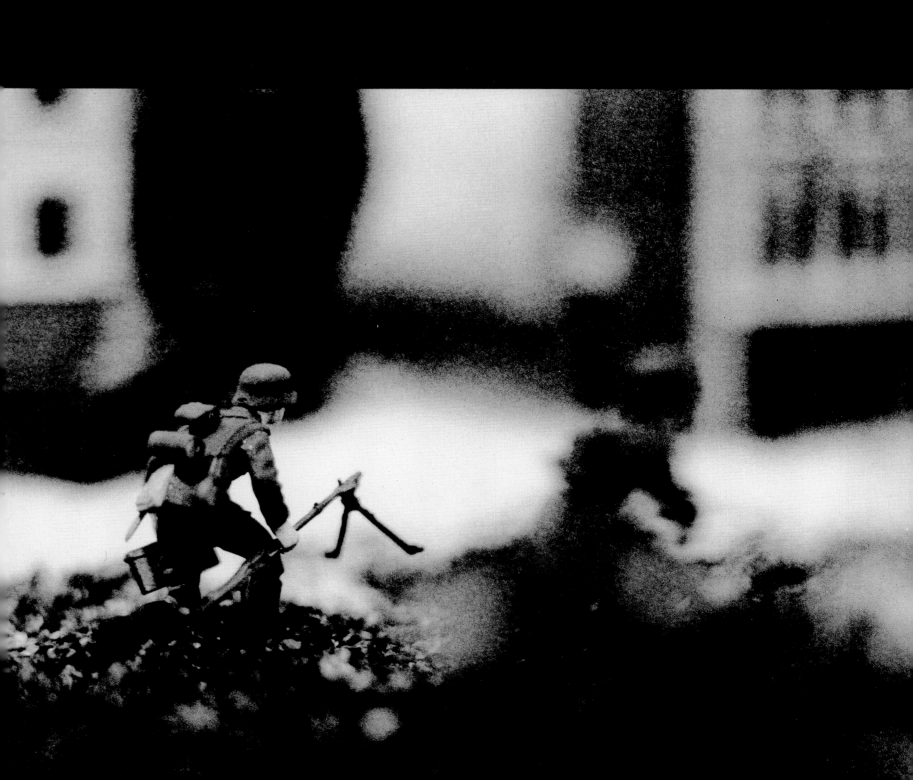

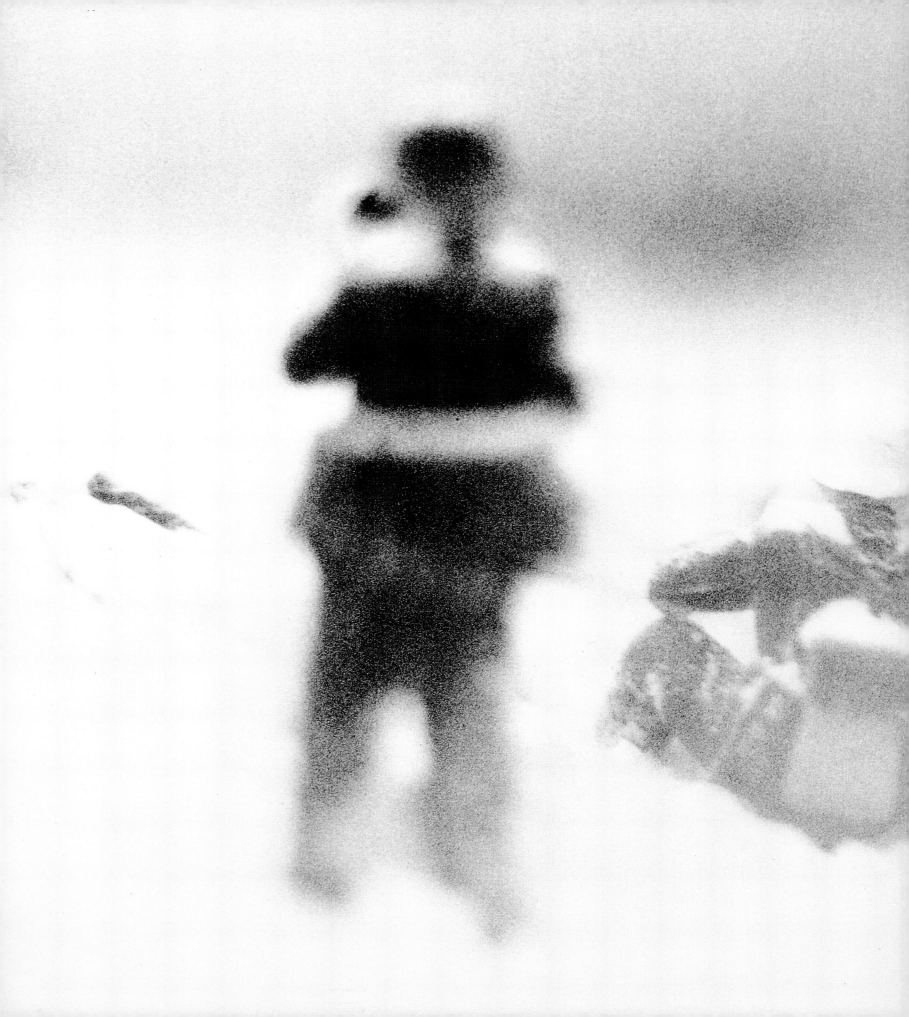

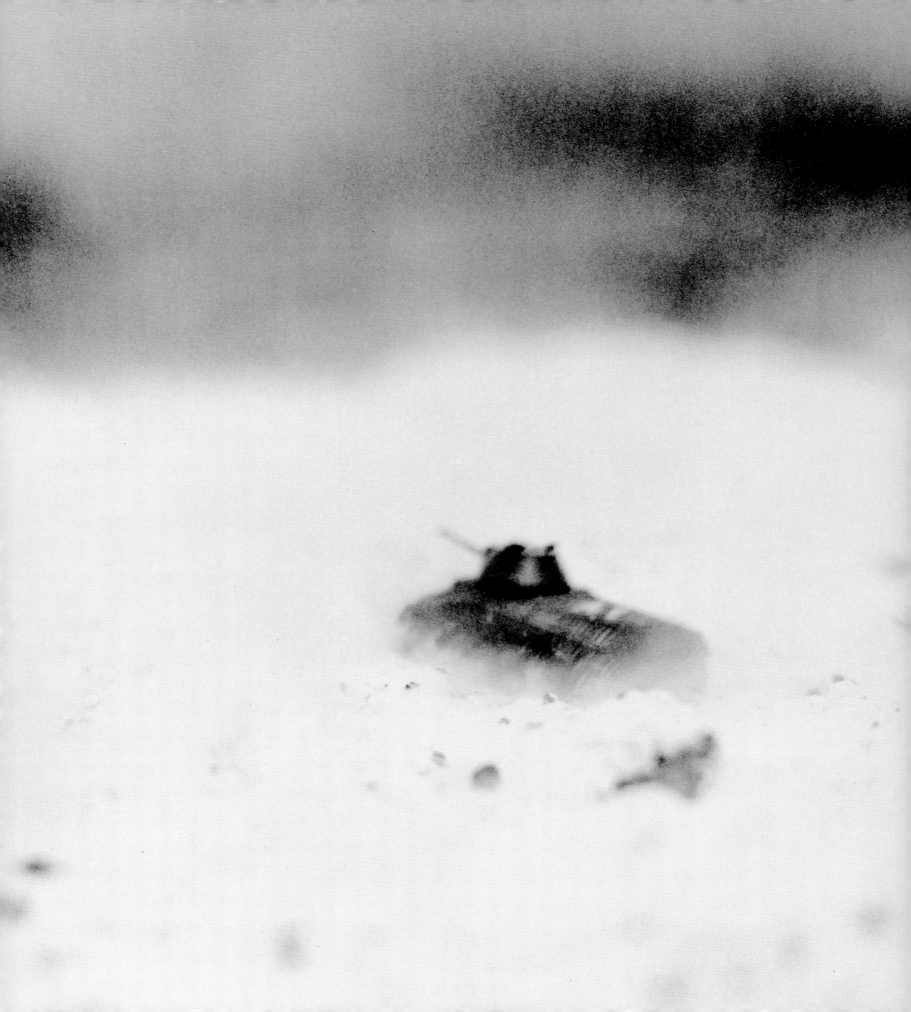

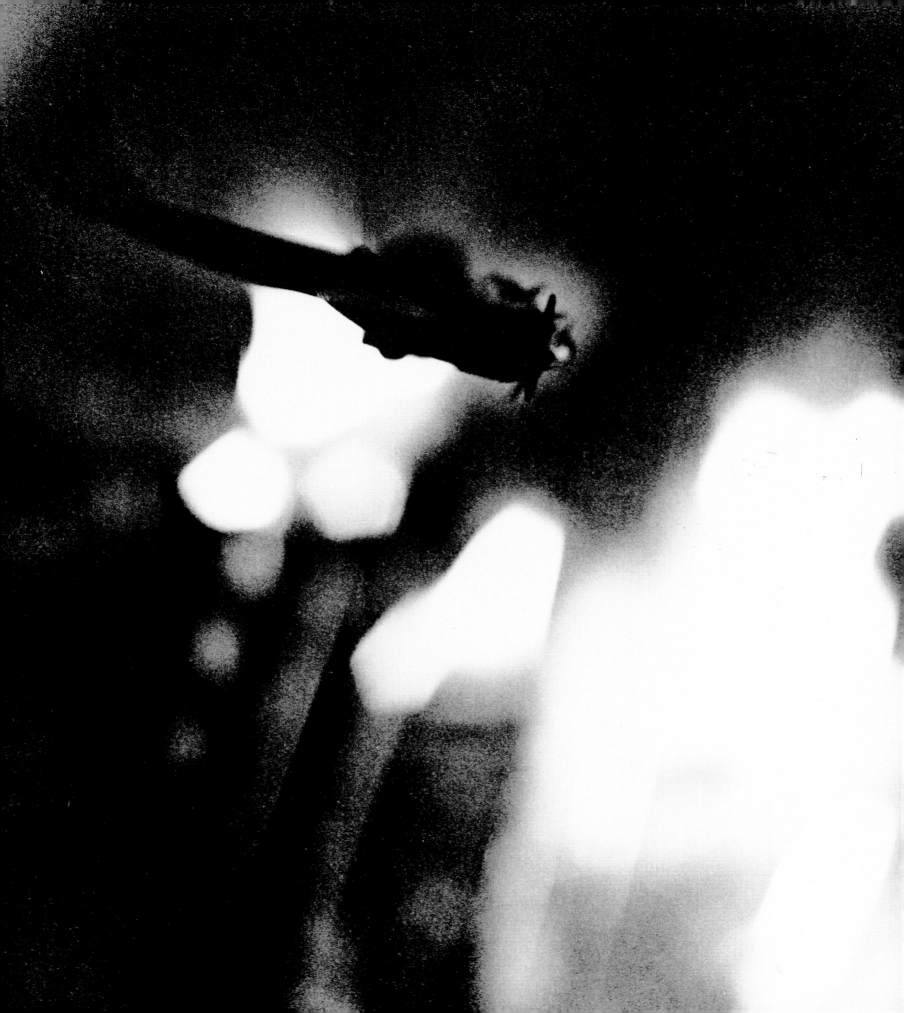

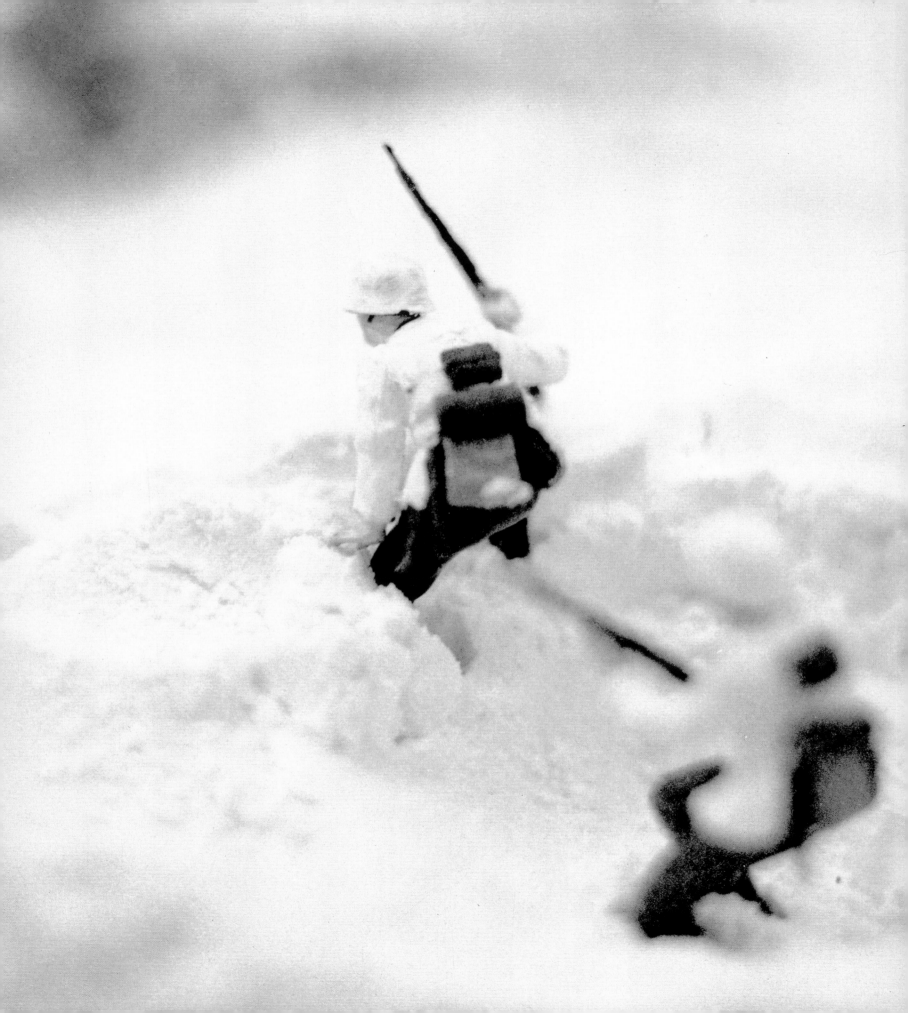

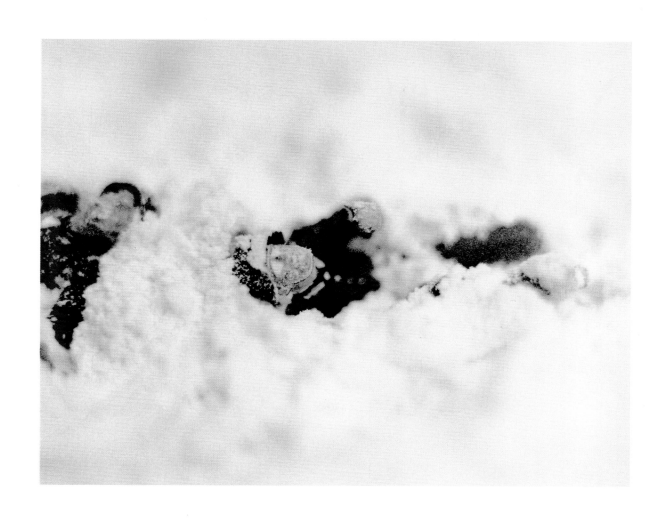

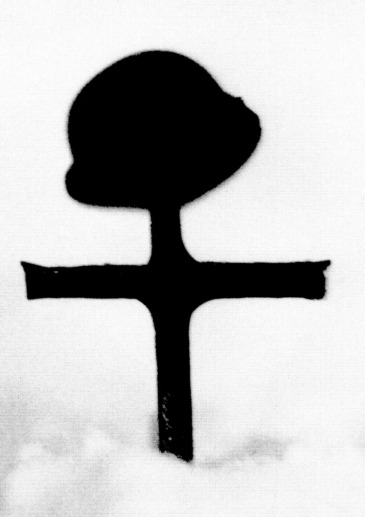

Modern Romance, 1984-86

RW: Oftentimes historical photographs, whether by W. Eugene Smith, Robert Capa, or Mathew Brady, are captioned. There's an explanation, a story that directs the viewer. Is it there in your work too, or do you allow the viewer to bring his or her own interpretation?

DL: All the objects in my photos, particularly in my most recent works, have a history. I suppose I require the viewer to know a little about that history— not of the object, but of the time it represents. If I look at "Modern Romance," for example, the series that followed "Hitler Moves East," I see Edward Hopper, and I see America in the '30s and '40s. I see a country in transition.

RW: So you make pictures about pictures and about the way we read the signs to construct a narrative. But your pictures are also about the ideology of history—the winners and the losers and who keeps score.

DL: They are. Our world is so much about pictures that talking about the world means talking about pictures. I was always fascinated by artificial constructs, generally. Going to Disneyland is all about that—the small-scale architectural models, the blatant artificiality.

RW: You obviously like the special effects "wizardry" of photography.

DL: I especially like the Polaroid camera, because you can lose the sense of scale as completely as you do in a movie. Viewers have no idea what size the figure actually is. The "Modern Romance" series is the best example of that. The figures are tiny, but because I photographed them off of a video screen they almost look like film stills.

CS: Is "Modern Romance" the only series taken entirely indoors?

DL: Some of the images were taken in an outdoor setting, but most of it was shot in a closed space. I wanted to create Hopper-like rooms with shadowy corners. The imagery is based almost entirely on film noir and Hopper. Somebody once said to me that my work reminded them of a film still in which something had happened and something is about to happen. The photograph is that moment in between.

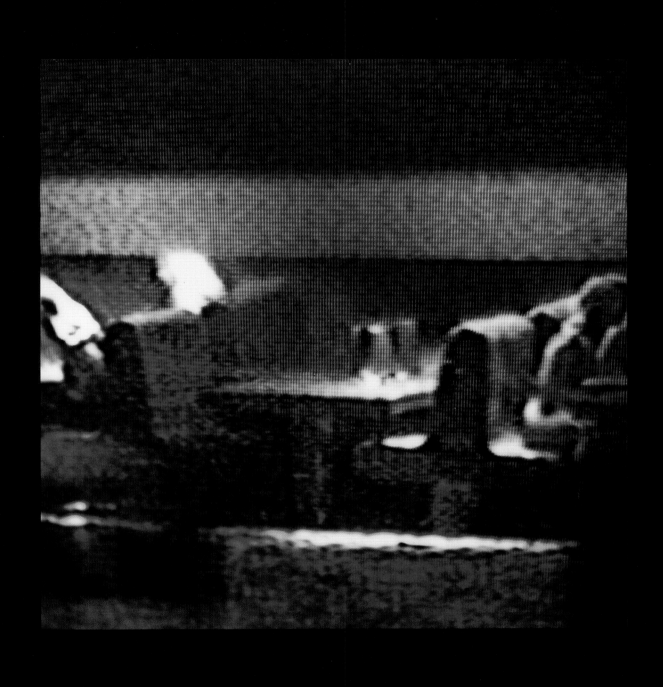

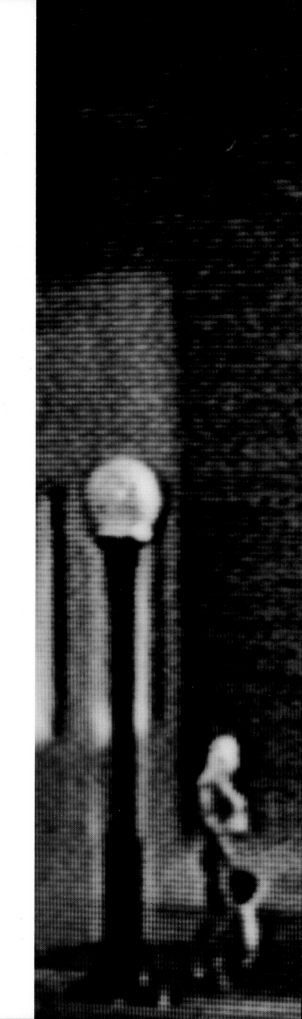

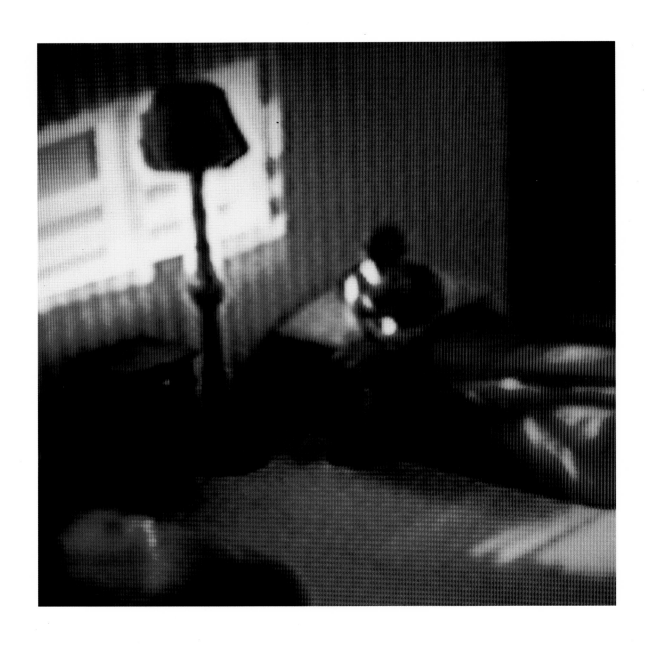

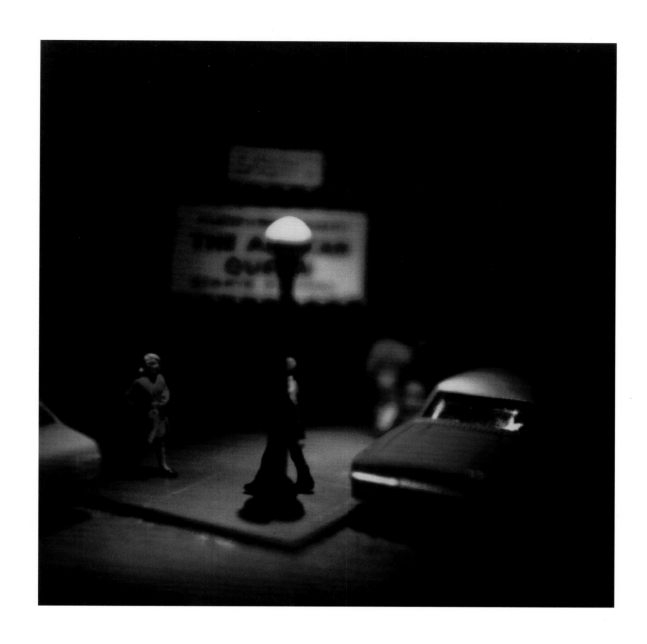

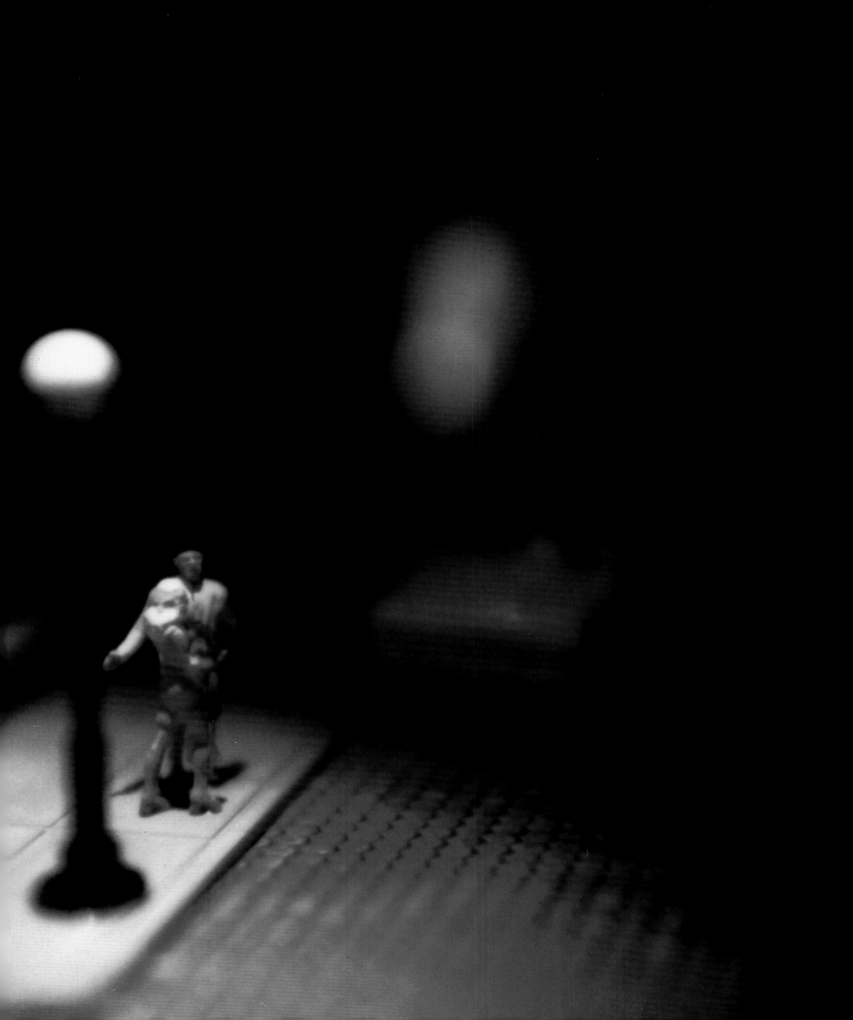

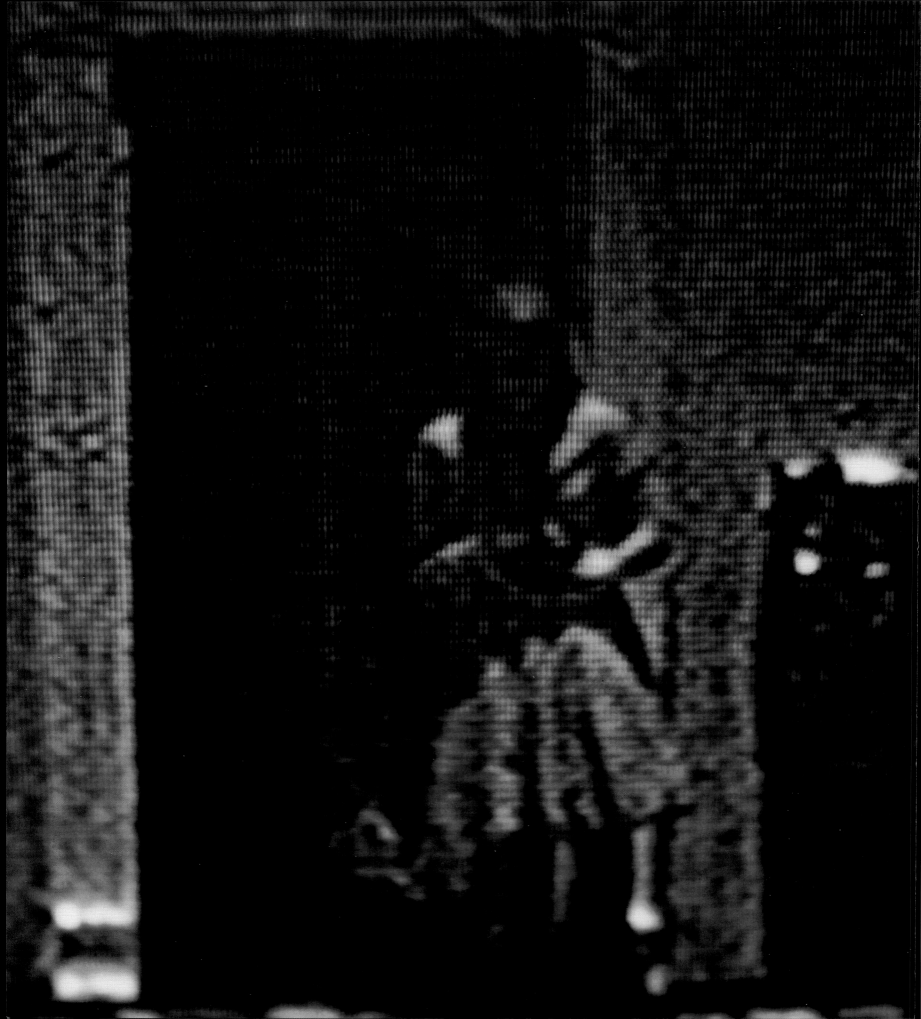

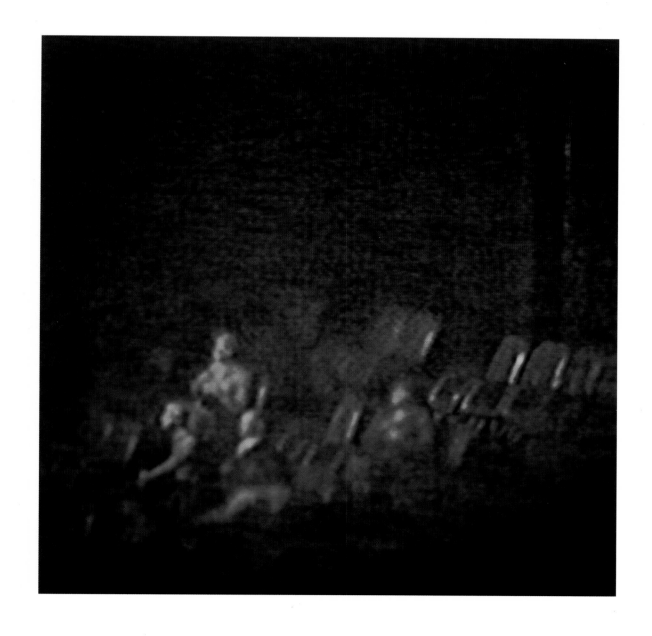

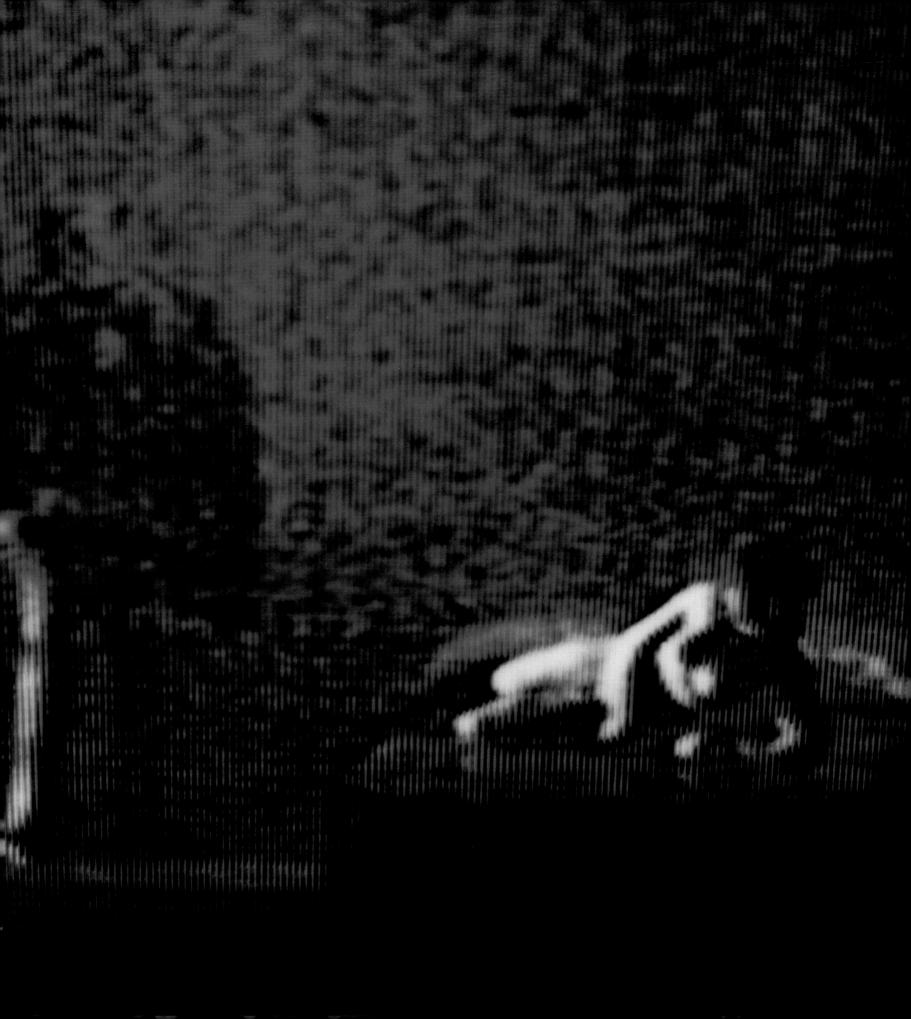

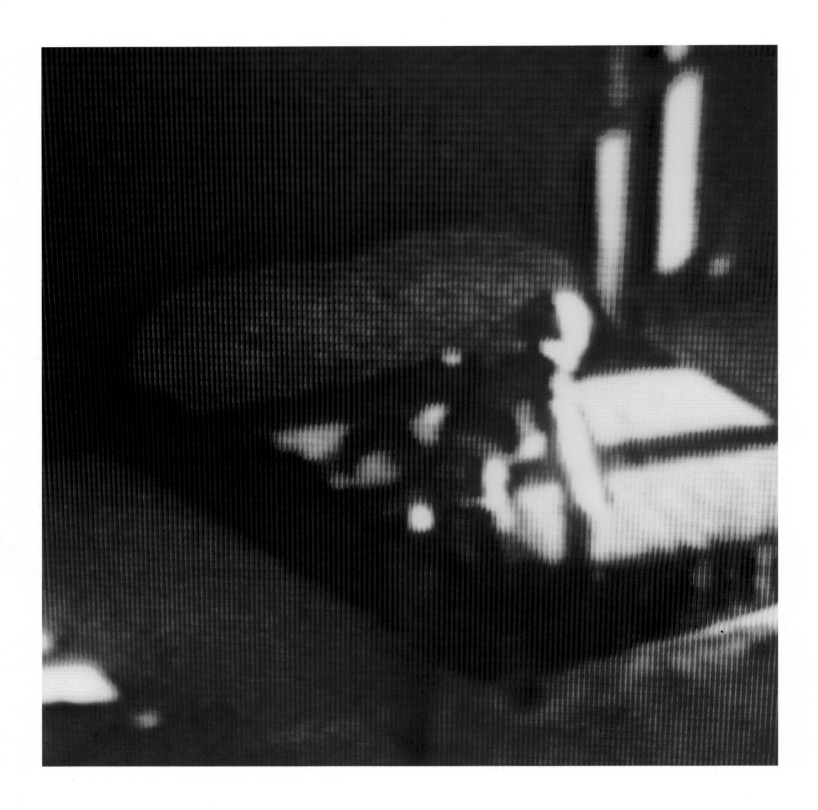

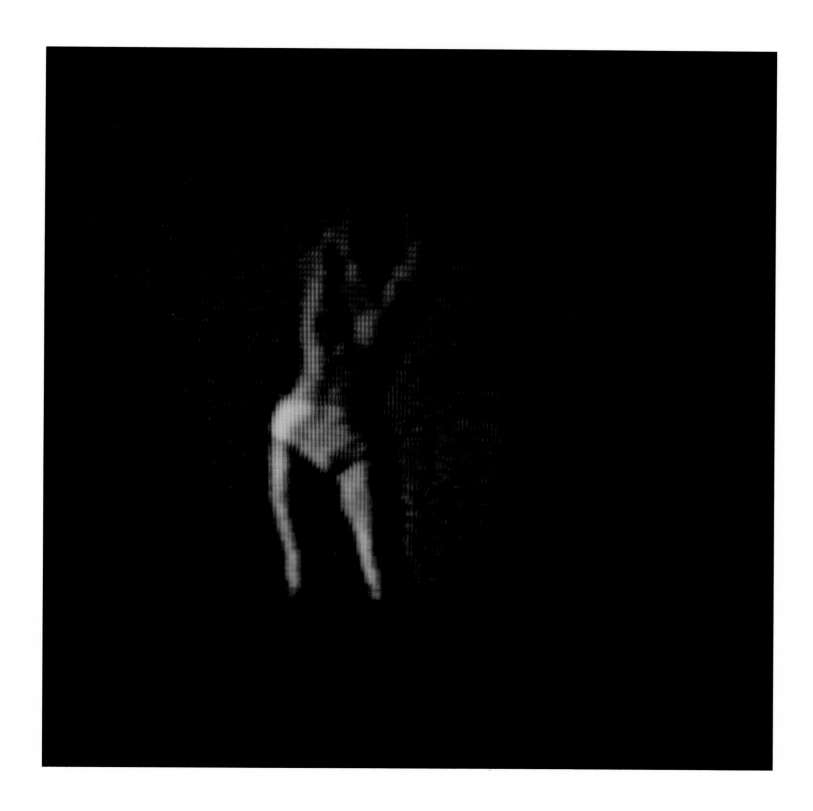

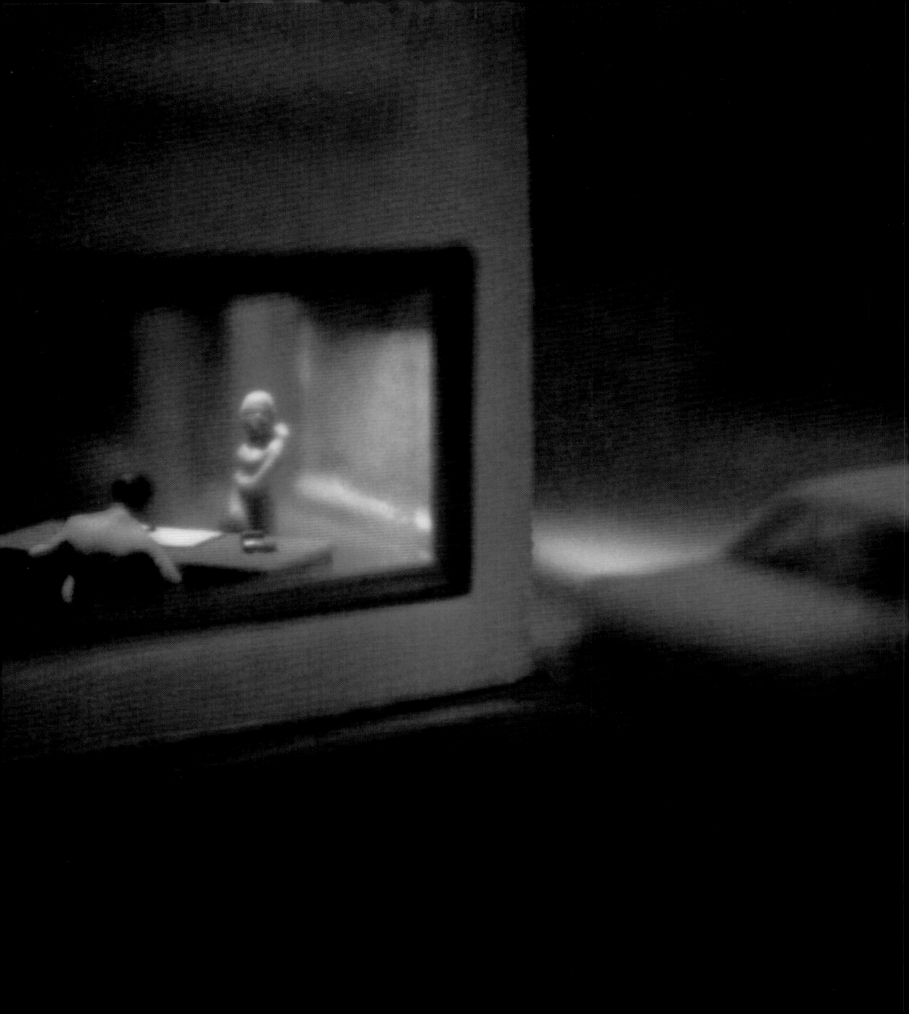

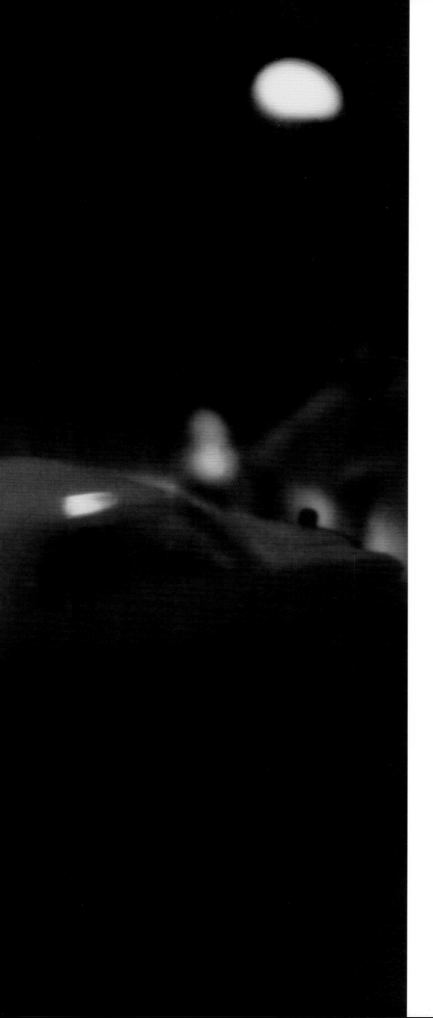

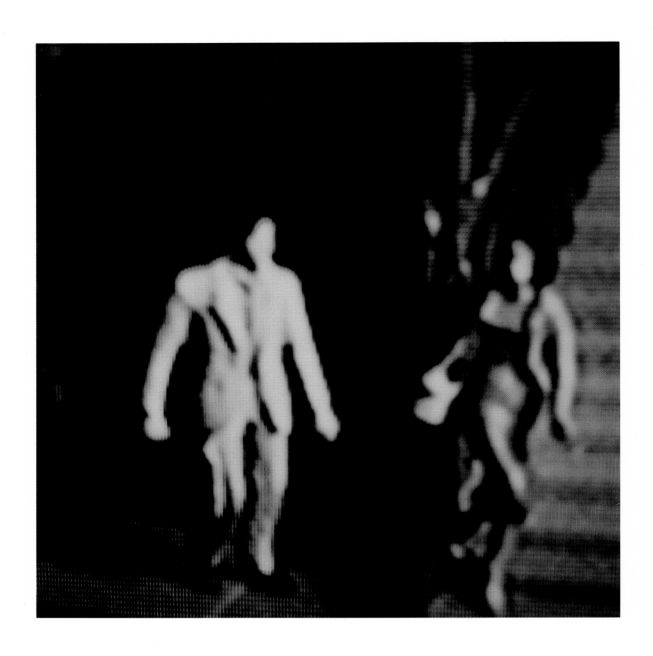

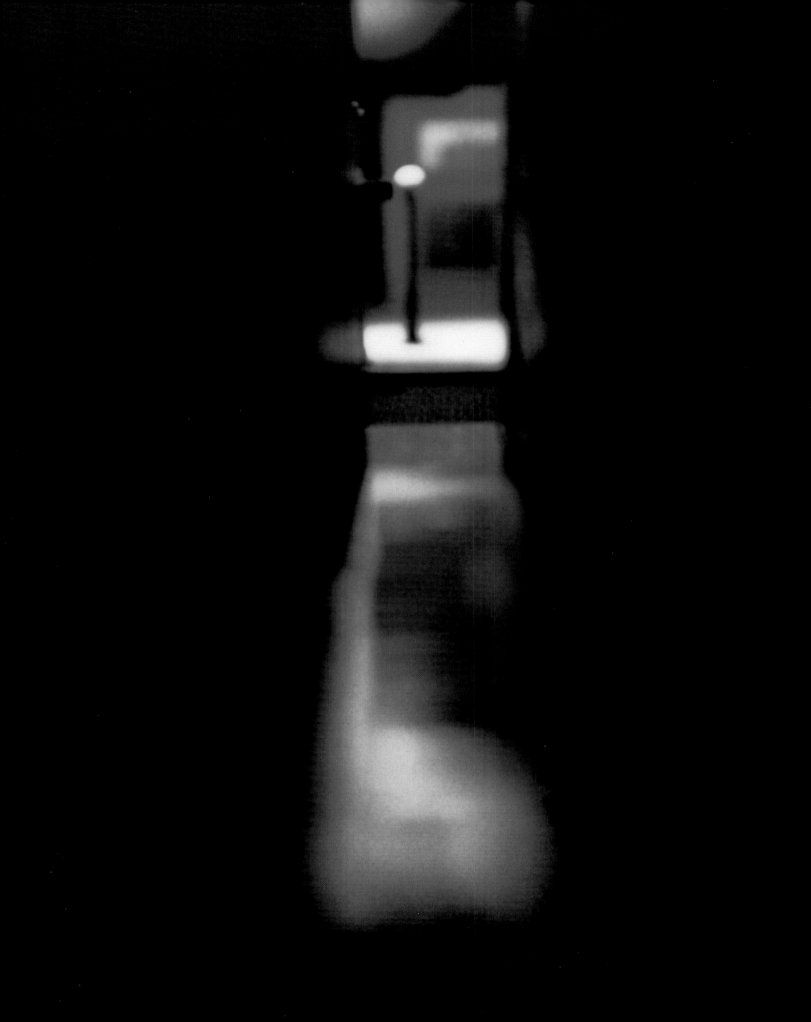

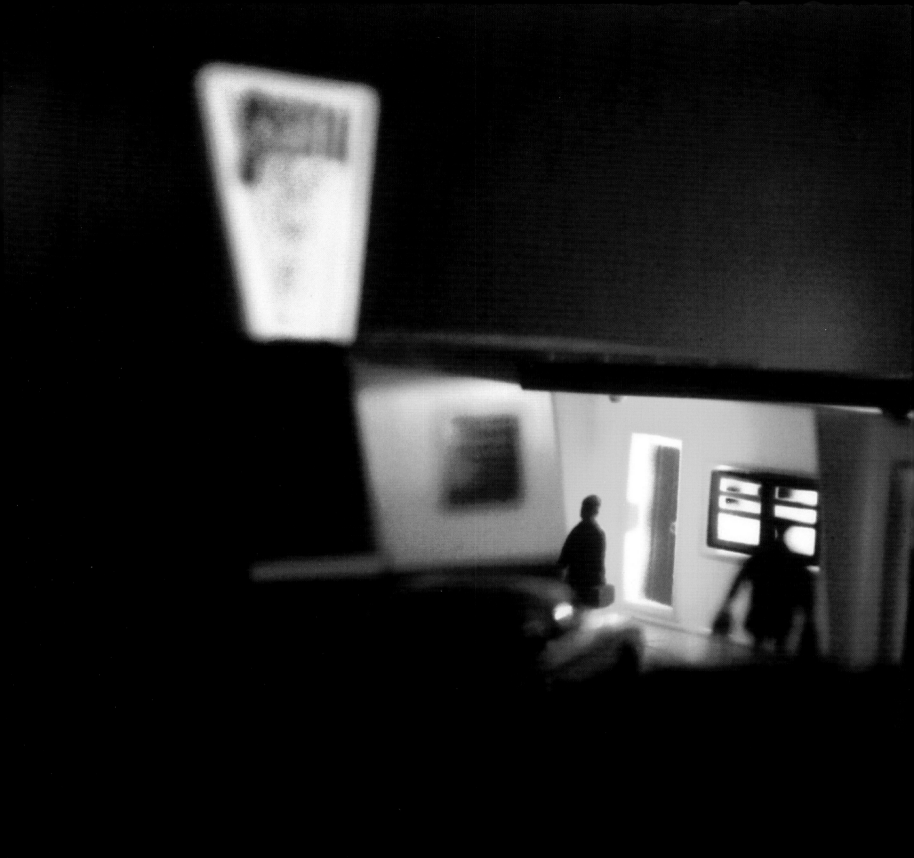

THE WILD WEST, 1987-89

RW: Photography is so much about facial expression, the head shot. Yet you almost never show the face.
Does showing the face of a toy figure dispel the illusion?

DL: They look better if I don't show the faces. It's an aesthetic question. In some works I generated images that were both sensuous and horrible with dolls whose faces were so badly done that I couldn't have photographed them clearly. The cowboy series became at once more abstract and more active by not photographing the faces. The figures are standing still, of course, yet they have such a sense of movement. It really looks as though the cowboy's lasso is whipping around, or the cowboy on horseback is galloping across the plain.

CS: In the "Wild West" series you, in a sense, restore the viewer's faith in the product.
We've all learned that the toys are never going to be as animated as they look on the box,
then you come along....

DL: I make them look the way we imagined them, or hoped they would look. The little boxes of plastic soldiers advertised on the back of comic books look so colorful, and then you get them and there are only two colors of plastic: the colonials are blue and the British are red and that's it. I'm supplying the life. I'm animating them, they become as real as any documentary on television.

RW: We were talking once about a photography show that was going to feature artists and their muses—
Stieglitz and O'Keeffe, Paul and Rebecca Strand, Harry and Eleanor Callahan—and you said, only half-flippantly,
that if you were ever included in this pantheon of couples, the show would have to feature pictures of you
with your television set.

DL: Too true, I'm afraid. (Laughs.) I've always said that I'm a voyeur. I was born in 1949 and I'm part of that generation that grew up with television as more than just a novelty. It was omnipresent. I remember watching kids' shows before I went to school and then coming home and, after playing outside, watching some more TV. I think my "Wild West" series reflects the pervasiveness of the Western myth during that time on television.

RW: For you, it doesn't come out of Remington paintings, at least not directly.

DL: No. It was from Saturday afternoon television. During the '50s, half of the top-rated shows were Westerns. They still had serials in those days. Or look at the toys in Sears catalogs from the '50s, with page after page of holster sets—Hopalong Cassidy, Roy Rogers, and the generic ones. The television culture was very important to me.

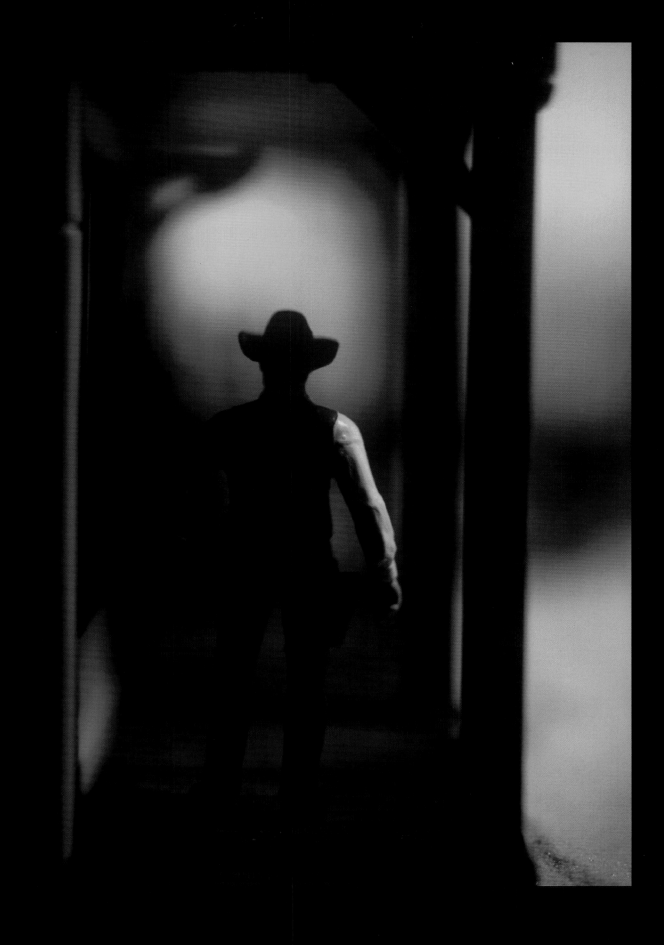

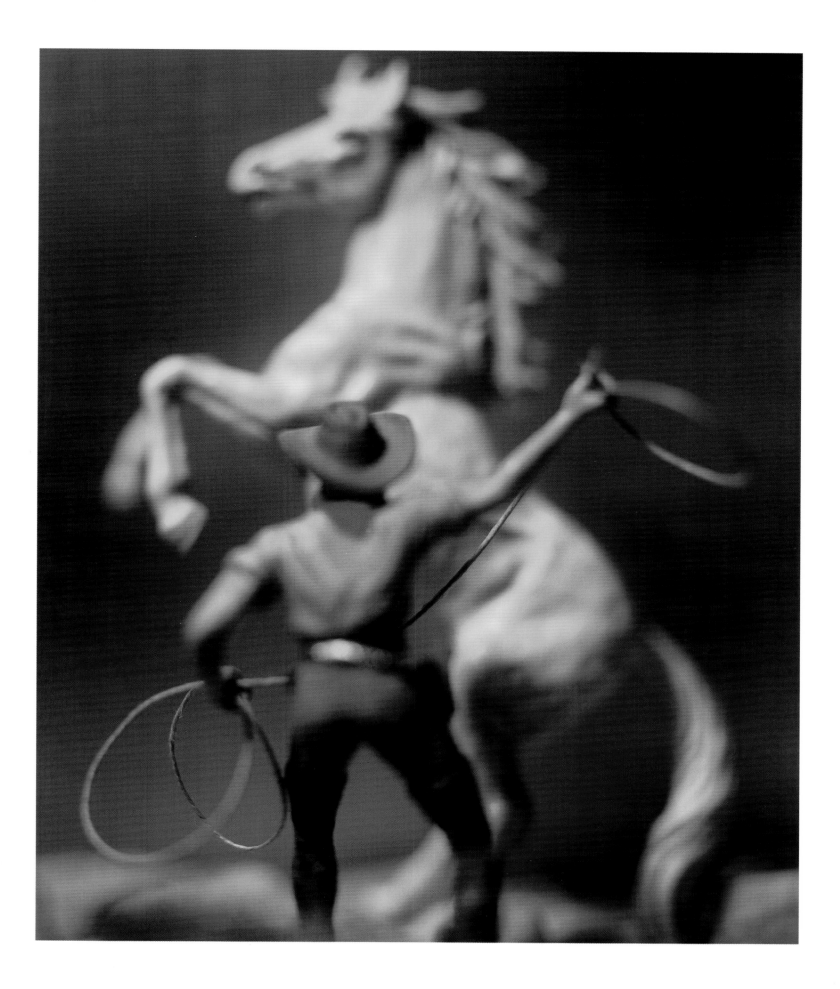

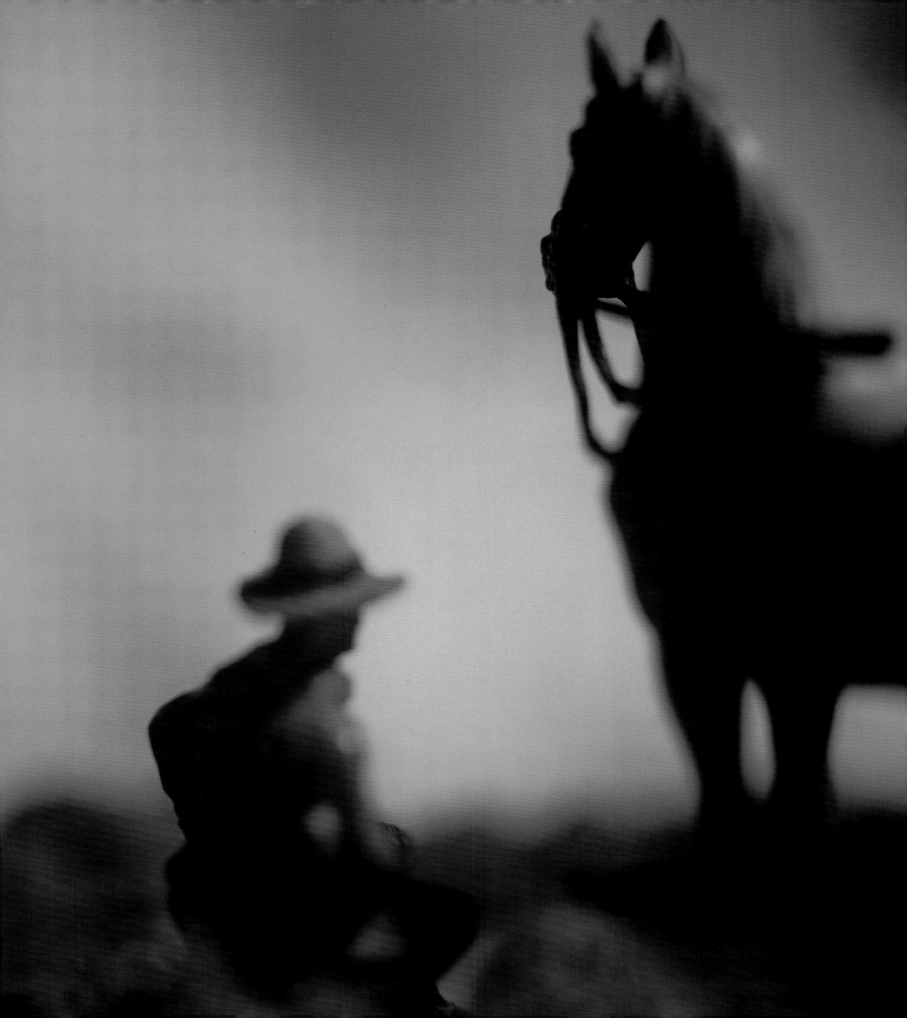

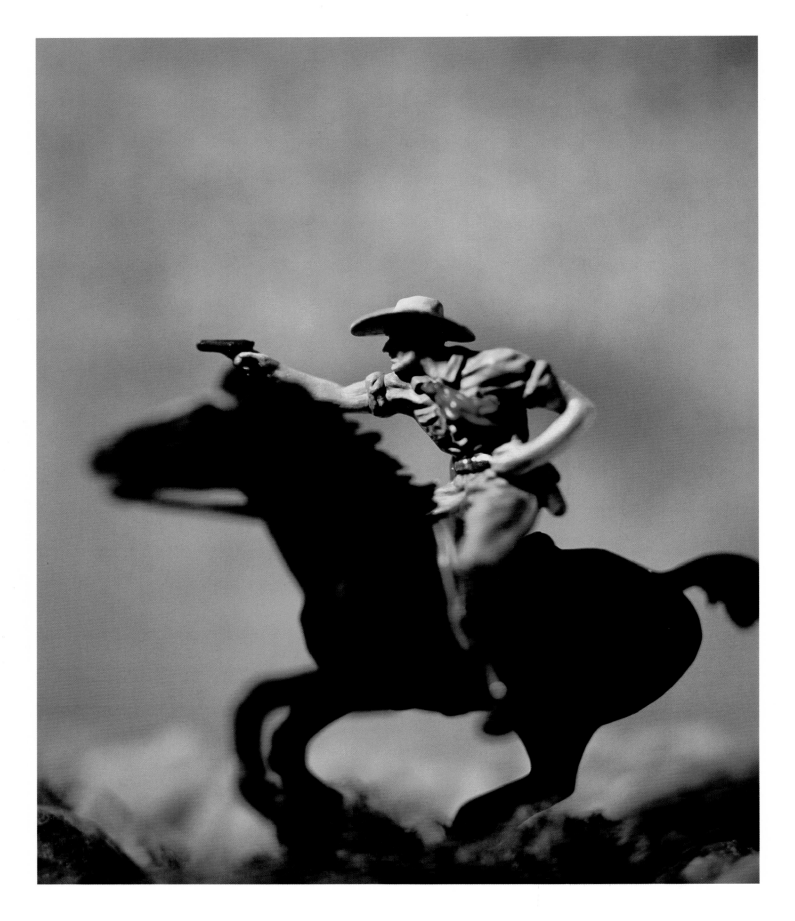

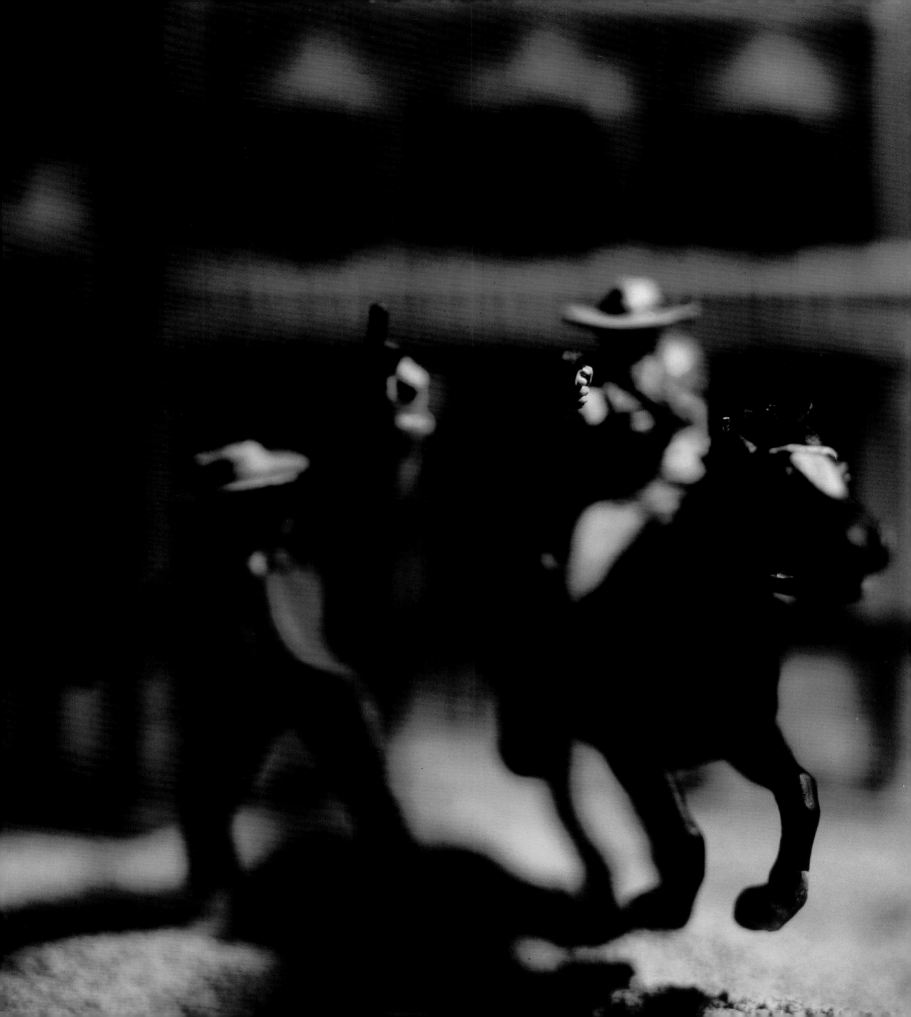

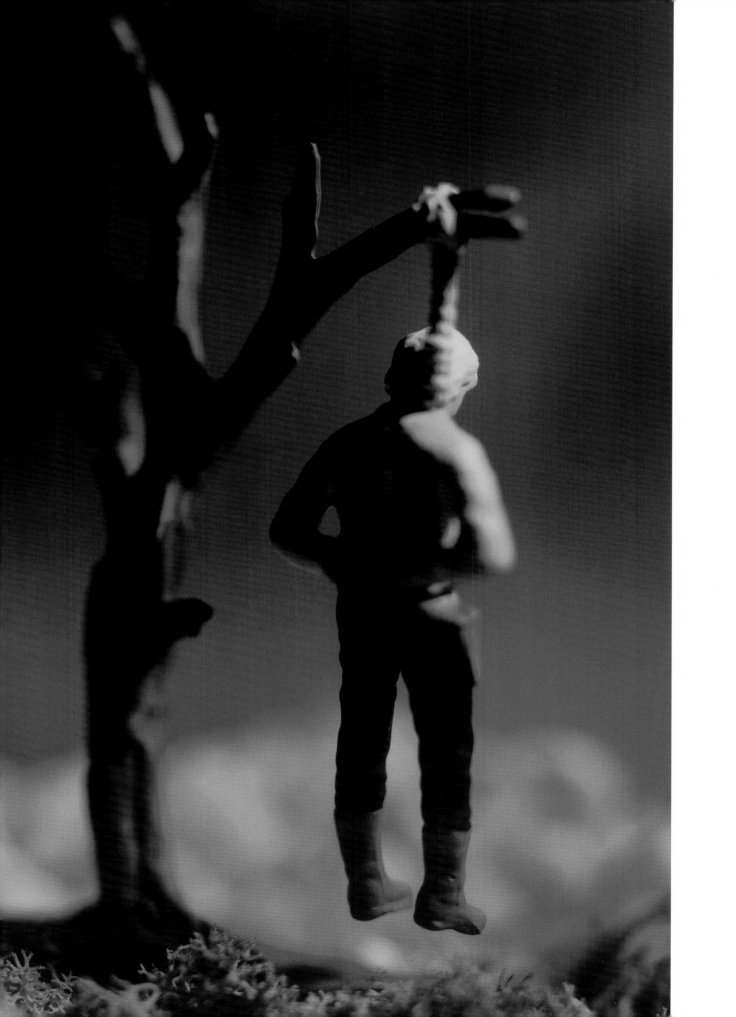

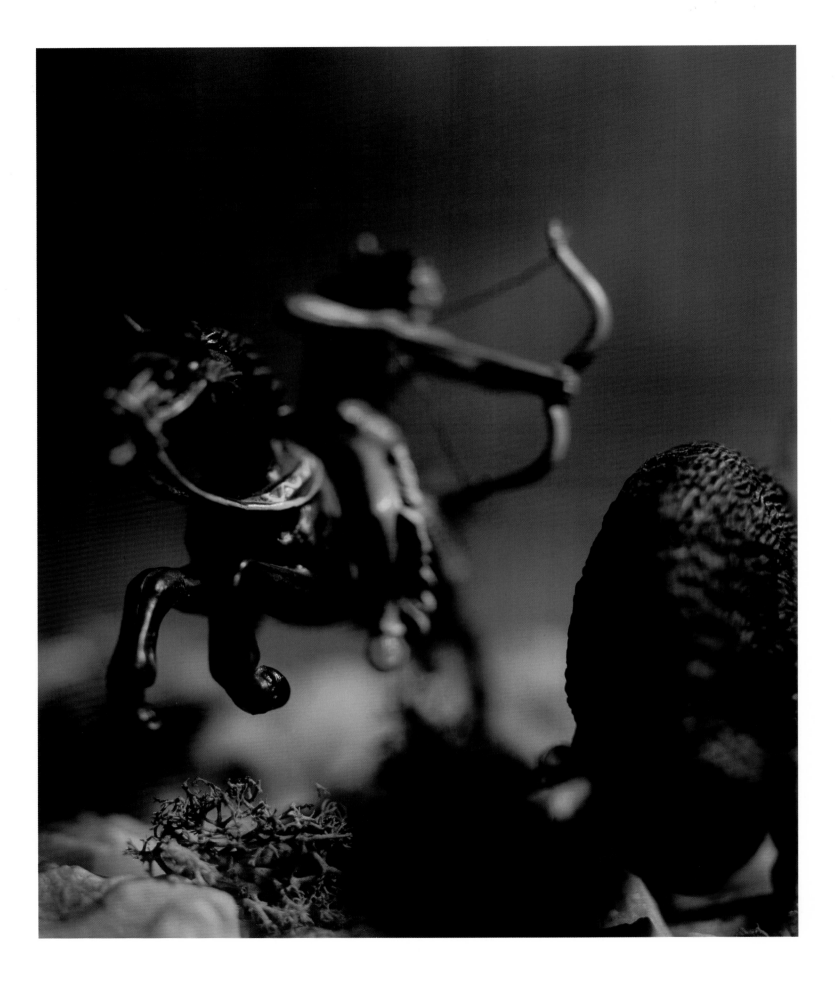

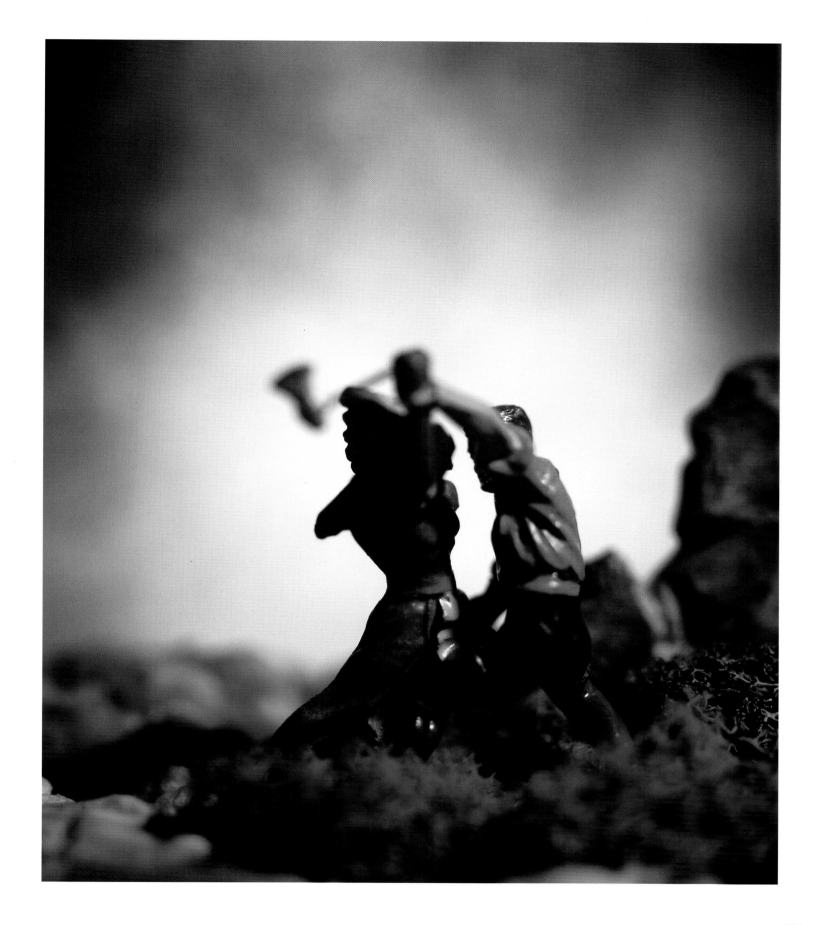

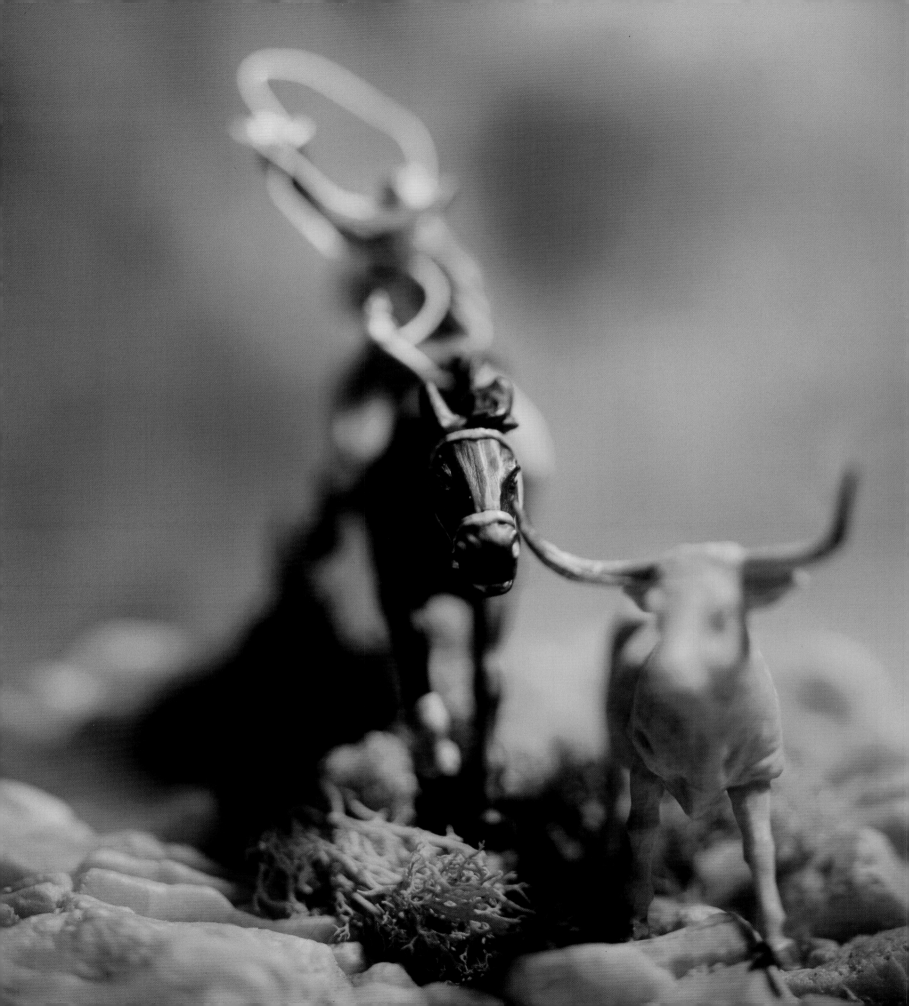

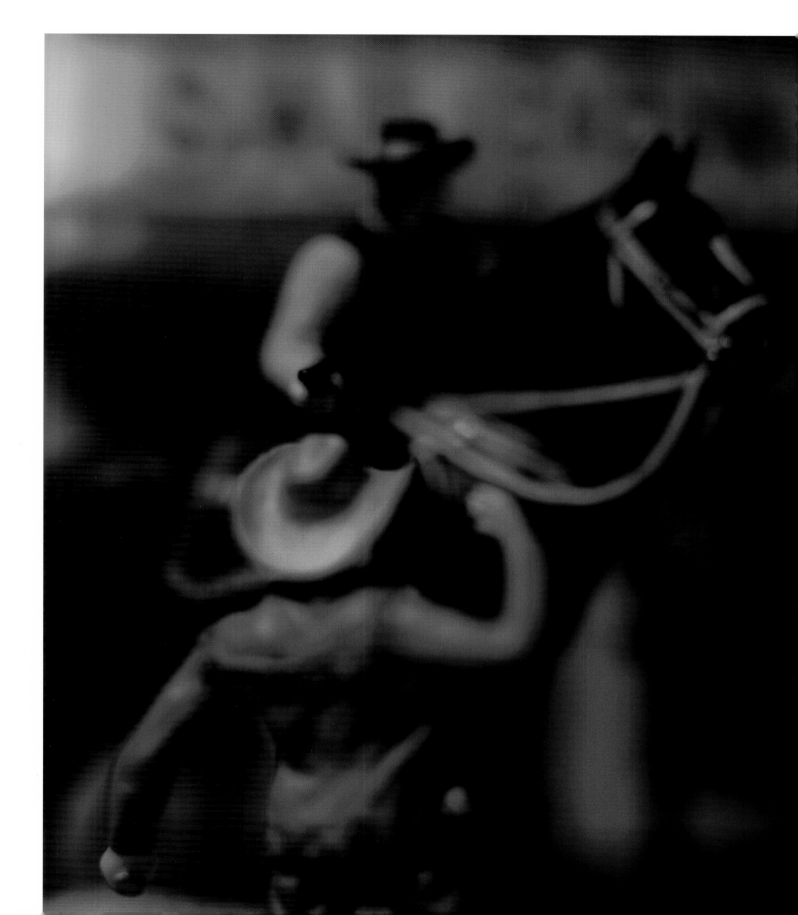

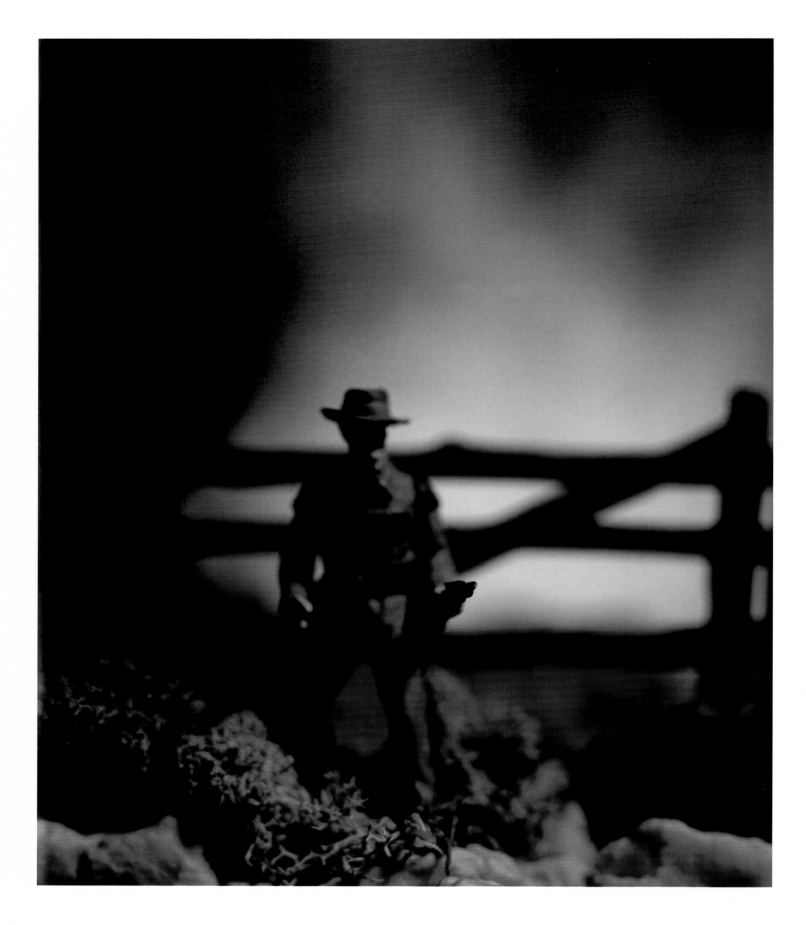

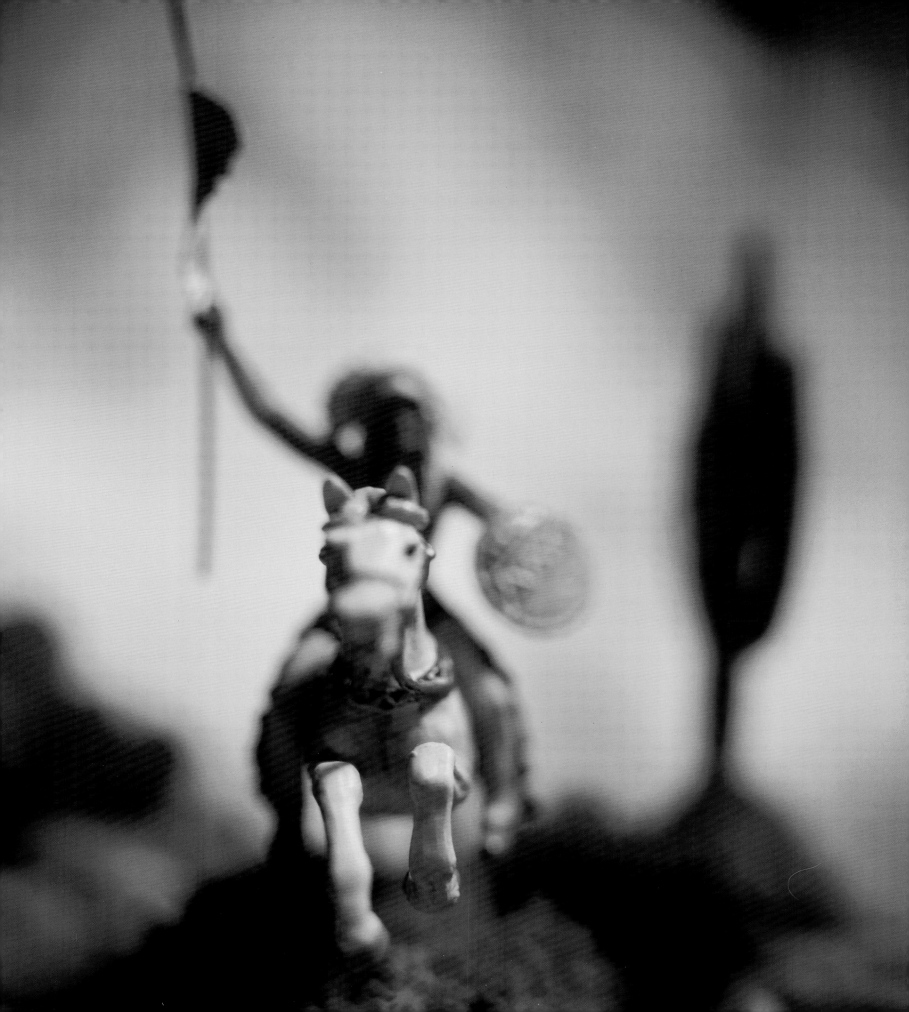

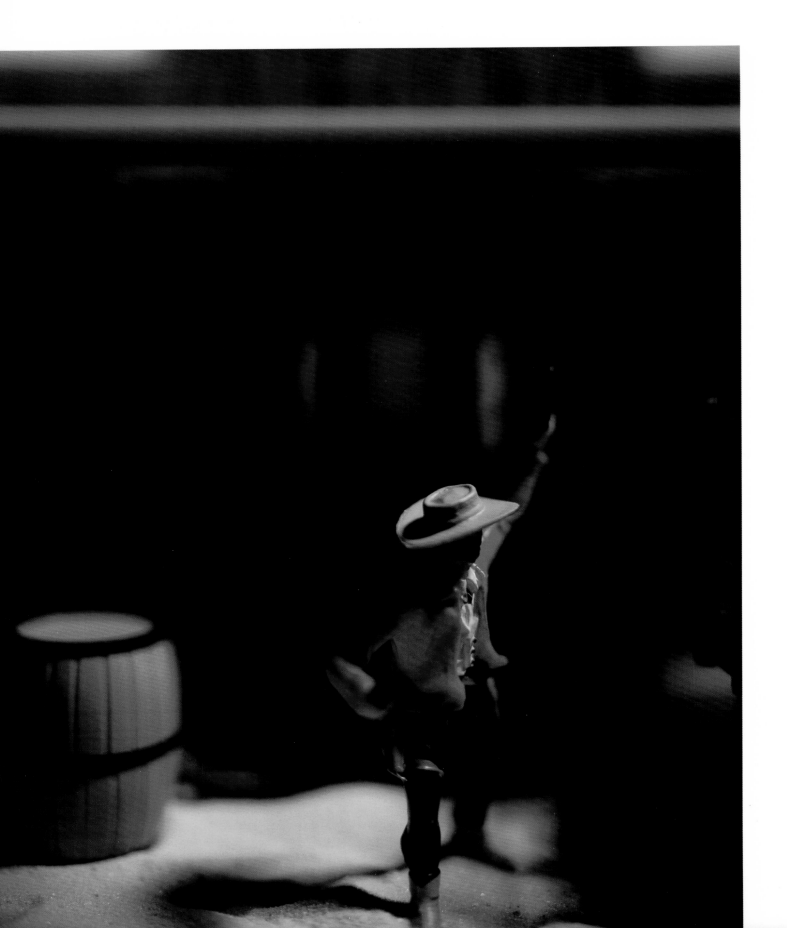

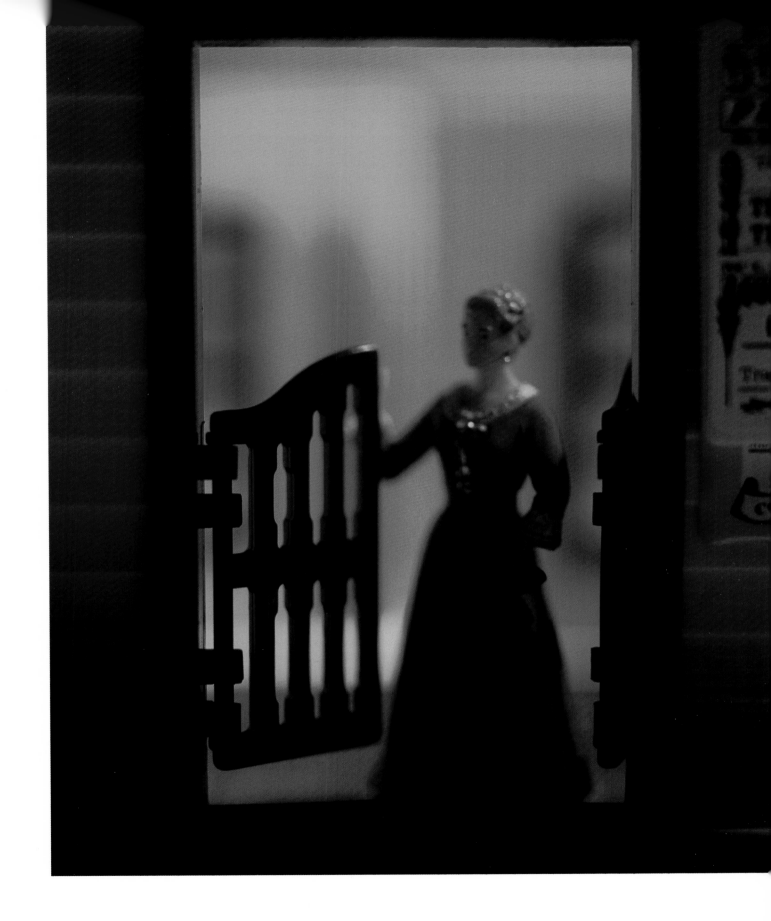

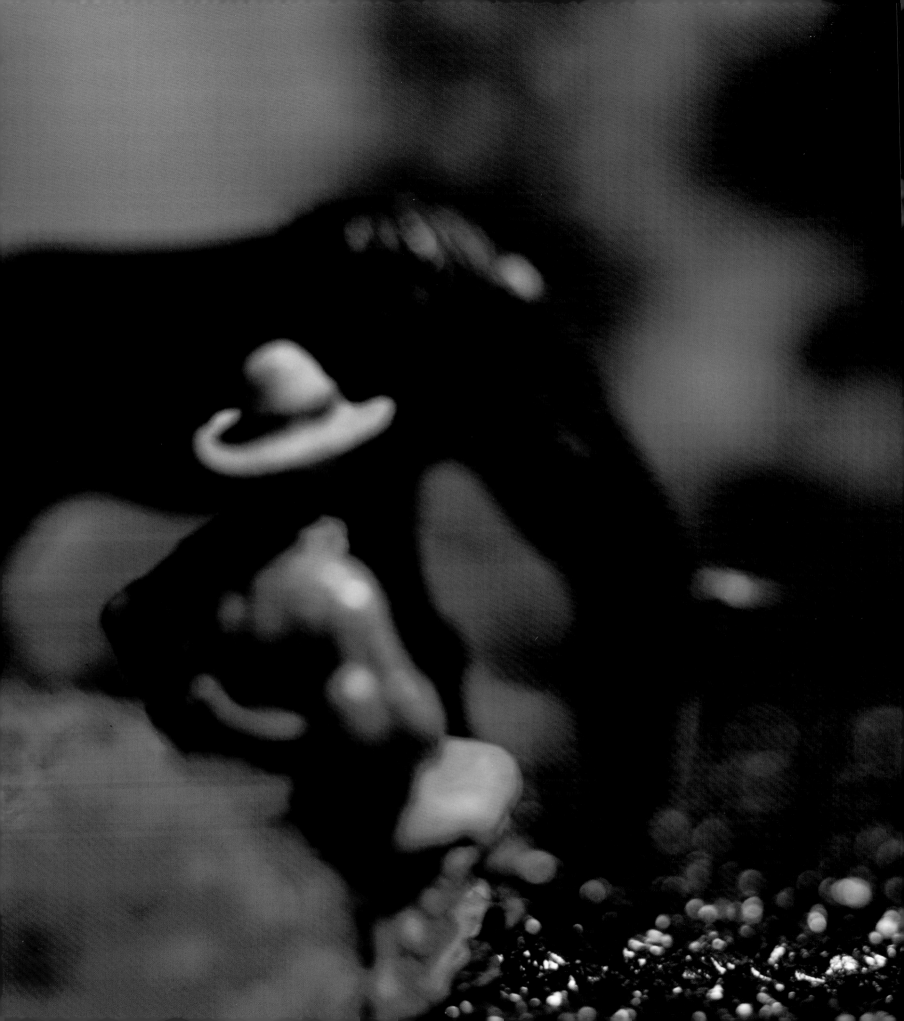

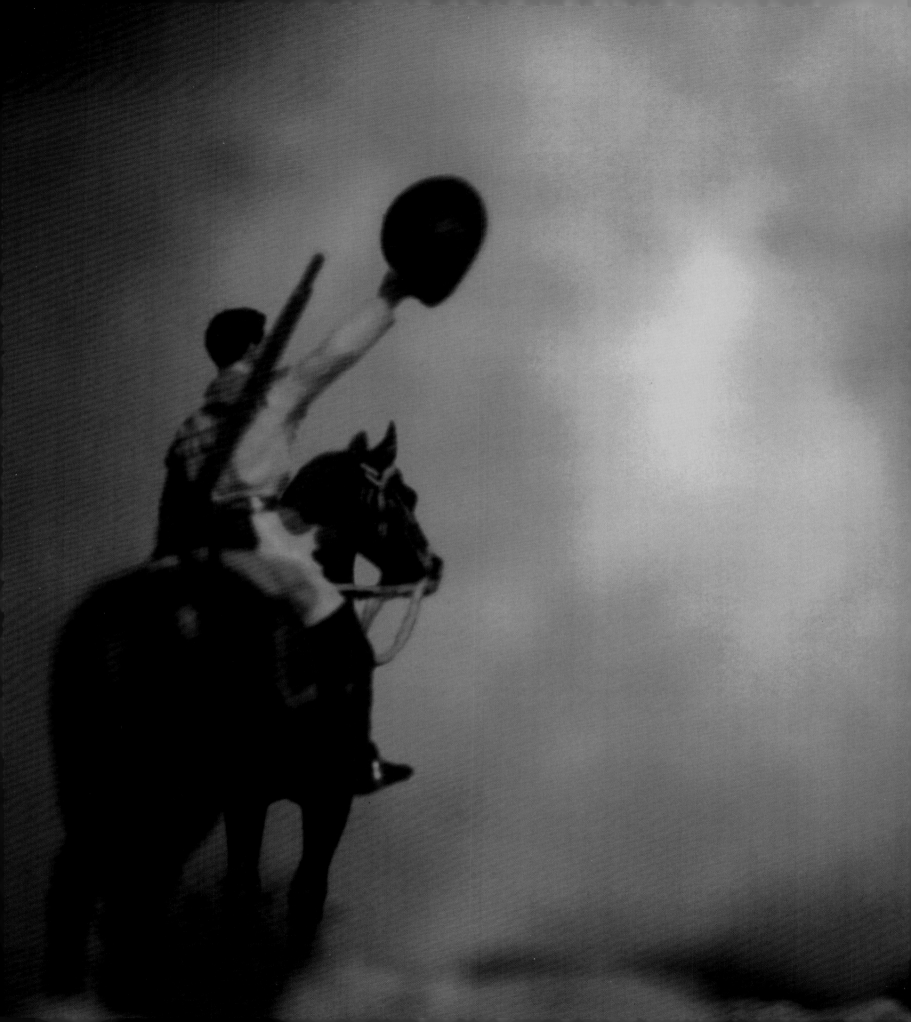

American Beauties, 1989-90

RW: Describe the origins of "American Beauties."

DL: I found one of the figures in a flea market, got a few more from a dealer, then they sat in my toy inventory for about a year. One day, after I had finished shooting the cowboy material, I tried a couple of set-ups. I didn't know if they would work as images.

CS: You don't know, when you buy a figure, whether it will "come to life" as a photograph?

DL: No, in fact most of the toys in my collection have never found their way into my photographs. I had a group of figures called "Campus Cuties" that didn't work as photos; they didn't have the robust '50s sexuality of the "American Beauties."

CS: I find it interesting that you consistently choose to perpetuate the illusion rather than present the artifice. Your work resembles Cindy Sherman's film stills in this sense.

DL: I'm happiest when the line is blurred. I'm trying to submerge the toy-ness of the image, smooth it over. I want the viewer to get to the end of the series or book and realize they're all toys, then go back and look again, knowing they're toys the second time around.

Ellen Brooks and Laurie Simmons were working with toys in the late '70s, but they were dealing with the issue of the toys themselves, bringing out their artificiality. The toy-ness was very much a part of their imagery. I was doing the opposite.

CS: You've been appropriating cultural icons for the last twenty years. What do you think of being labeled a postmodernist and put in this group of people that shaped a period of time?

DL: I was certainly very flattered and gratified to find both Richard Prince and Cindy Sherman were fans of the *Hitler Moves East* book back in the '70s. I don't really spend a lot of time thinking about the historical context of the work in terms of art, though. Other work like it was made in the past, and there were certainly other photographers working with toys. But it was not a style that many people were familiar with.

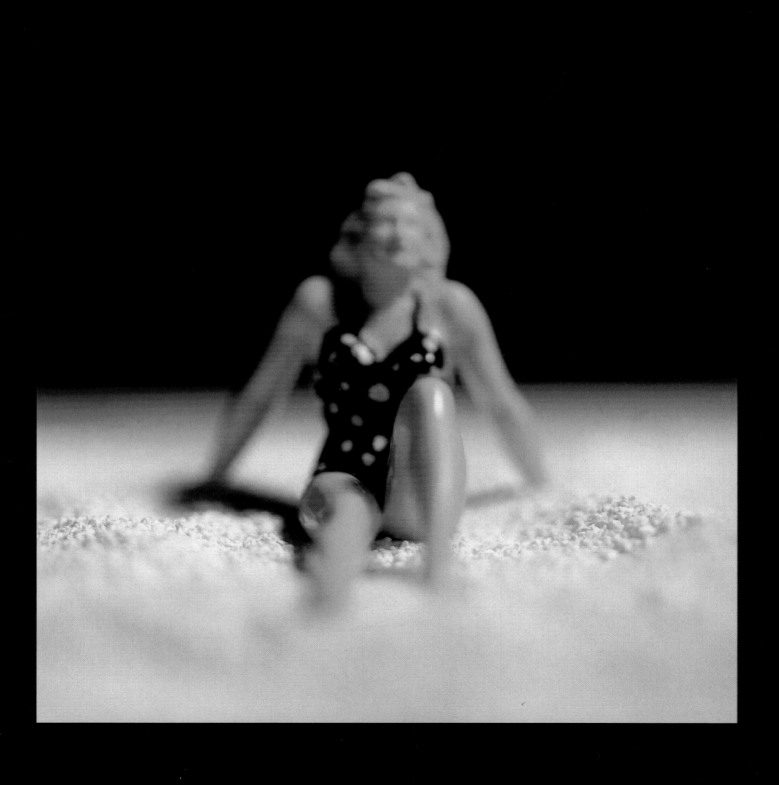

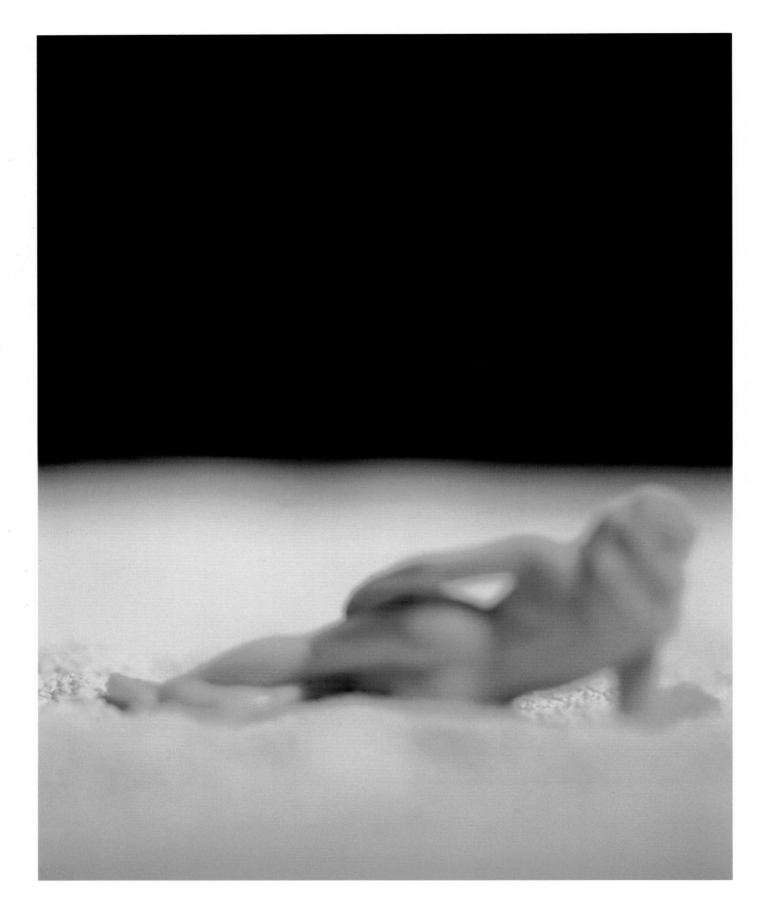

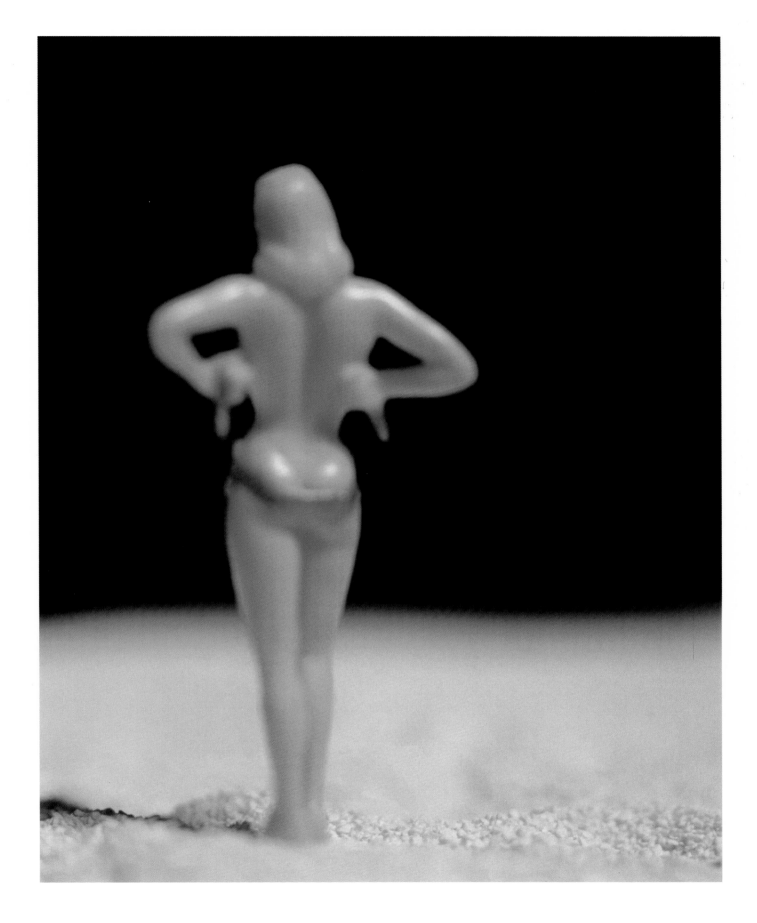

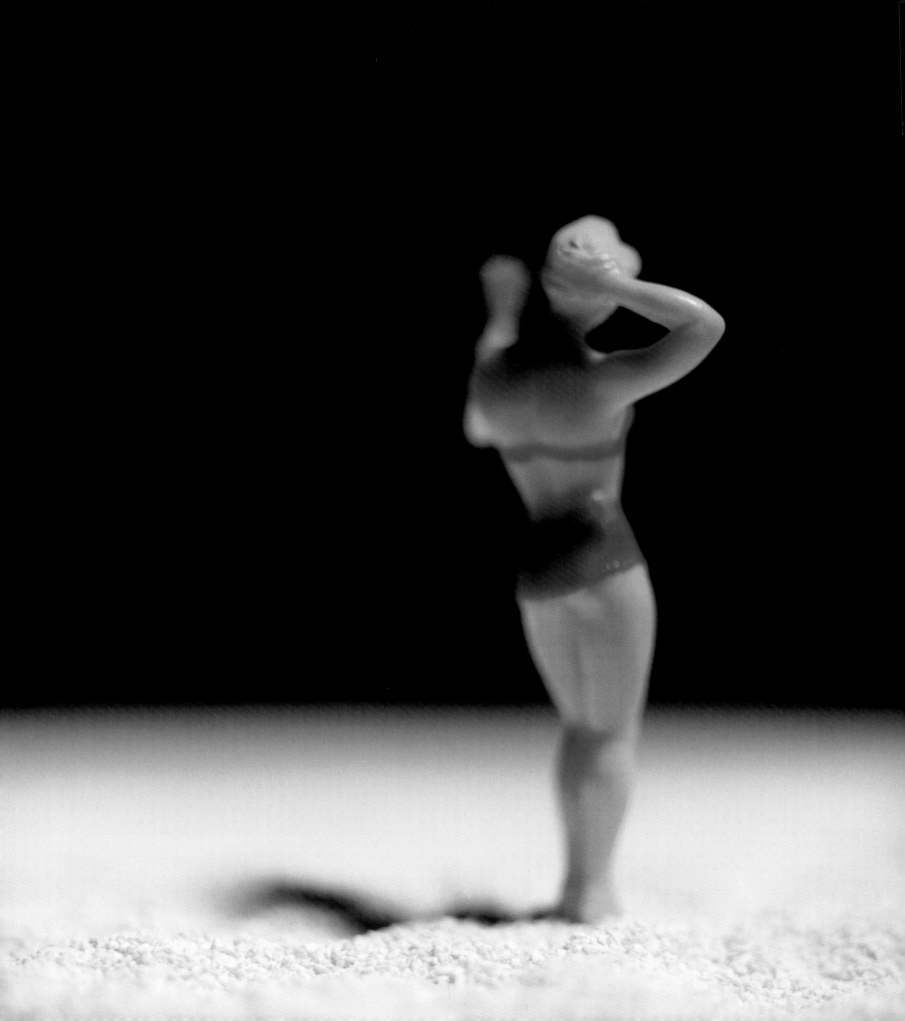

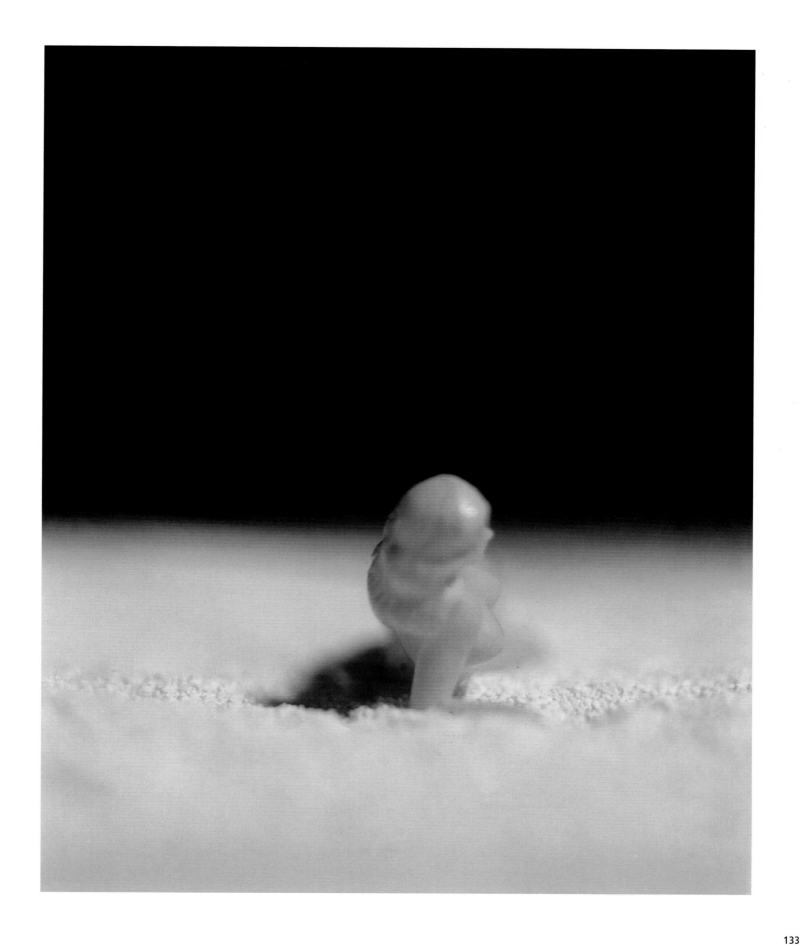

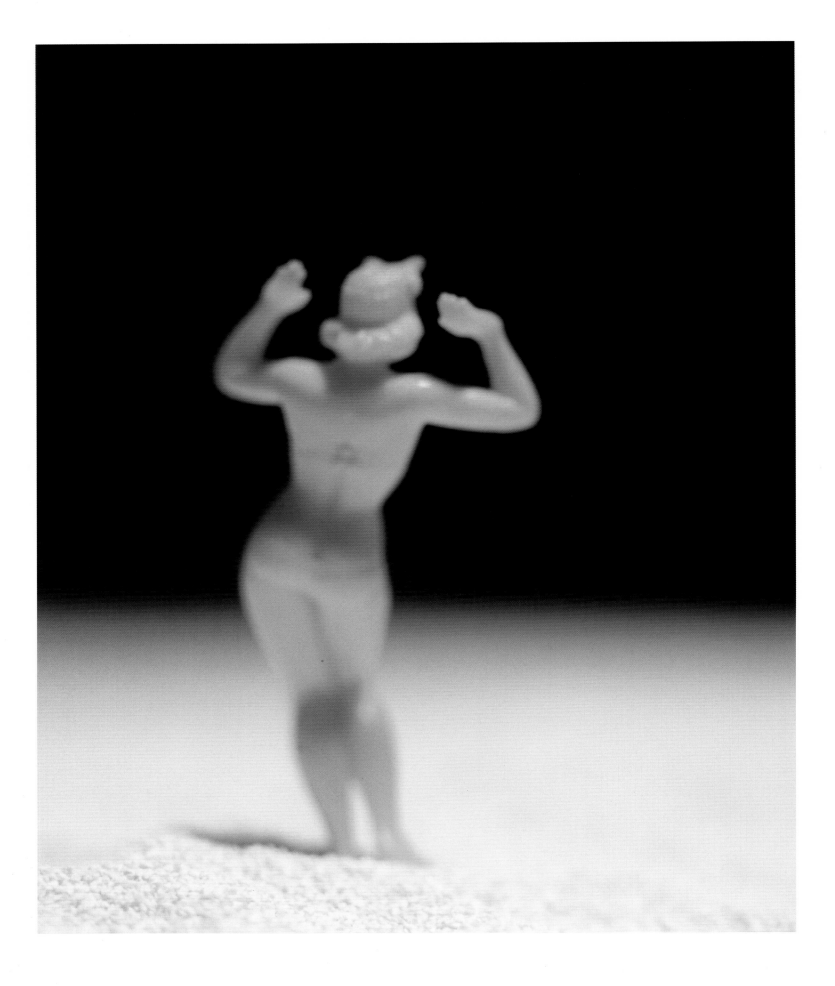

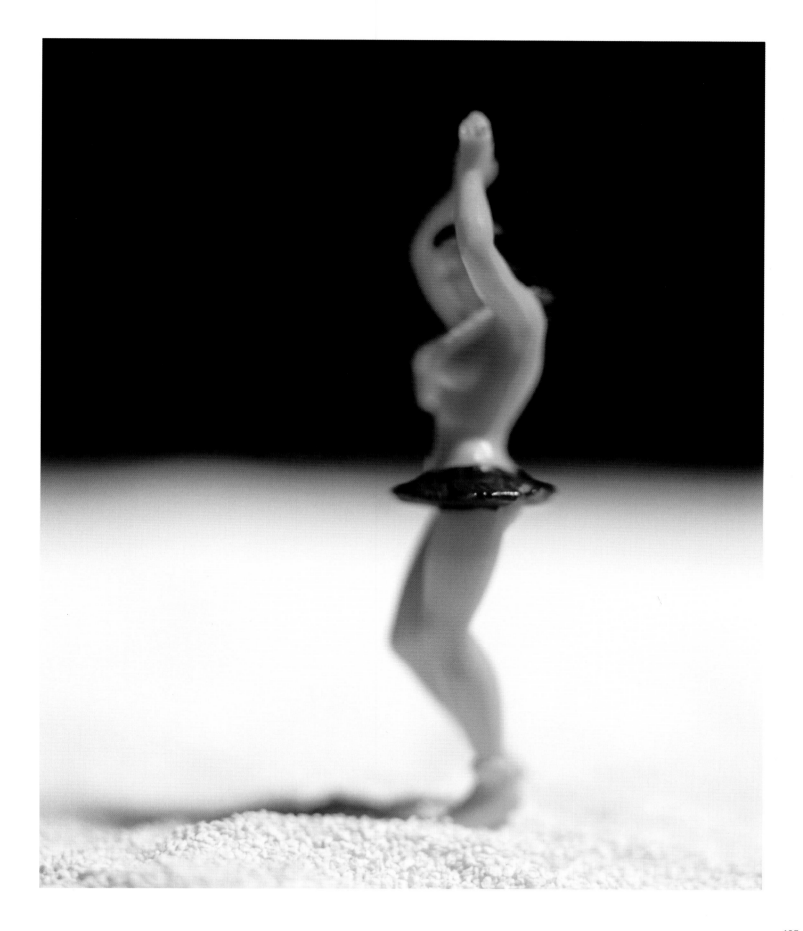

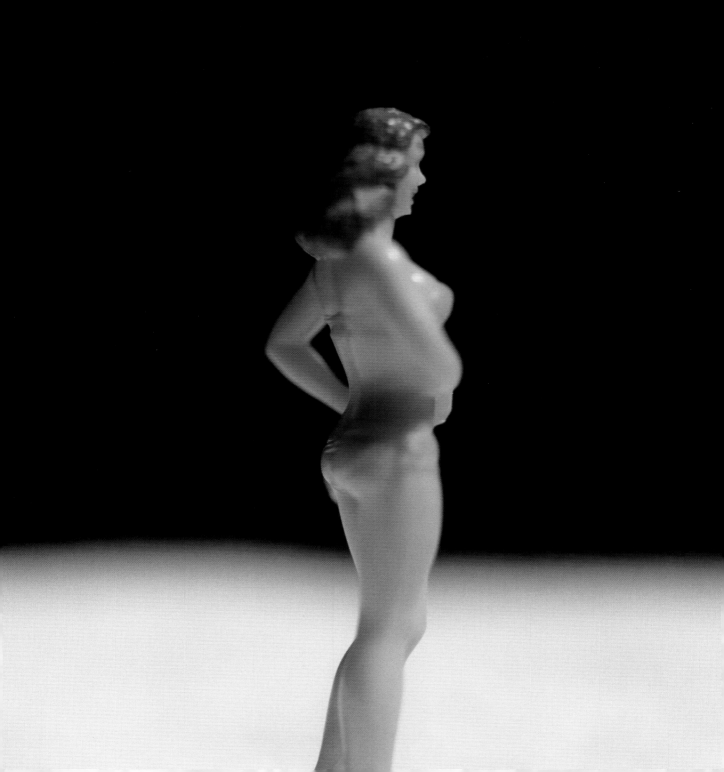

···

W: How did the "Desire" series originate?

DL: It was made in part as a reaction to the enormous proliferation of pornograp[
on the newsstands. Pornography used to be something at the back of Johnny's
Smoke Shop; now it's everywhere. Any bodega or deli has row after row of harc
core stuff. *Playboy* used to be edgy; now it's like *Ladies Home Journal*.

As I said earlier, toys serve as icons for what's going on in society. The
Japanese sex dolls in bondage that I used for this series would not have been
available twenty years ago. Even if the idea was germinating in men's minds,
it wasn't made manifest until recently. I'm reacting to those changes in society.

W: Of all the work you've done, did this series incite the strongest reaction?

DL: There was some negative reaction to the "Desire" series, but I had expectec
more. Of all my work, it was the most deliberately provocative. The imagery
triggers an immediate response from the viewer. You might be looking at the
"Desire" work and find that there is a sexuality or pornographic sensibility
emanating from it. At the same time, you're cognizant of the fact that these
are six-inch-high, badly detailed polyurethane figures from Japan of Caucasian
women in bondage. These two things are in conflict with each other, yet you're
drawn into the imagery the same way you're drawn into images of the West.
You know it's not representative of the West as we now understand it; nonethe
less, it is a reality that exists because it's part of our shared iconography.

CS: You're saying that people accept these myths, these manufactured images,
because they're accustomed to not knowing what is fact and what is fiction?

DL: Exactly. And when I take these stereotyping figures and photograph them
and make them monumental, am I adding to the perpetuation of a stereotype c
am I critiquing it? I feel I'm making a critique, a visual critique and a historical
critique. I know there are people who see it differently. I've always been aware
that people might find it offensive. In the "Wild West" series, the work could be
seen as perpetuating the stereotype of the American Indian; the "Desire" series
caters to sexual stereotypes.

RW: We know the photograph is not the teller of truth, but because you go to such lengths to produce these images, and obviously you are the creator of the images, people may attach the problem, whether it be the Holocaust or racism or sexism, to you. You're creating it, then making a photograph of it.

DL: I, by choice, am creating an image of a crematorium with a body being pushed into an oven.

CS: By choice you play with evil.

DL: I think I'm exploring boundaries. I sometimes think of my work in general as a kind of Rorschach test. I haven't made the scenes as meticulously detailed as possible; the viewer fills it in. The "Western scene" becomes a Western scene because it seems so familiar. The crematorium, or the people being shot in "Mein Kampf" seem to have a credibility because they mirror, in some ways, the documentary images we're familiar with. Ever since I began working with toys in '72, I've been intrigued with the idea that these seemingly benign objects could take on such incredible power and personality, simply by the way they were photographed; that suddenly a box of German soldiers manufactured in Japan could become the Sixth Army stranded in Stalingrad, simply by the way I fabricated the imagery, or that I could make a six-inch polyurethane object sexually alluring.

CS: You said earlier that the "Desire" series was your most provocative series. How would you compare it to your other work?

DL: In "Desire" I felt I was touching on important and sensitive issues. I'm a man, and I was photographing plastic figures of Caucasian women in bondage. Since both Laurie Simmons and Cindy Sherman were making work that dealt with similar issues, I hoped that my work would add another element to that discourse. My goal was to engender a discussion.

There are very few elements in the work, really. We looked at some of the "Modern Romance" pieces. There may be three or four little objects, at most, in a frame, so the viewer is required to fill in the gaps, so to speak. In the "Desire" work, the viewer imagines a scene the image may have come from.

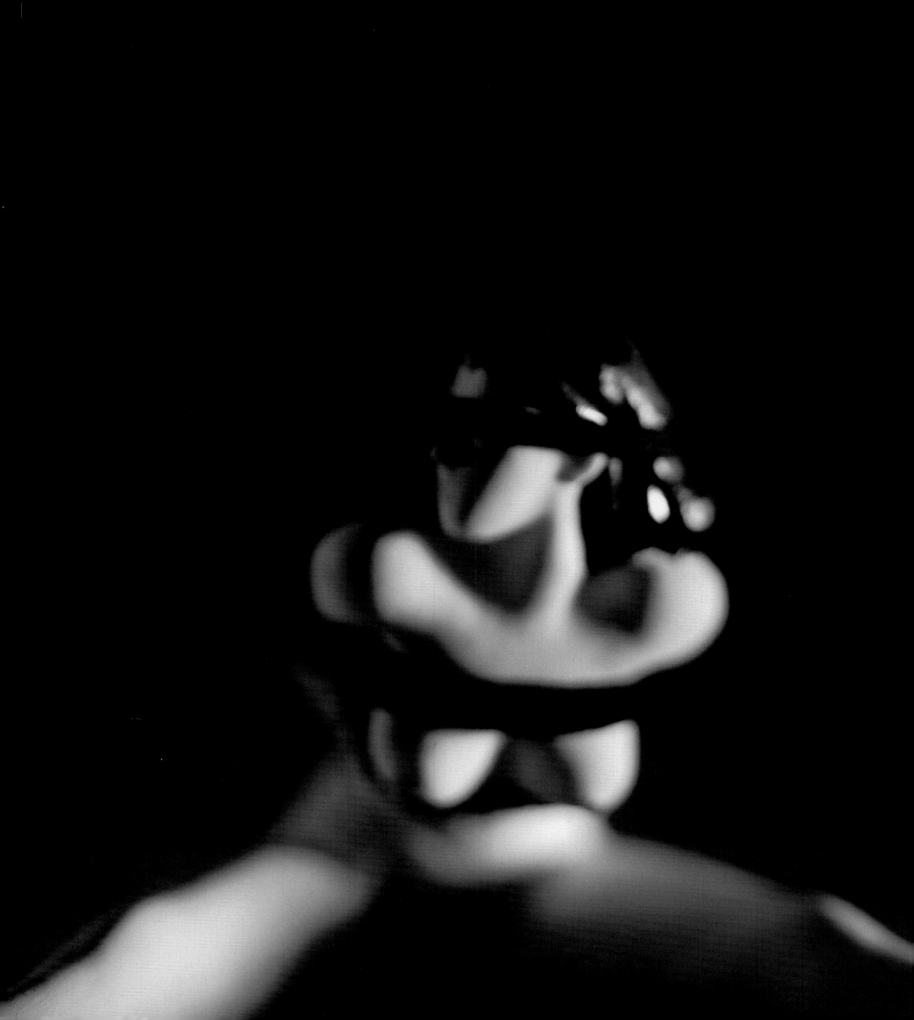

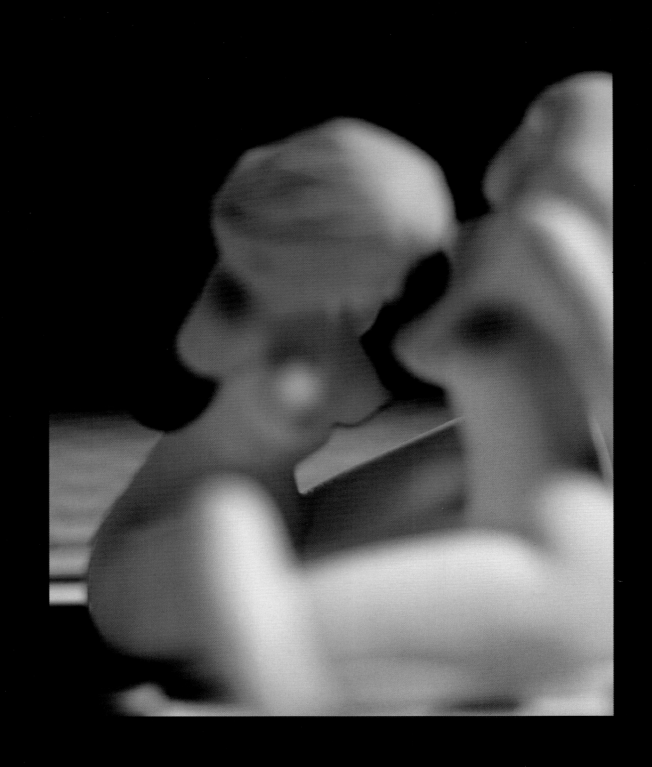

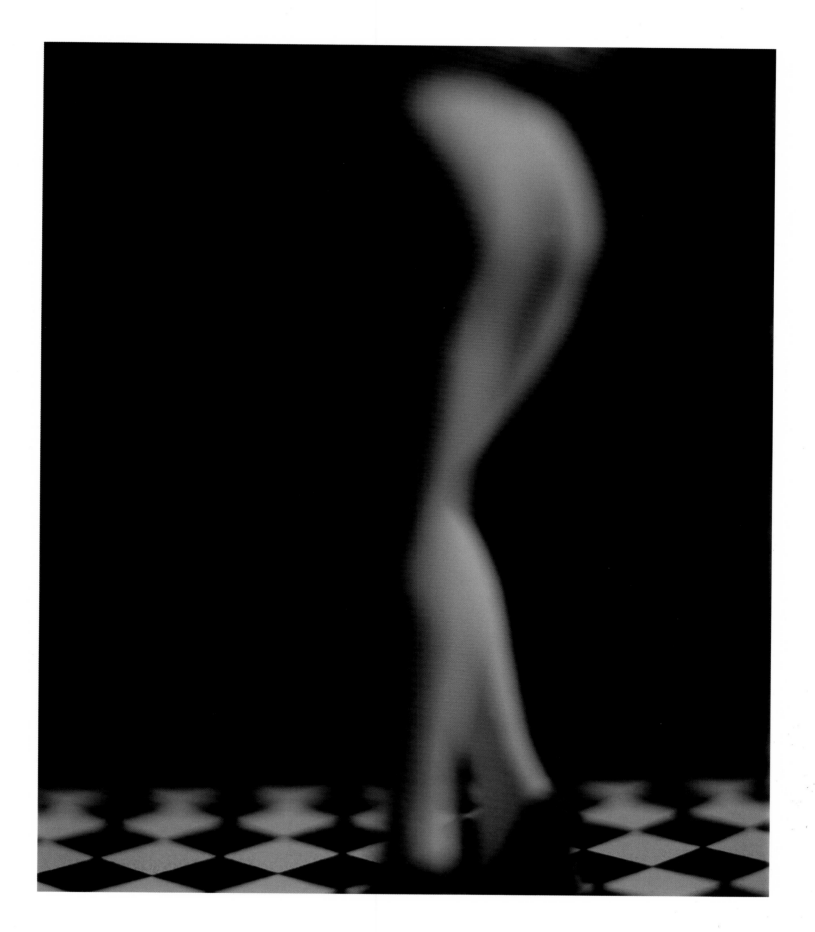

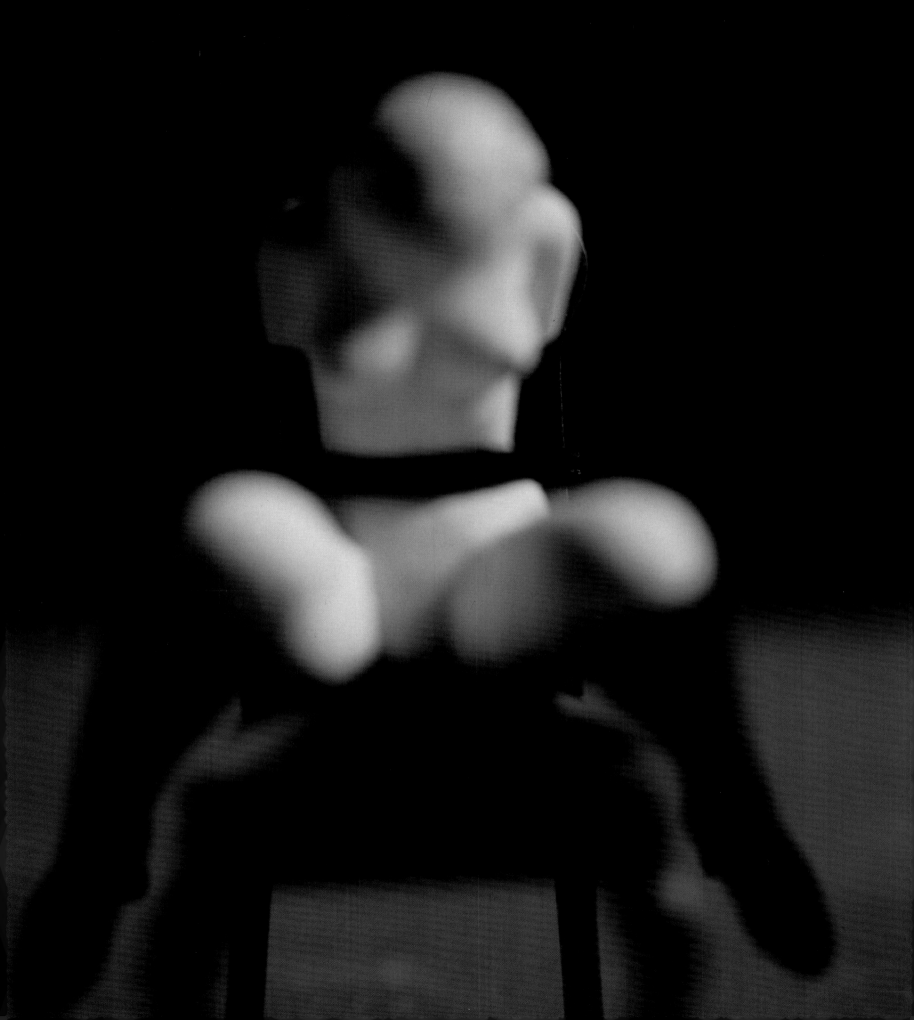

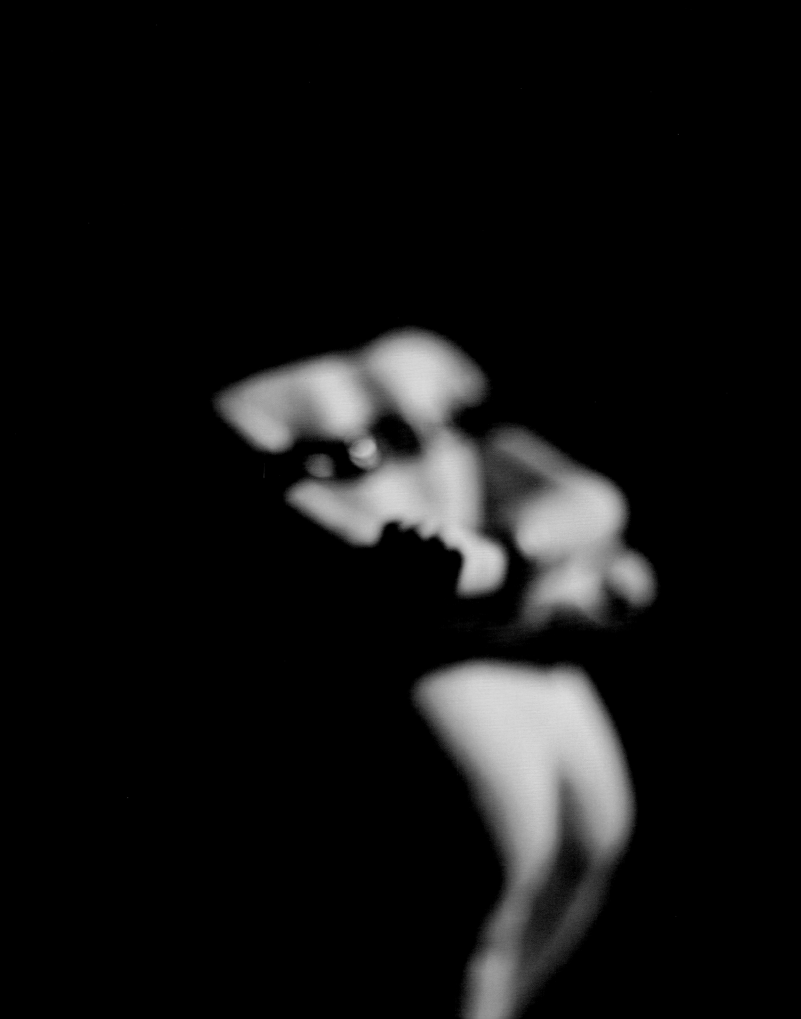

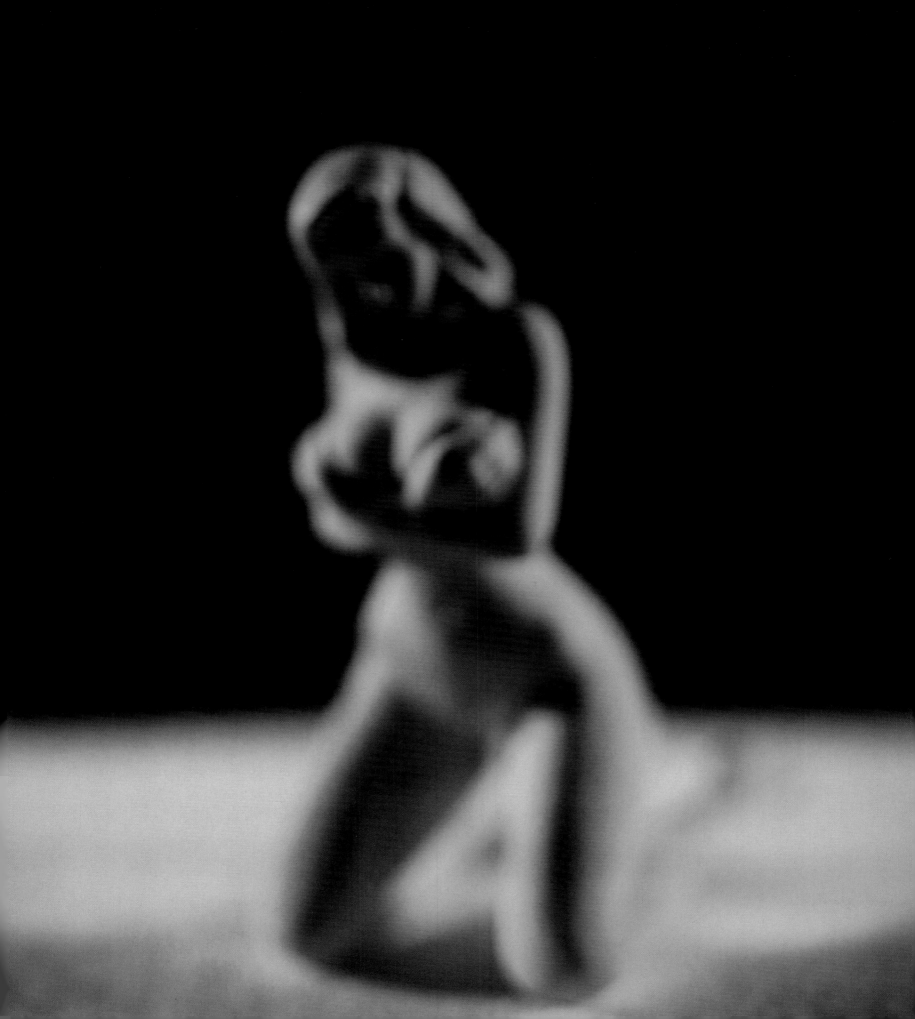

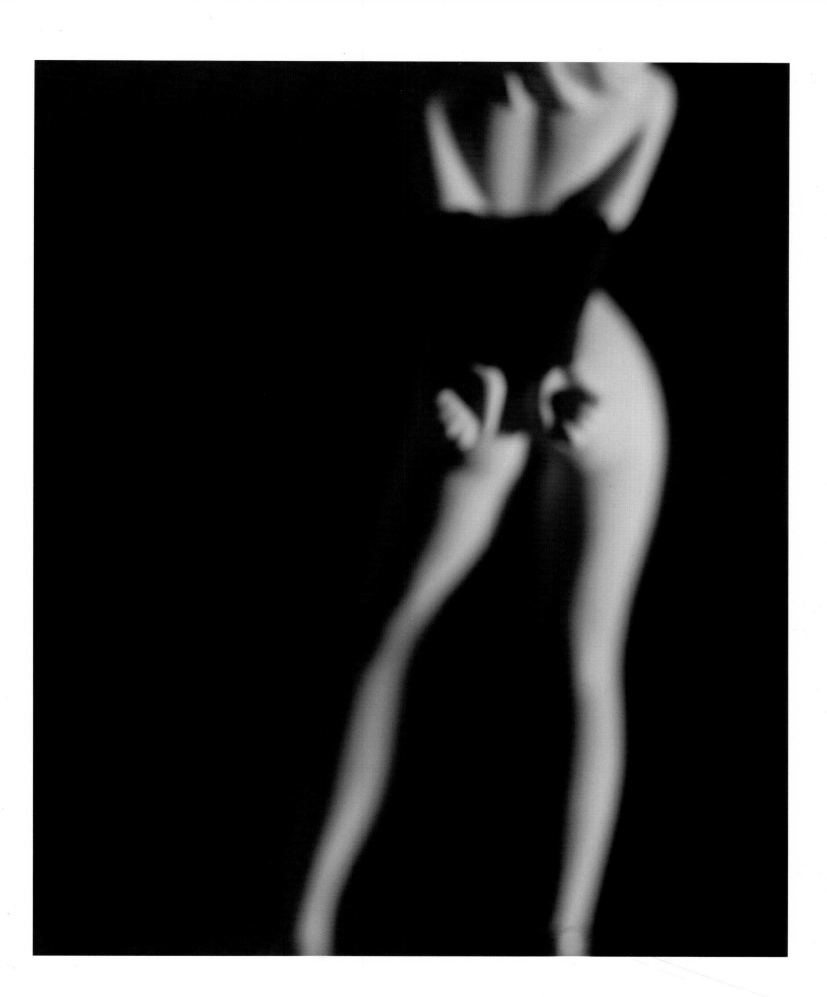

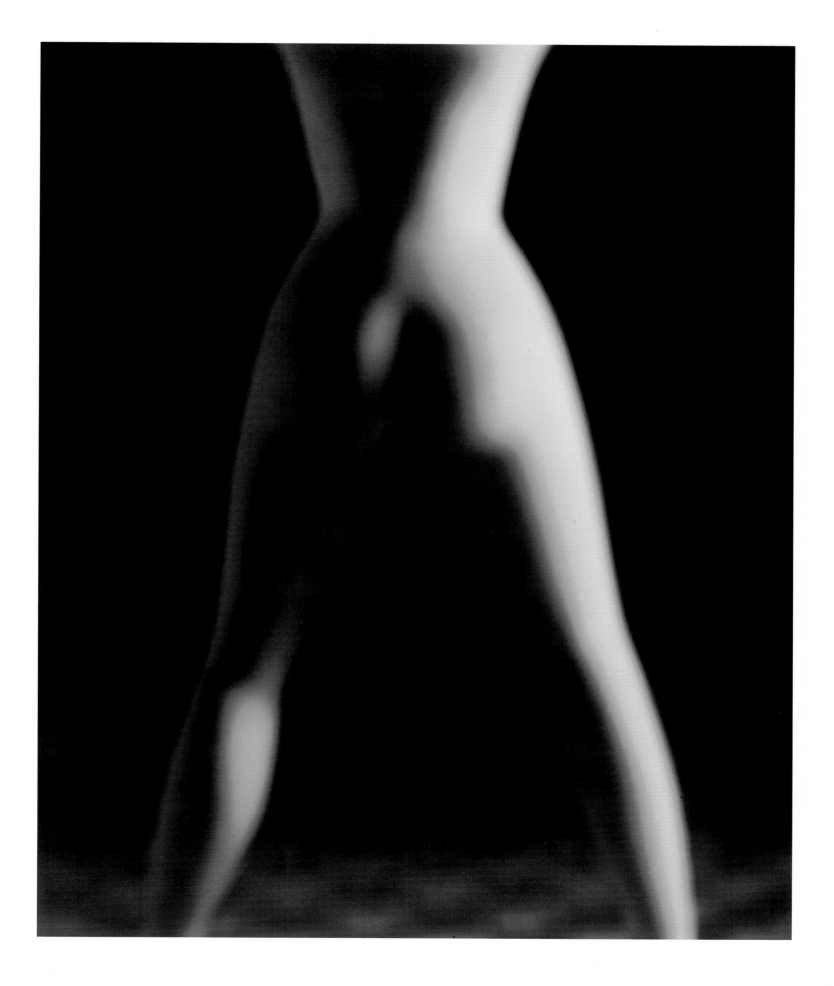

Mein Kampf, 1993-94

DL: Some people were convinced that the figures in the "Desire" series were real women. I told them I didn't know anyone who would pose for me in those positions. The "Mein Kampf" series, on the other hand, is obviously toy-like, but the emotions are so powerful that for most viewers there is a suspension of disbelief.

RW: When you made the Holocaust pictures for "Mein Kampf" you must have been aware that you could hardly find a more loaded subject. Did you choose it because you hoped it would be controversial?

DL: The Holocaust pictures evolved from others I was making. My original idea was to make August Sander-like portraits of toy figures of German leaders, but that didn't work. So I started putting these figures in Leni Riefenstahl-type settings, marching them in front of the Brandenburg gate and so on. Later, I made a photograph of three women as seen from over the shoulder of the SS officer as a response to an image I had seen over and over again in my research; an image of women being herded across a field at Birkenau on their way to the crematorium. The photo had such a strong impact on me that the work just took off. I started looking more closely at other Holocaust imagery, wondering how I could encompass it in this work. I knew it was emotionally charged, but I had so much momentum going in the series that I wasn't judging the work.

CS: What was the driving force of the work? The Holocaust has been exhaustively researched and interpreted, unlike the Eastern Front.

DL: Some of it was personal. I always read a lot before I start a series, and when I started reading up on the Holocaust I realized how little I knew. The Disneyesque version of the Holocaust was "The war ended. We discovered these camps. We were shocked because it was so horrible." In reality we knew about the camps and did nothing.

RW: In "Mein Kampf," once again, you show an abiding interest in Nazism, and again you have produced a body of work that is based not on personal experience but on the emotional impact of certain images on you. Your work is both exorcistic and voyeuristic.

DL: The absorption of images and the distancing that later takes place is part of voyeurism. But I'm also trying to confront and draw out from the viewer childhood memories that have an emotional residue.

RW: Do you think that's why virtually all of your photos take place in the past?

DL: I think I create a window that allows the viewer to come into an image that appears to be more complete than it really is. It becomes complete when the viewer becomes a participant and fills in the missing details.

CS: I'm reminded of formative childhood moments—the smell of grandma's house, the flood of remembrances and information carried in the mind's eye, the subconscious. I think what bothers people about "Mein Kampf" as well as "Desire" and "Blackface" is the role of photography in fetishizing loaded images, glamorizing them in big beautiful prints.

DL: I think the horror can also be beautiful. Think of Goya's paintings. In a sense I was doing that with "Desire." The scenes are horrific, but the imagery itself is quite beautiful and seductive. If something is beautiful, you're seduced by it a little bit. Then you think, oh my God, this is what I've let in. It's like letting the genie out of the bottle. I enjoy making beautiful work, but that doesn't in any way limit me from dealing with horrific issues or subject matter. In fact, I think it gives me more power.

The same is true of my "Mein Kampf" series. Leni Riefenstahl's *Triumph of the Will* was seductively beautiful; *Schindler's List* is simultaneously beautiful and horrible. The "Mein Kampf" work, particularly those images that deal with the pageantry of the Nazis, is seductively beautiful, as were the actual pageants.

CS: What's the difference between "Mein Kampf" and "Blackface" and Andres Serrano's *Piss Christ*? Obviously, Serrano pushed things to an extreme to provoke a response. But you glamorize provocative objects in your work....

DL: The issues these works raise are extremely important. They go beyond simple beauty, or mimicking documentary photography, or creating seductive images. I don't feel I've glamorized them, so to speak.

CS: There is a sense that you're using dolls, or you're using toys, for sinister purposes. These works are about things that are far from child-like.

DL: The catalogue of my show in London was called *Dark Light*. The curator saw what he called a dark strain running through all my work, and I think it's true. But at the same time, I'm playing with toy figures. Those two things are going on at the same time. Childhood play can have a real darkness around it. I enjoy bringing that out.

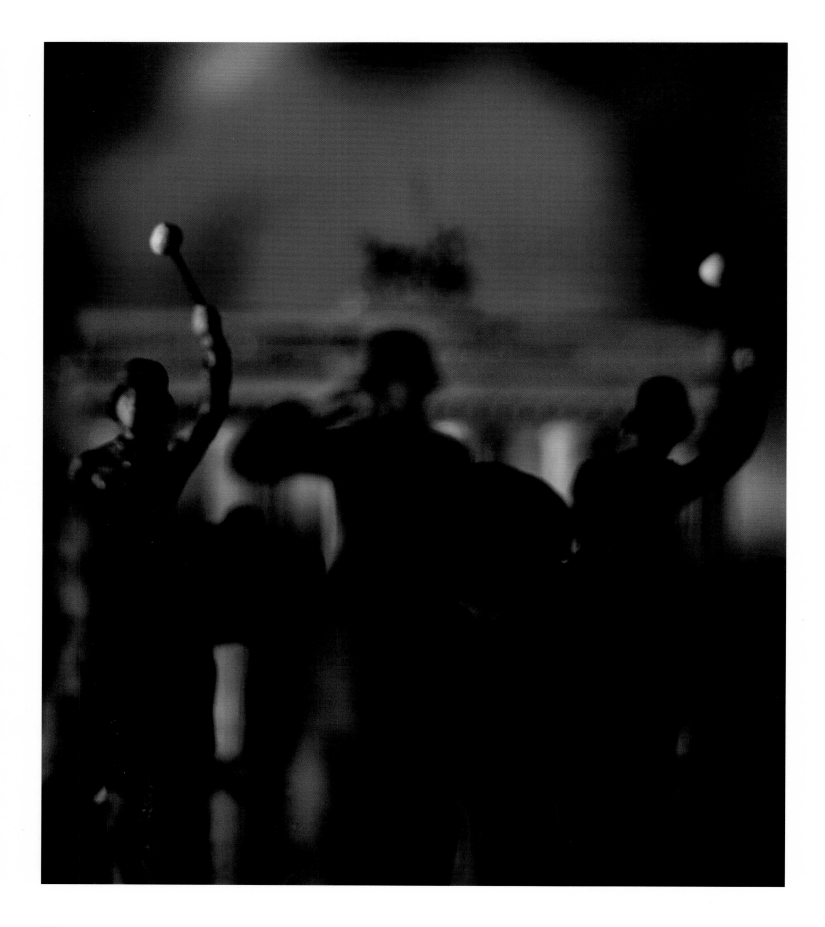

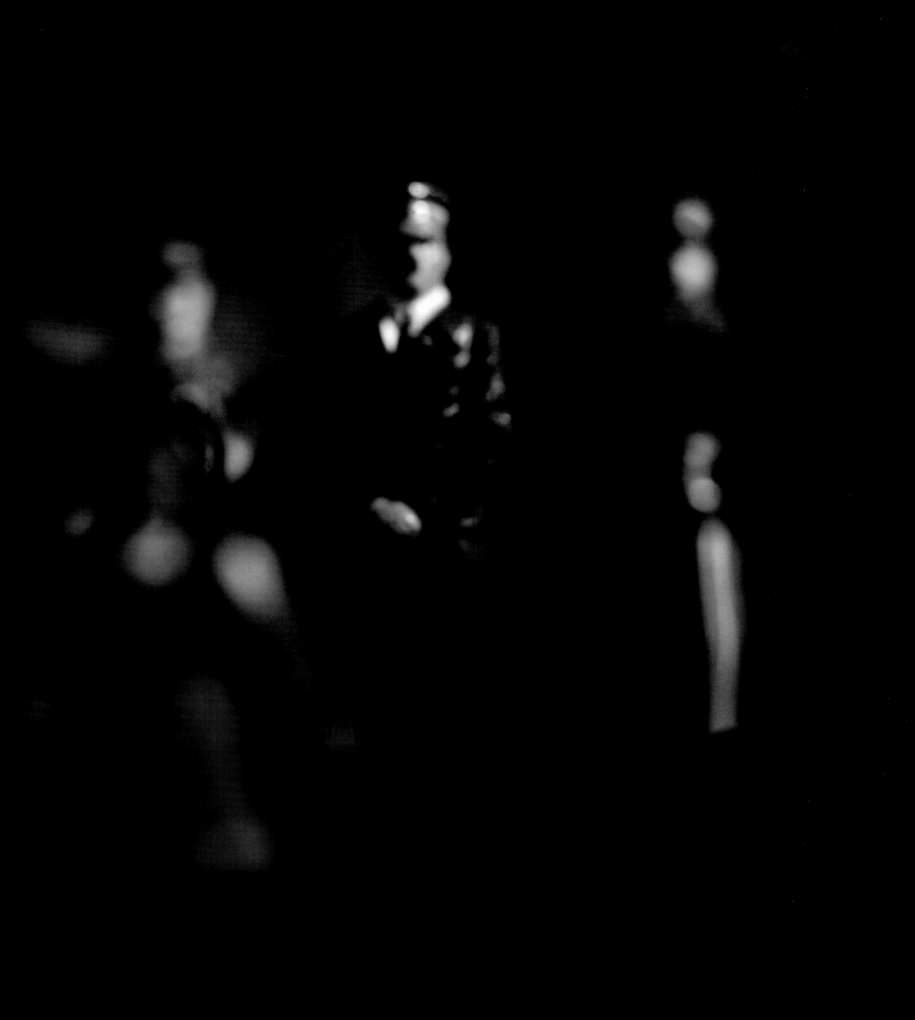

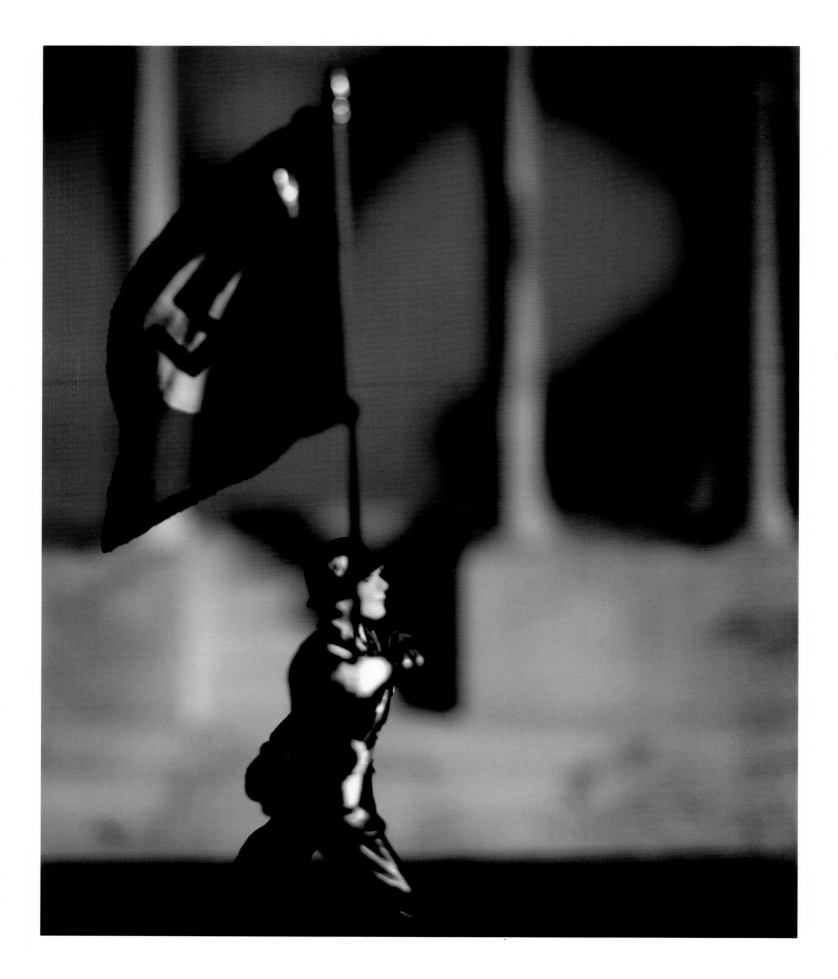

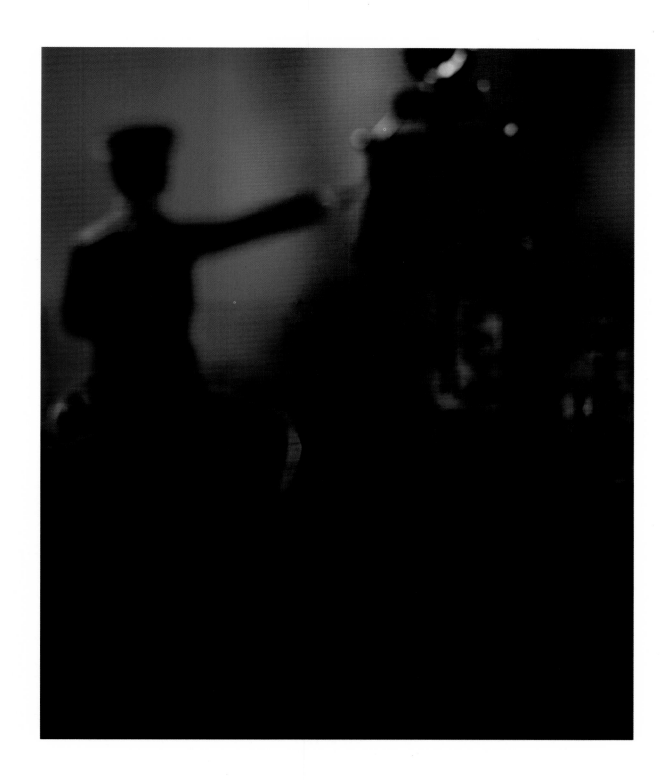

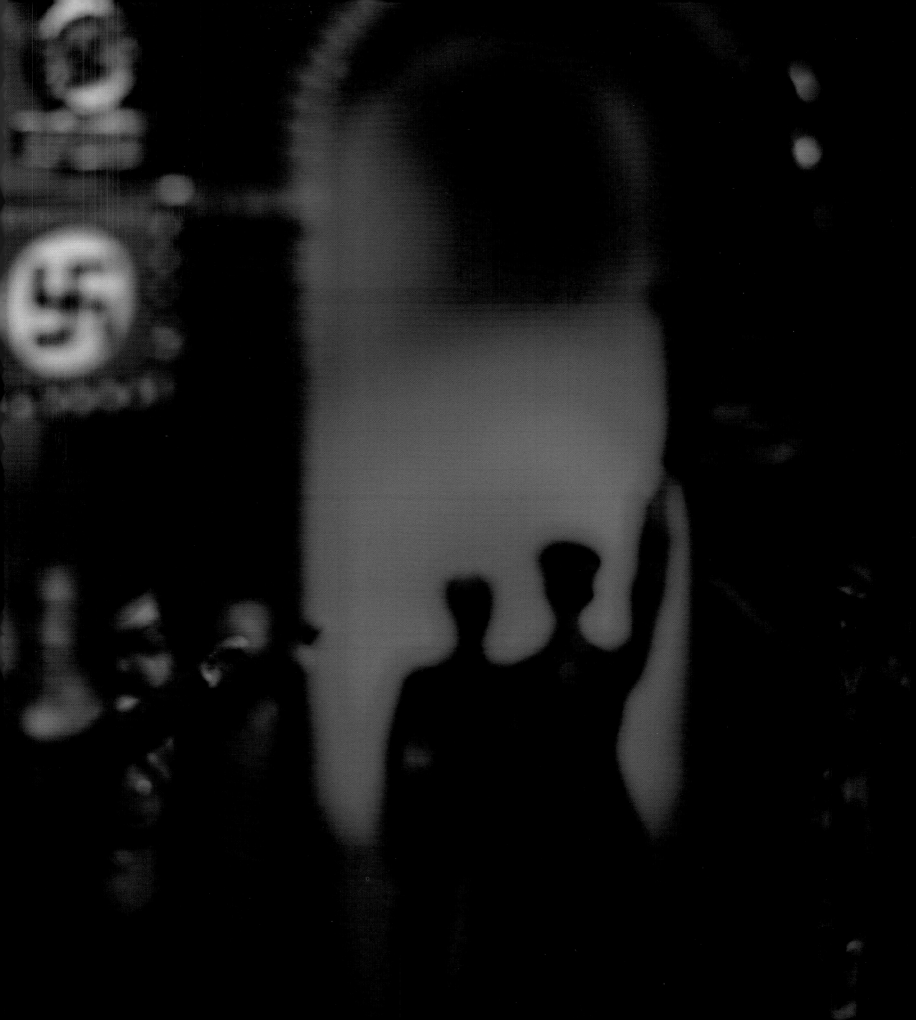

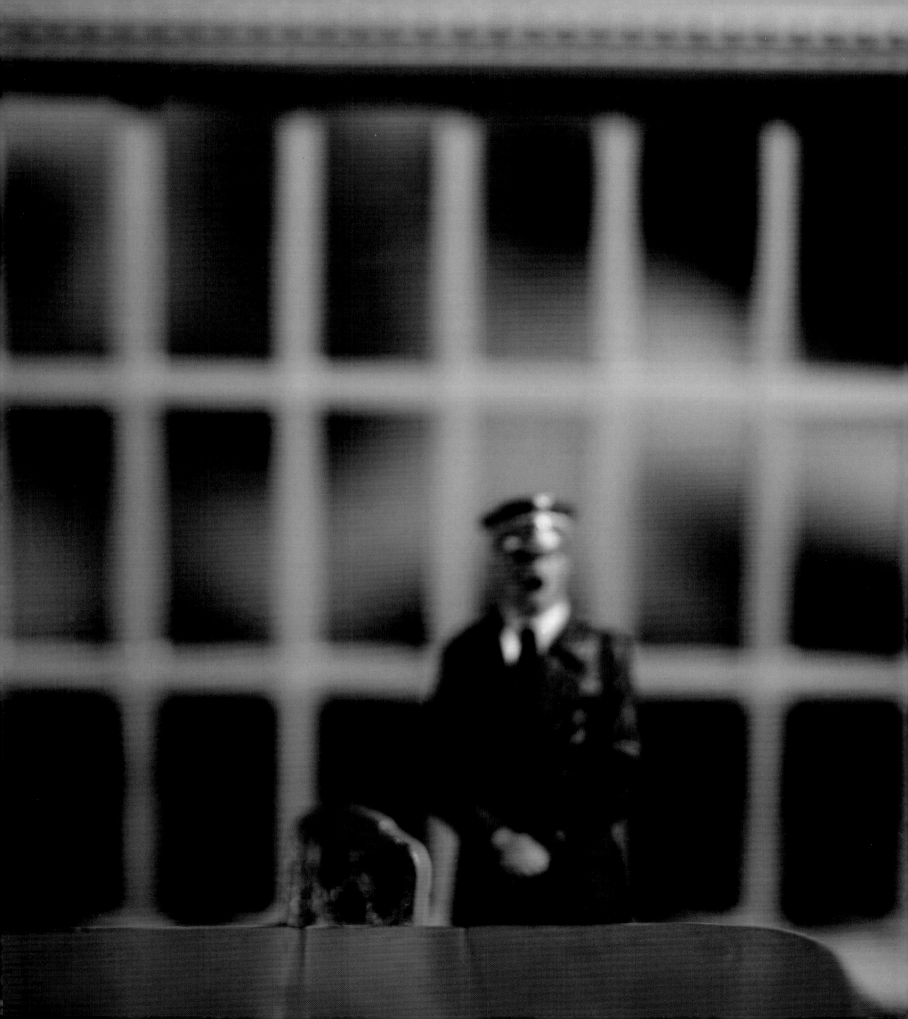

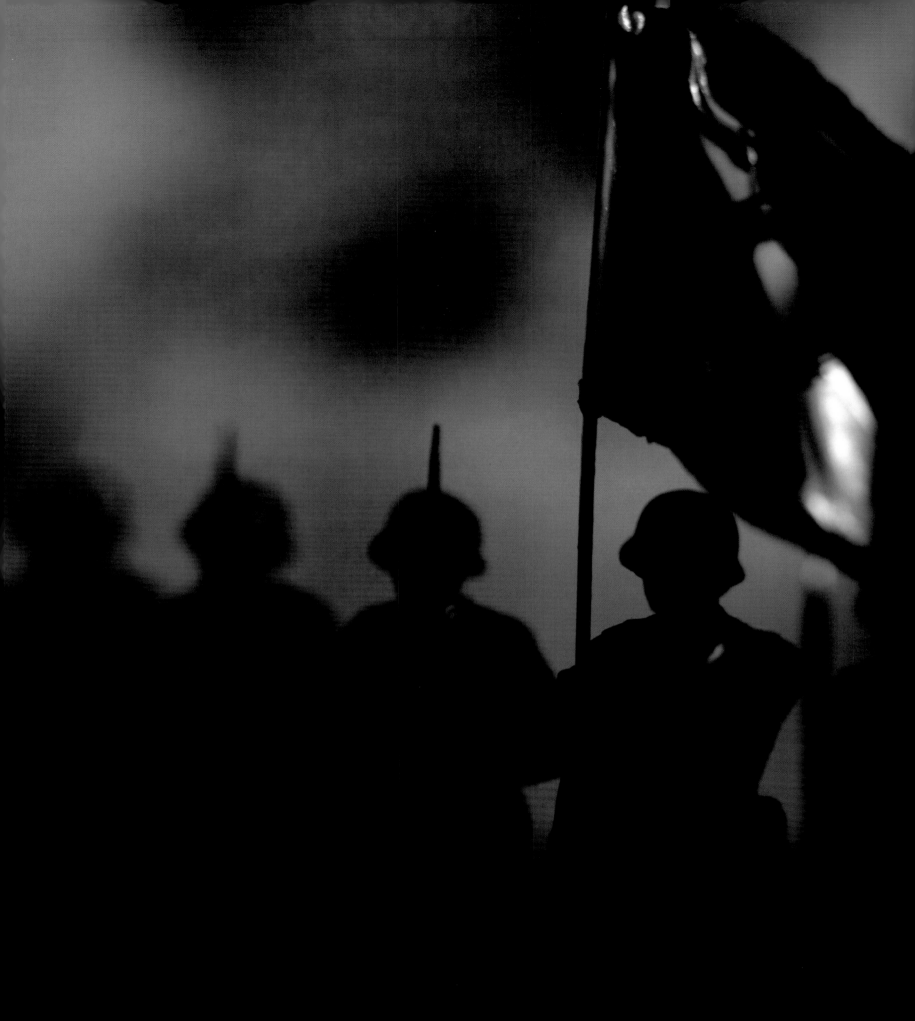

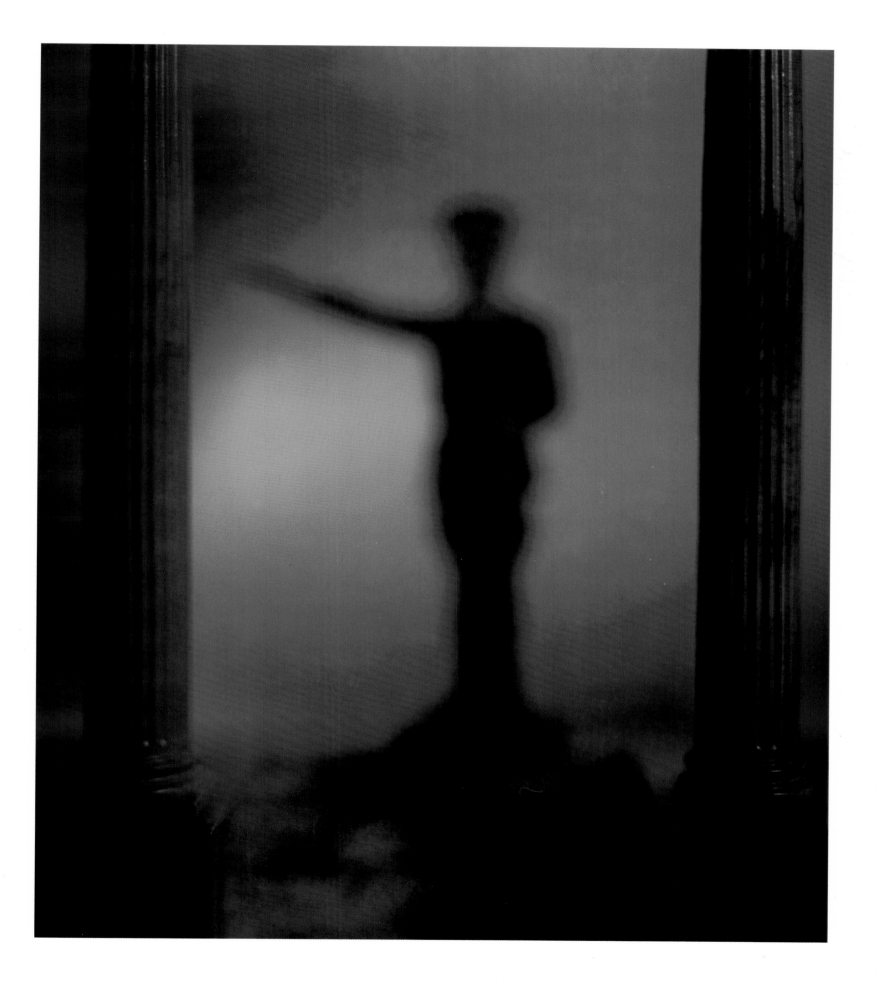

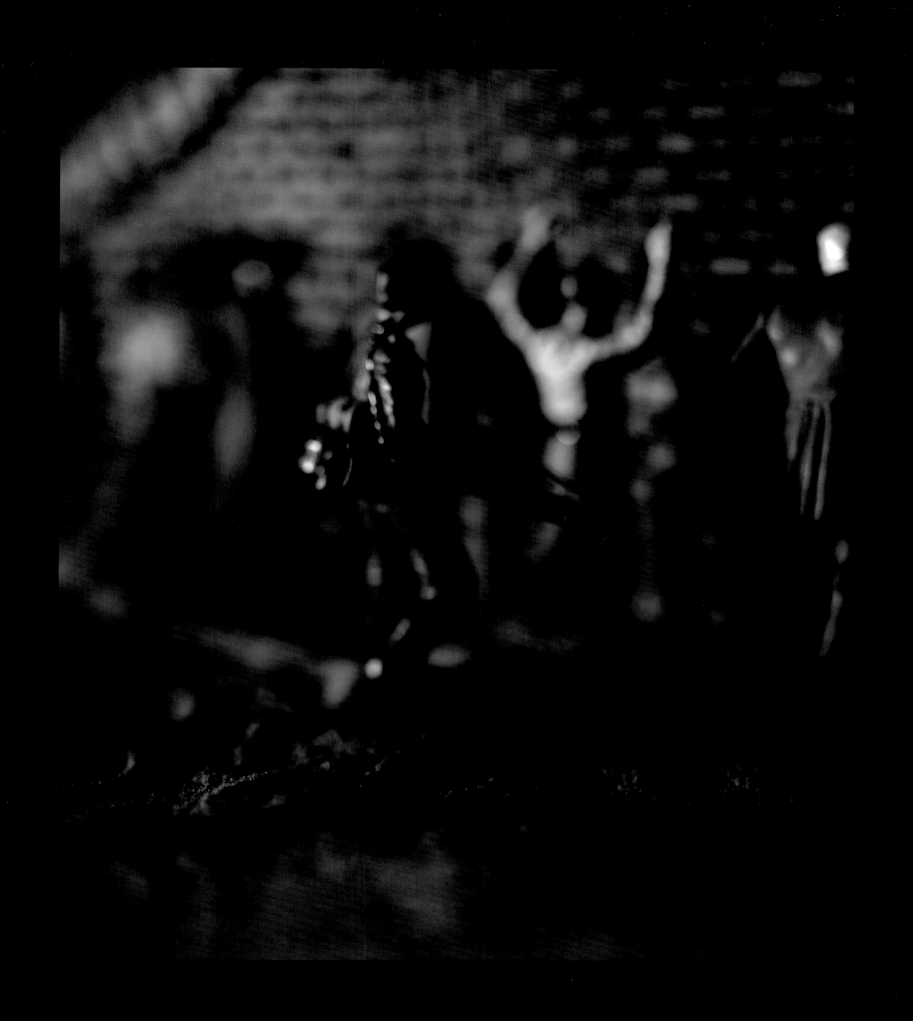

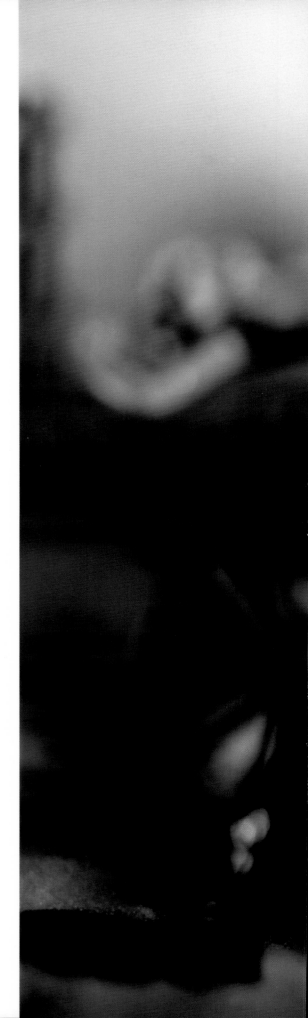

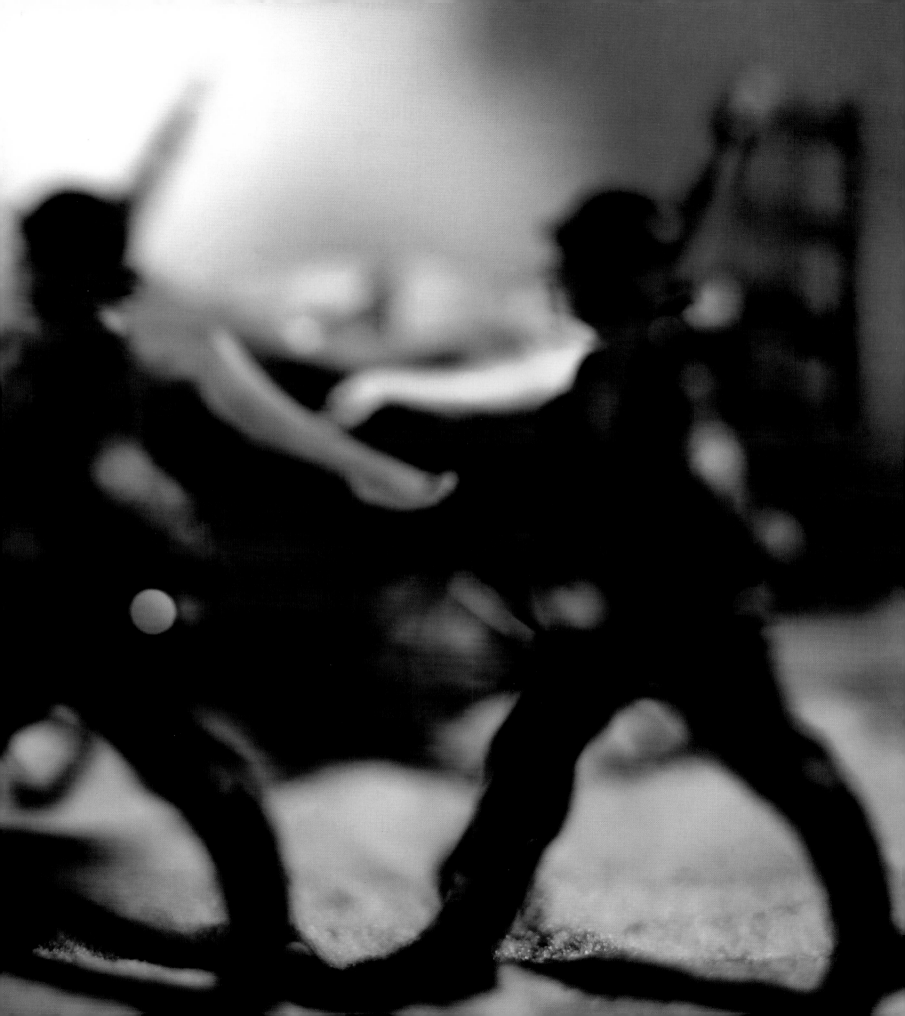

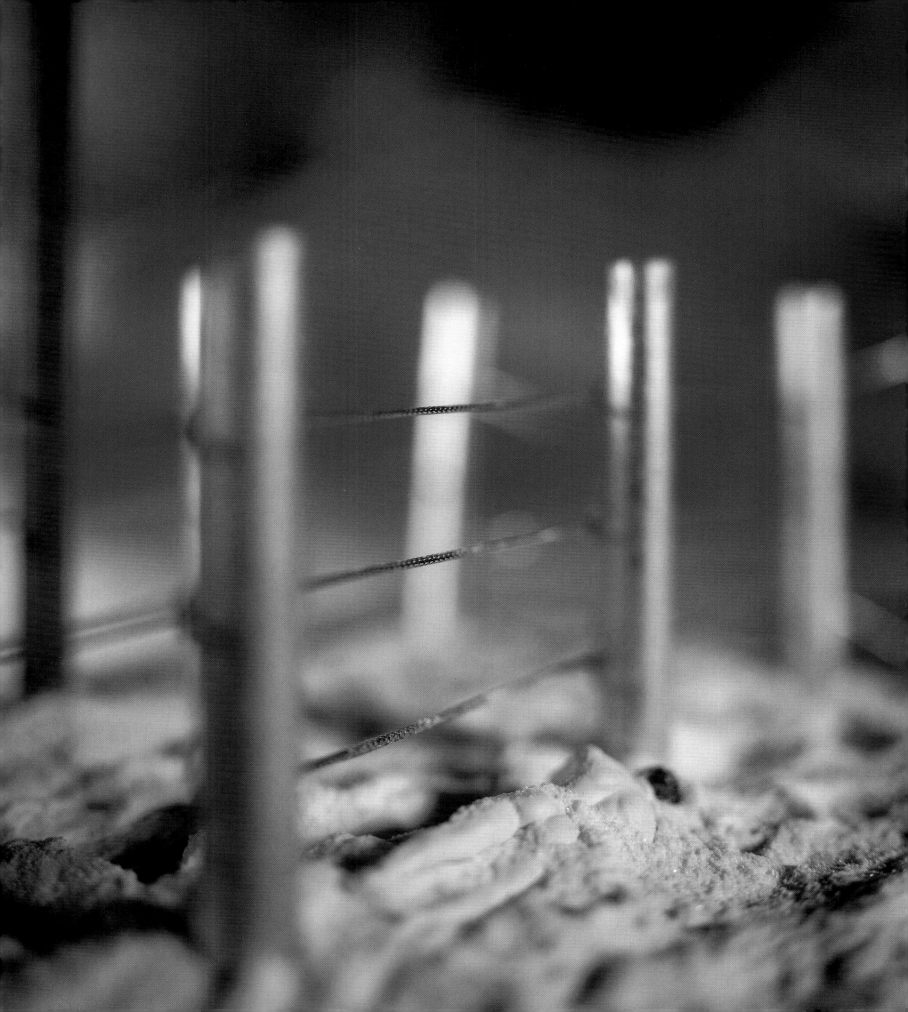

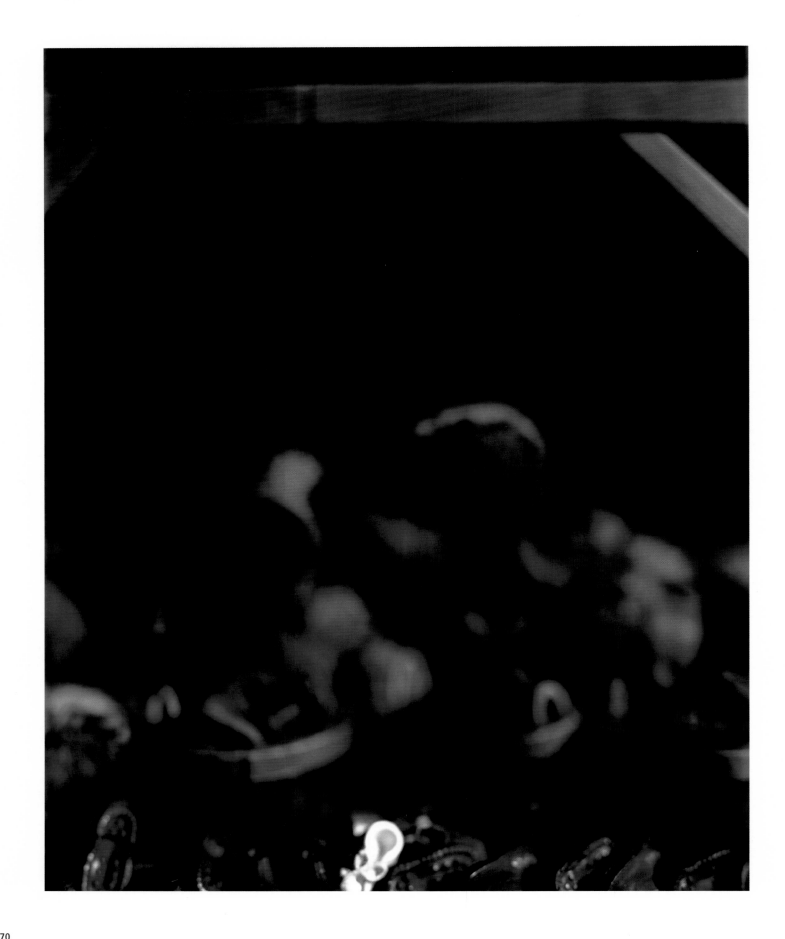

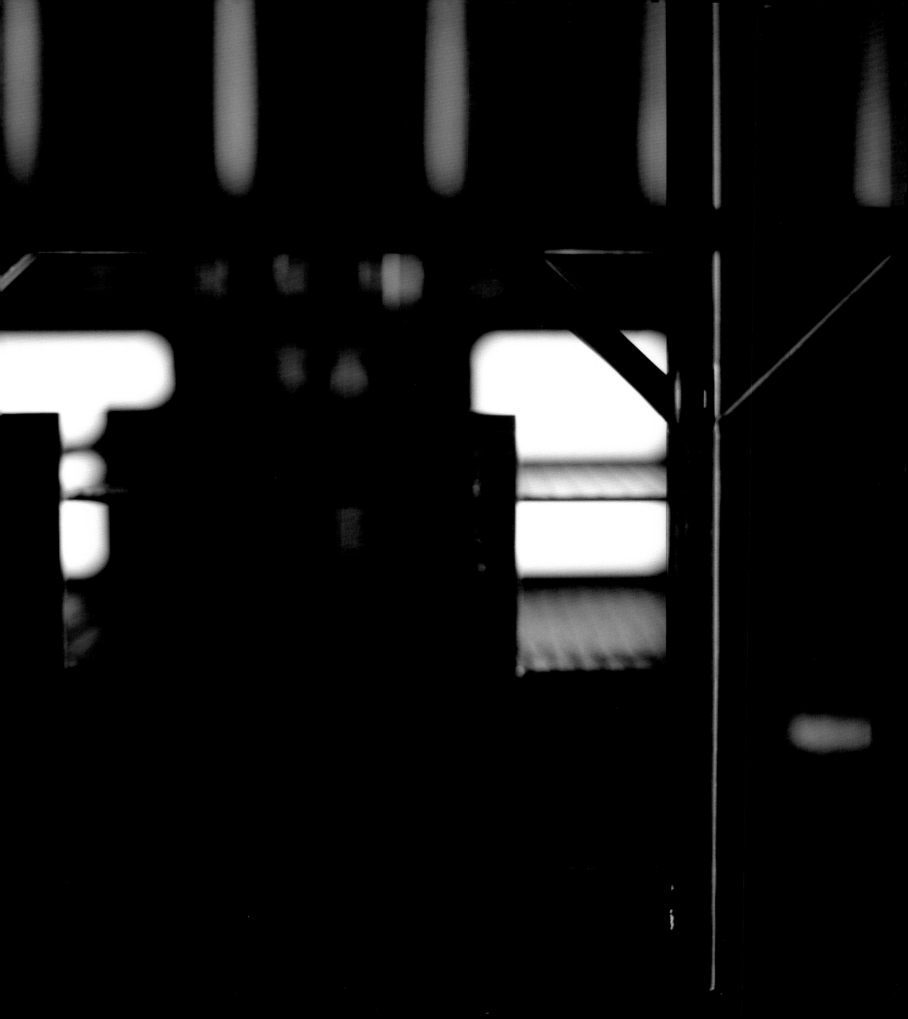

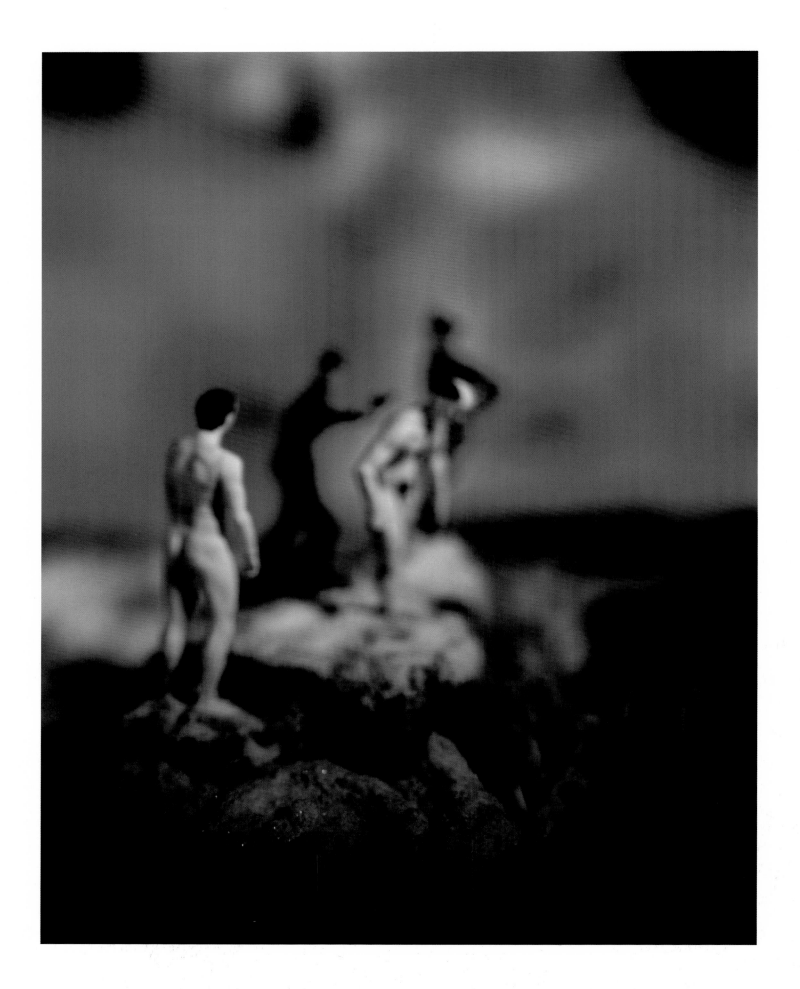

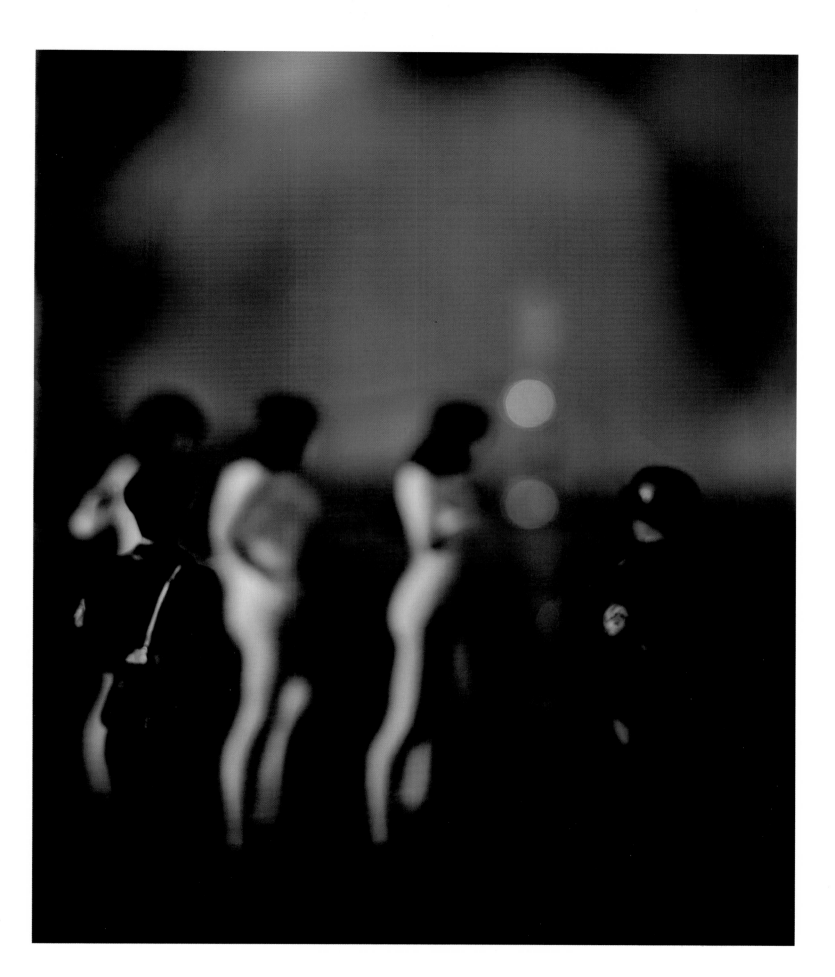

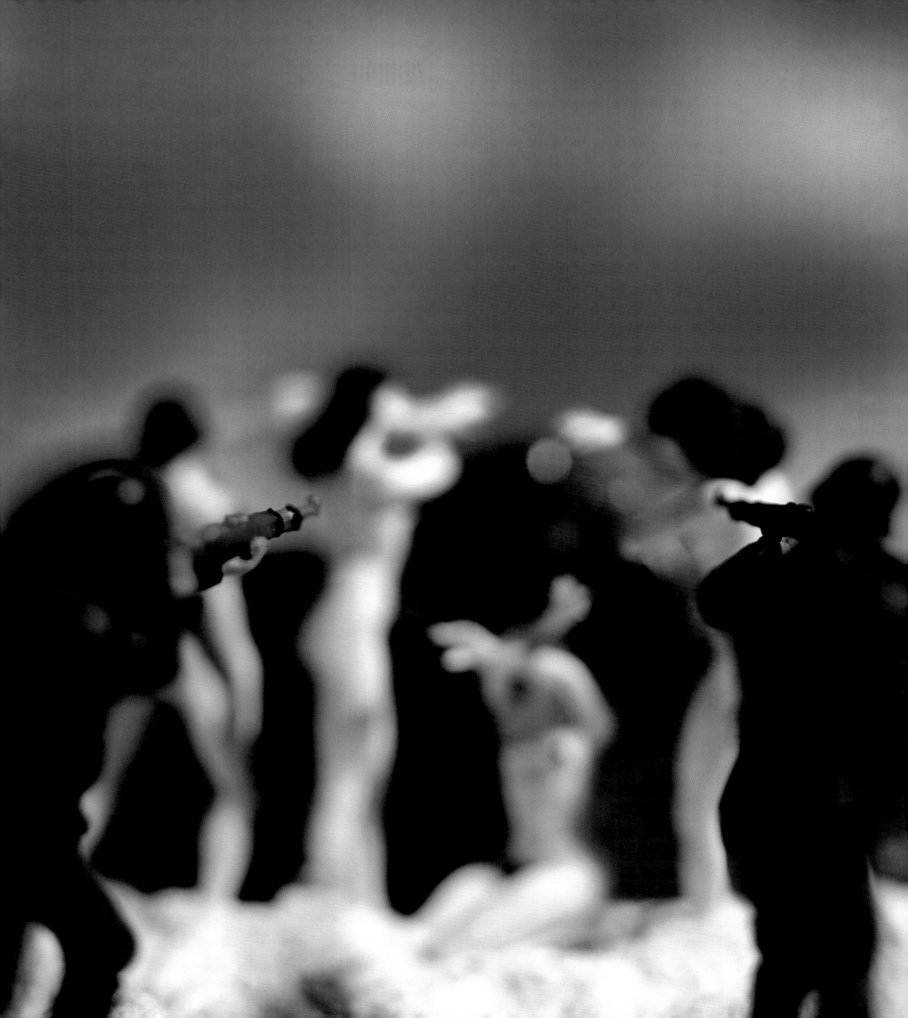

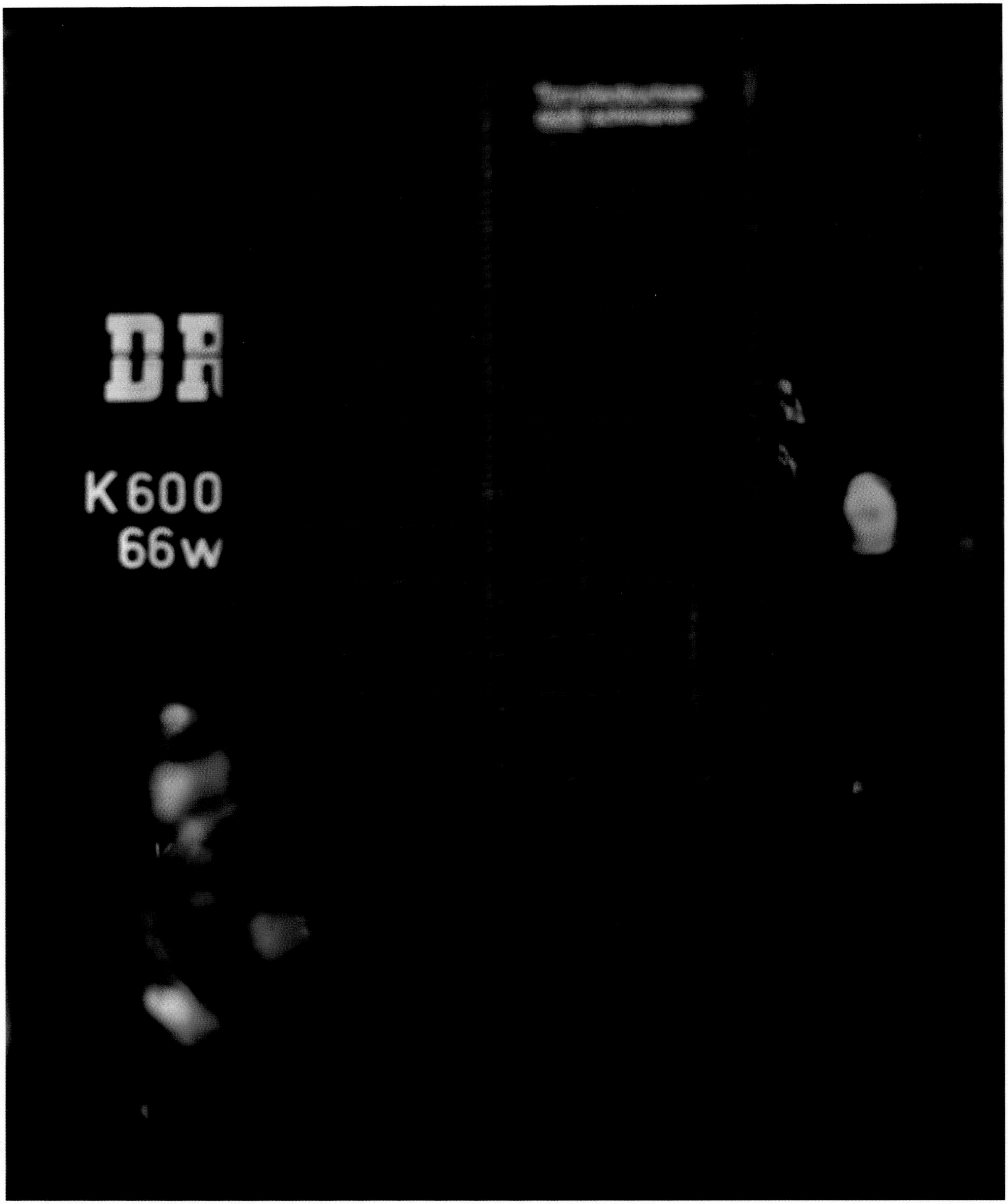
DR
K600
66w

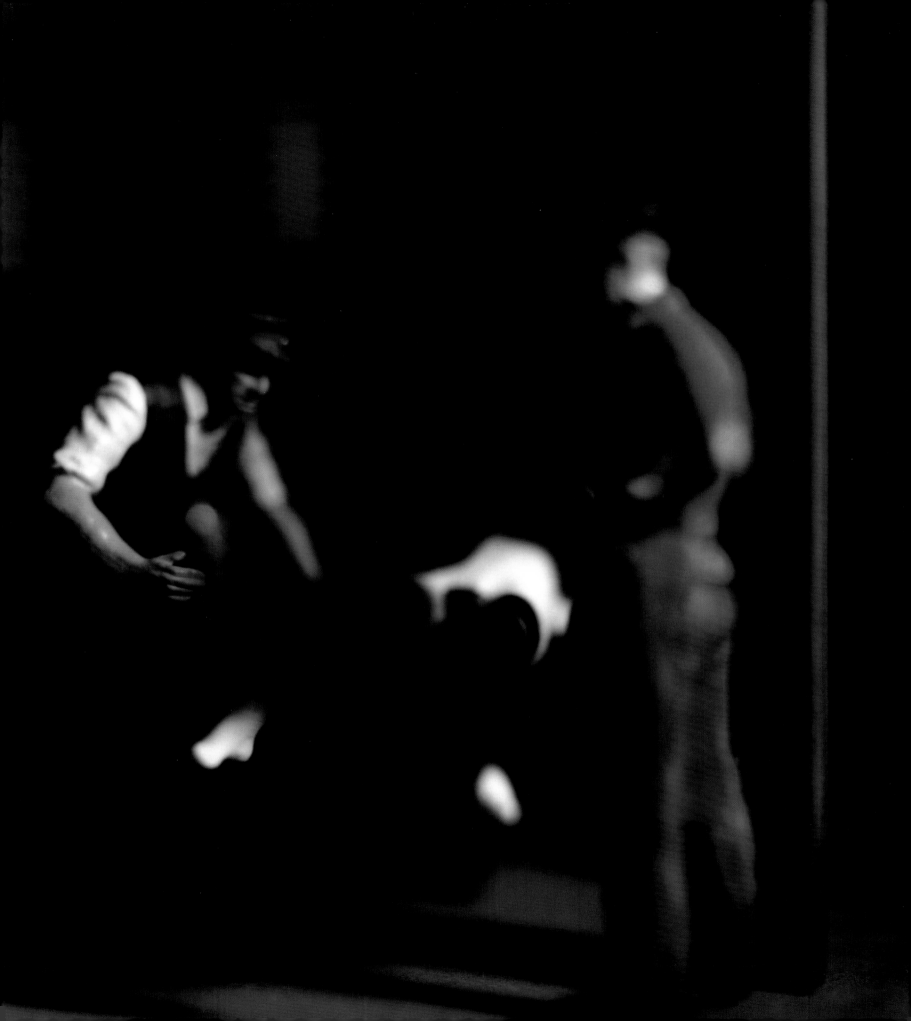

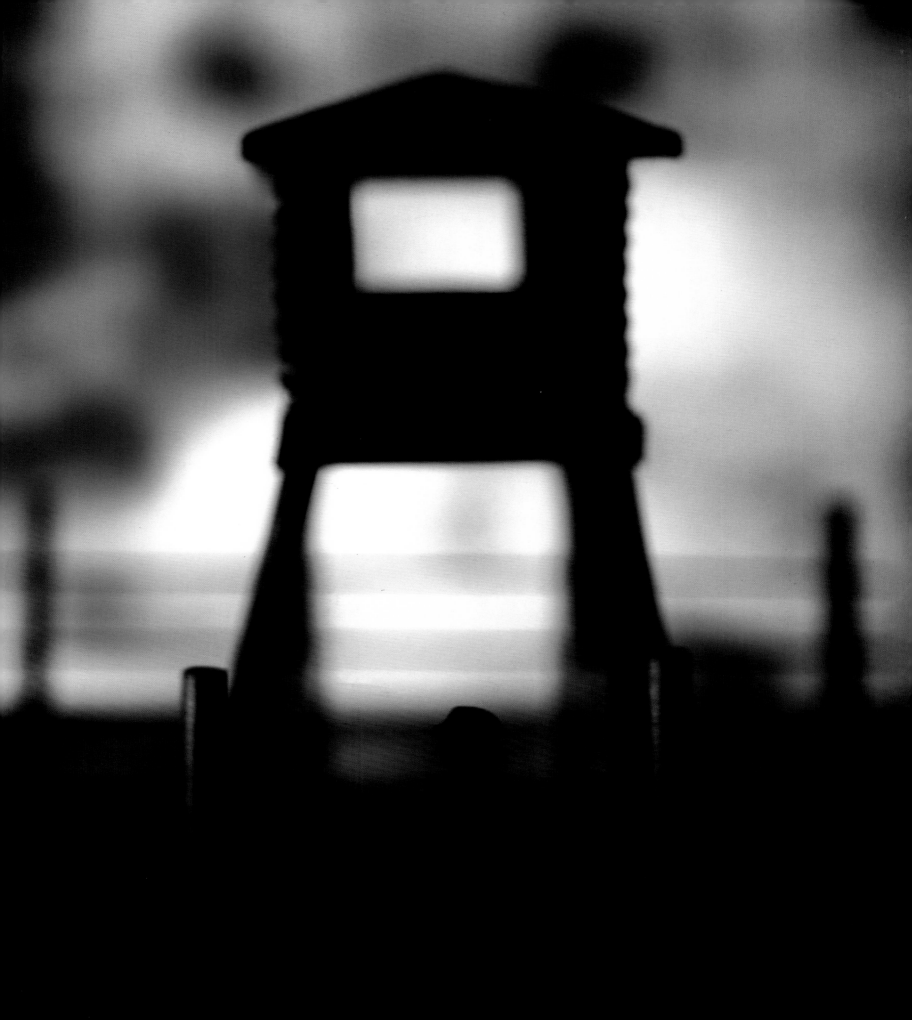

BLACKFACE, 1995-96

RW: Do you see your most recent series, "Blackface," as a logical or inevitable development from the work you were doing earlier?

DL: As the artist, I'm in the worst place to give perspective on my work. That said, I think each body of work deals with stereotypes of iconography. Given this country's cultural history, perhaps the most formidable stereotype that we have is that of race. The iconography of the objects in "Blackface," some of which have a history of well over one hundred years, might present the greatest challenge. The issues I dealt with in the "Desire" series are certainly very important. But nothing that I've addressed previously is as pervasive as the issue of racism.

I look at the "Blackface" work as, in many ways, a culmination of my work to date. It encompasses several issues from previous series: the idea of history, found in "Wild West," "Hitler Moves East," and "Mein Kampf"; issues of sexuality, as in both "Desire" and "American Beauties"; issues of alienation, which also arose in "Modern Romance." There are elements of all these in the "Blackface" series, in part because of the nature of our society's relationship to stereotypical images of blacks, and the concept of African American culture.

RW: Unlike previous work, however, you photographed these images straight. You did not create a tableau.

DL: "American Beauties" was also photographed without any sort of tableaux. I photographed the Amos and Andy figures in two ways, first as full figure, then head and shoulder shots. If you look at the figures, then look at the final photographs, there's a tremendous transformation of the object. I take the object as a starting point and I work with it. In the "Wild West" series, I created a scene around the object. Here I'm really editing—in this case, within the object.

CS: Yes, you're editing by deleting significant information from the picture.

DL: I'm also making information clearer. In other words, you see the face of the Amos and Andy figure far more clearly than you would if you were simply looking at the toy. The head itself is many times larger. It takes on a very powerful aura when seen in such detail.

I thought about using backgrounds for the "Blackface" figures, as I had in other series, but the diversity of objects made it more elegant to simply use black velvet. It's as if the figures emanate from that blackness. It's the same technique that I used with the "Desire" figures, actually; there it created a sense of sort of mystery and foreboding. While I wasn't looking for mystery in "Blackface," there is a sense of foreboding. Sometimes the objects merge with the blackness of the background to create a certain ambiguity.

CS: Again and again I'm struck by the fact that these photographs basically document fine objects, but you inject something into the image making them loaded and provocative.

DL: The times are more loaded. Back in the '30s, the most popular radio program was Amos and Andy—two white guys speaking in Blackface.

CS: You said earlier that you do a lot of reading to prepare for a project. What reading did you do for "Blackface"?

DL: I started by reading about the objects themselves, which meant finding books about collecting this material. I was fortunate to come across a fascinating book by Professor Patricia A. Turner at the University of California, Davis, titled *Ceramic Uncles & Celluloid Mammies: Black Images and Their Influence on Culture*. Hers was a very academic, intellectual look at the objects and the history surrounding them. I've probably read twenty to thirty books on the subject of black history and culture—with twice as many more that I still plan to read.

The more reading I've done, the more fascinated I've become. The history of African Americans in this country is not a history that can be dropped on top of what we've been taught, as a sort of parallel history. It's all woven together, and every time I peel away a layer I see another layer. The way things were reported—or not—reveals so much about our history and ourselves.

CS: I think it has a lot to do with photography, too. As a culture we attach so much significance to photographs.

DL: I never imagined that the "Blackface" work would provoke such intense controversy. Then again, race is probably one of the rawest nerves in our society. I hope that the work itself becomes a catalyst for reflection and discussion.

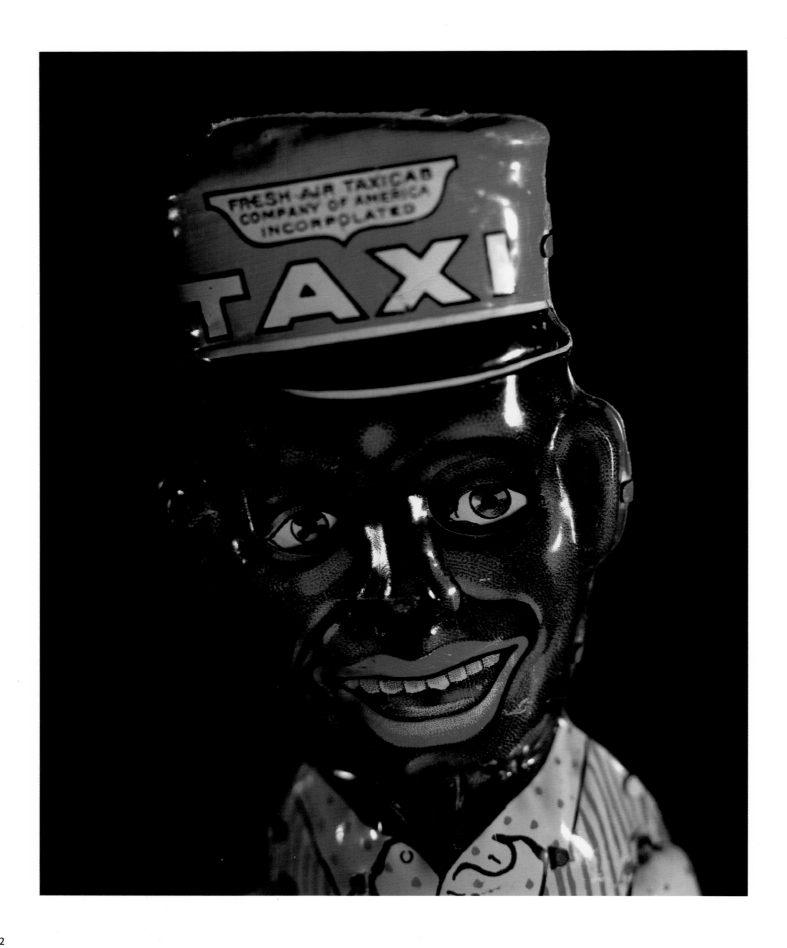

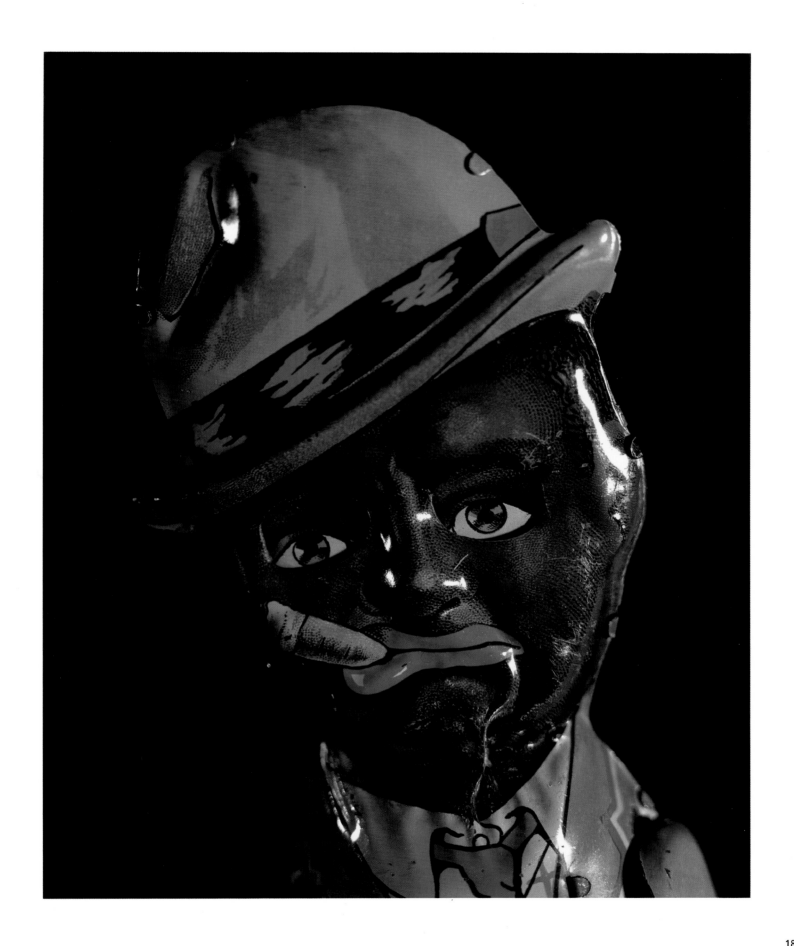

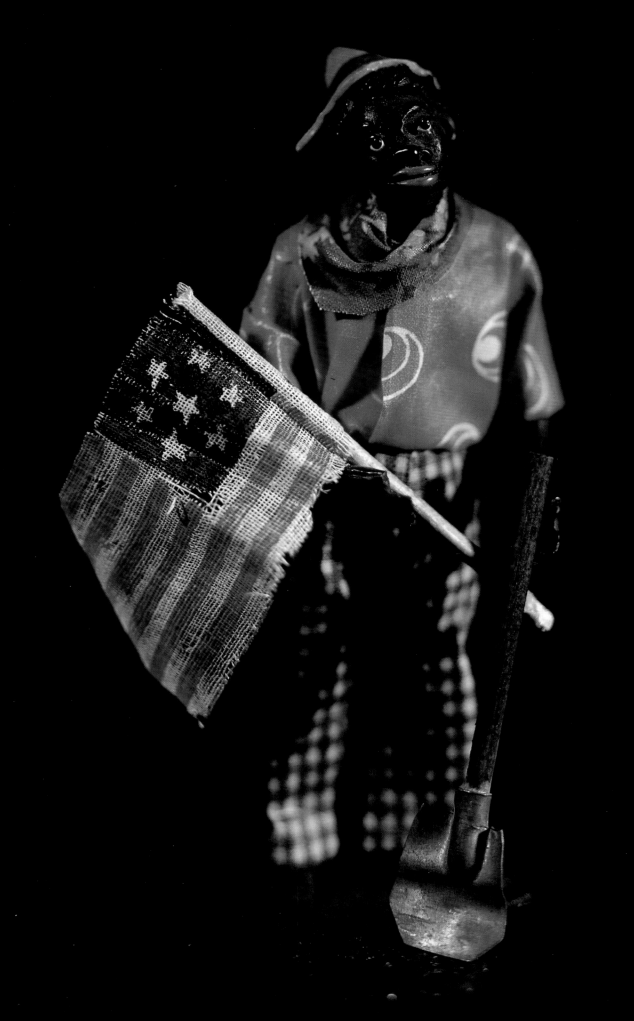

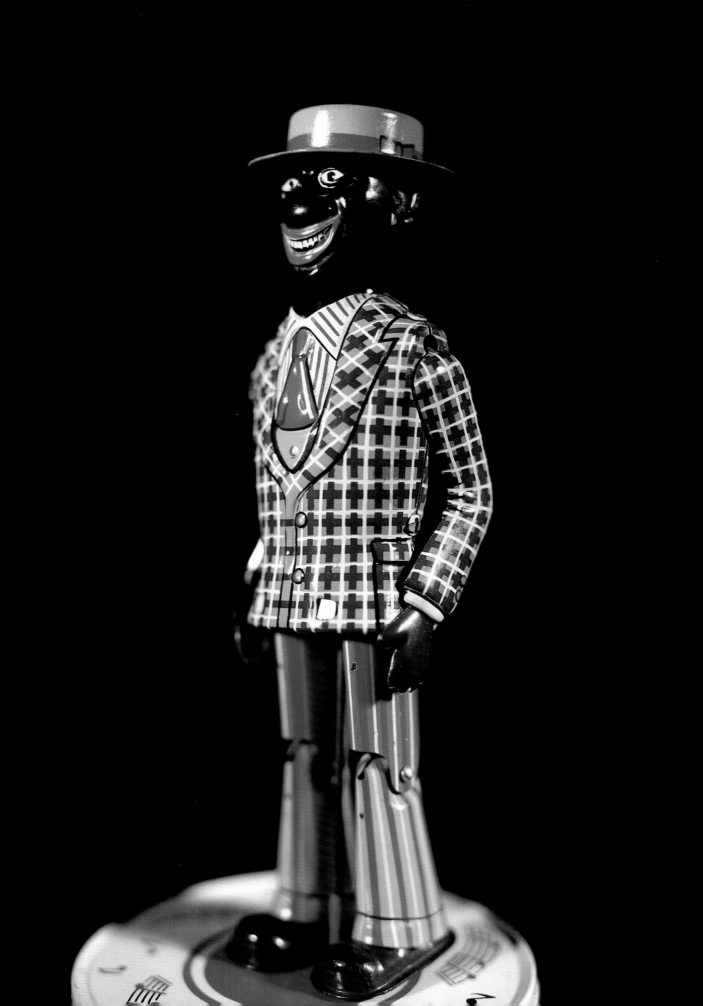

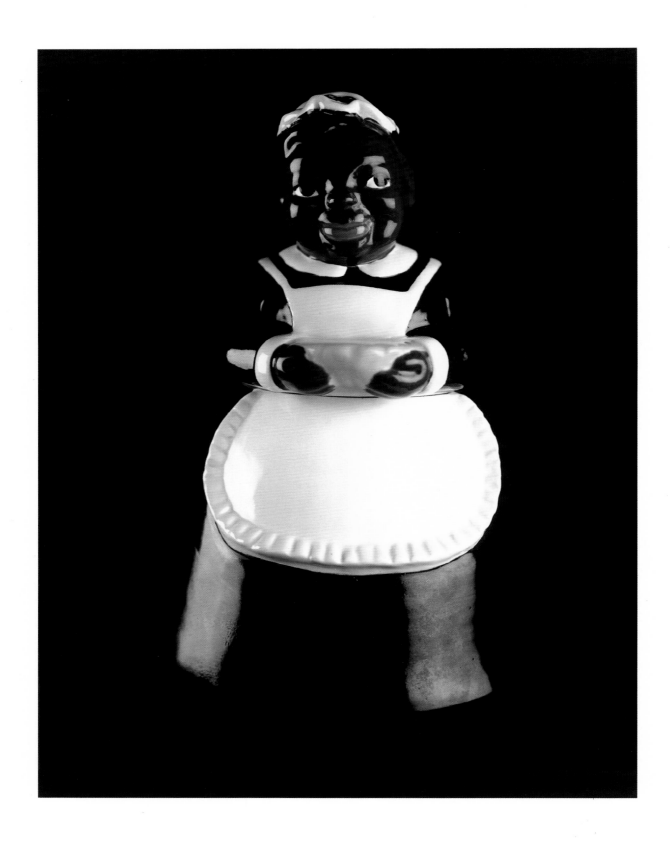

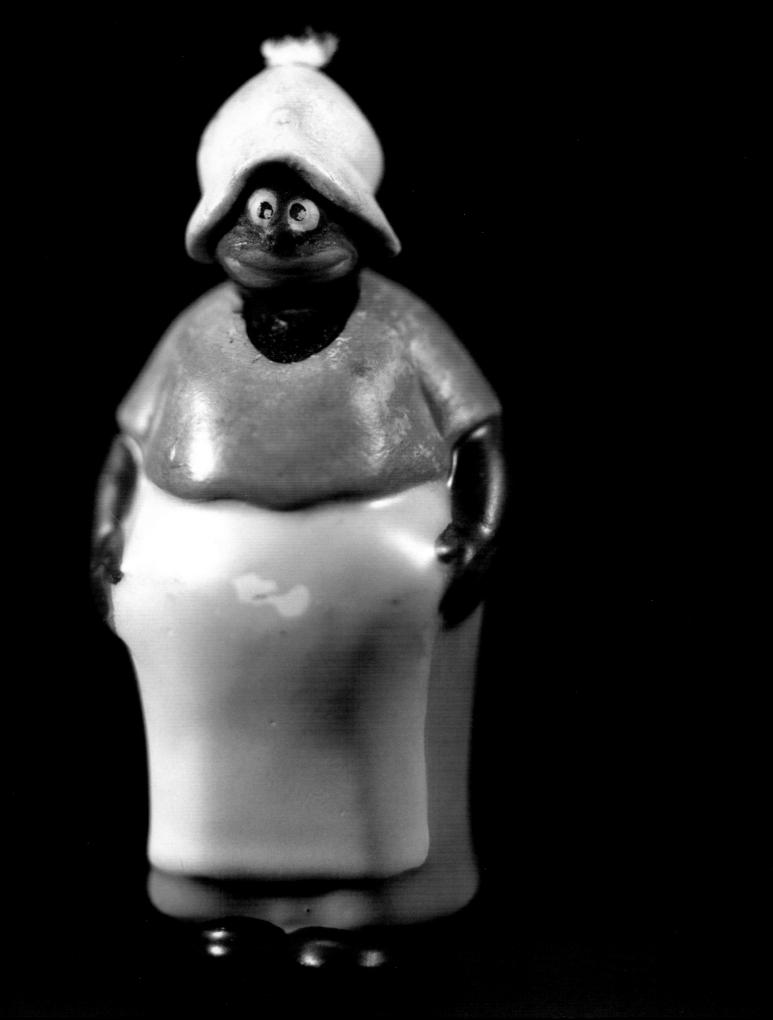

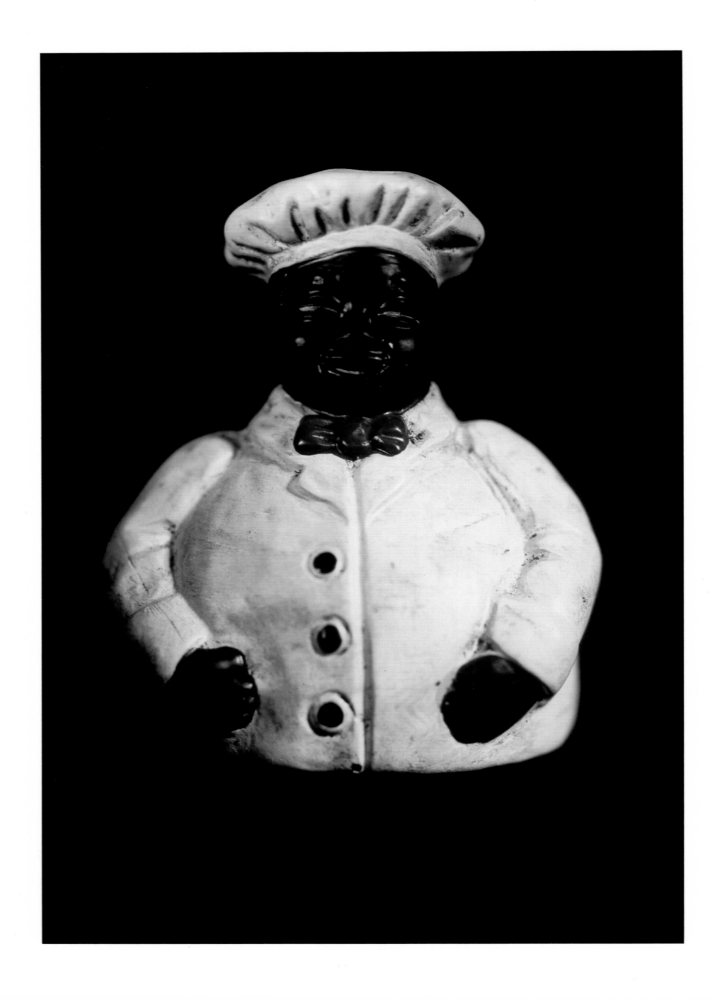

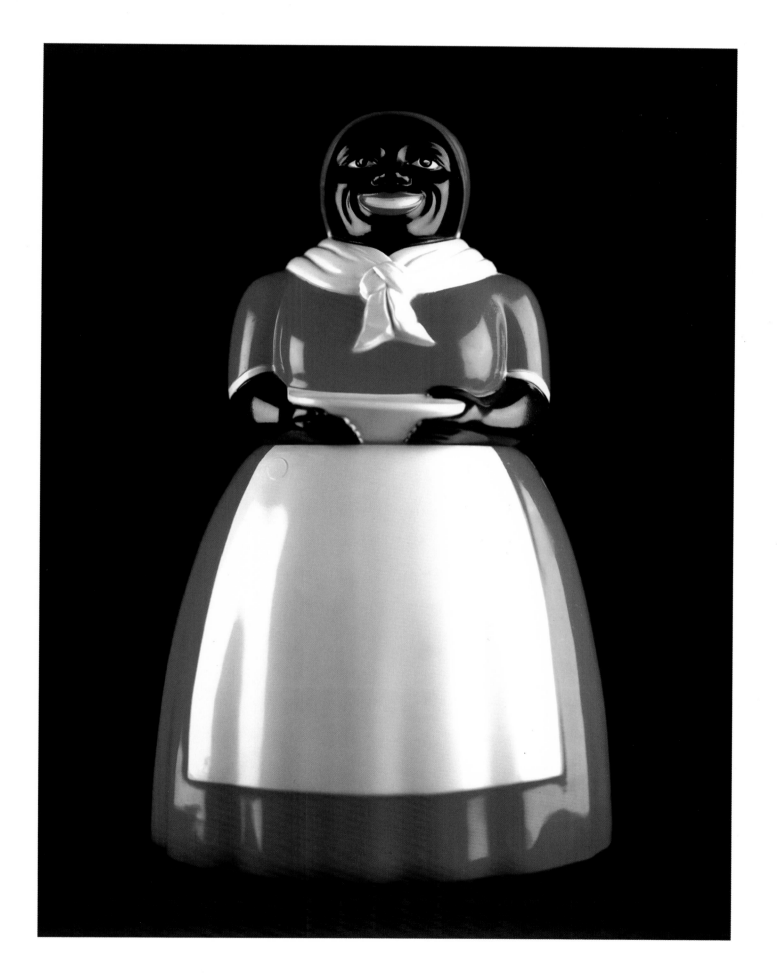

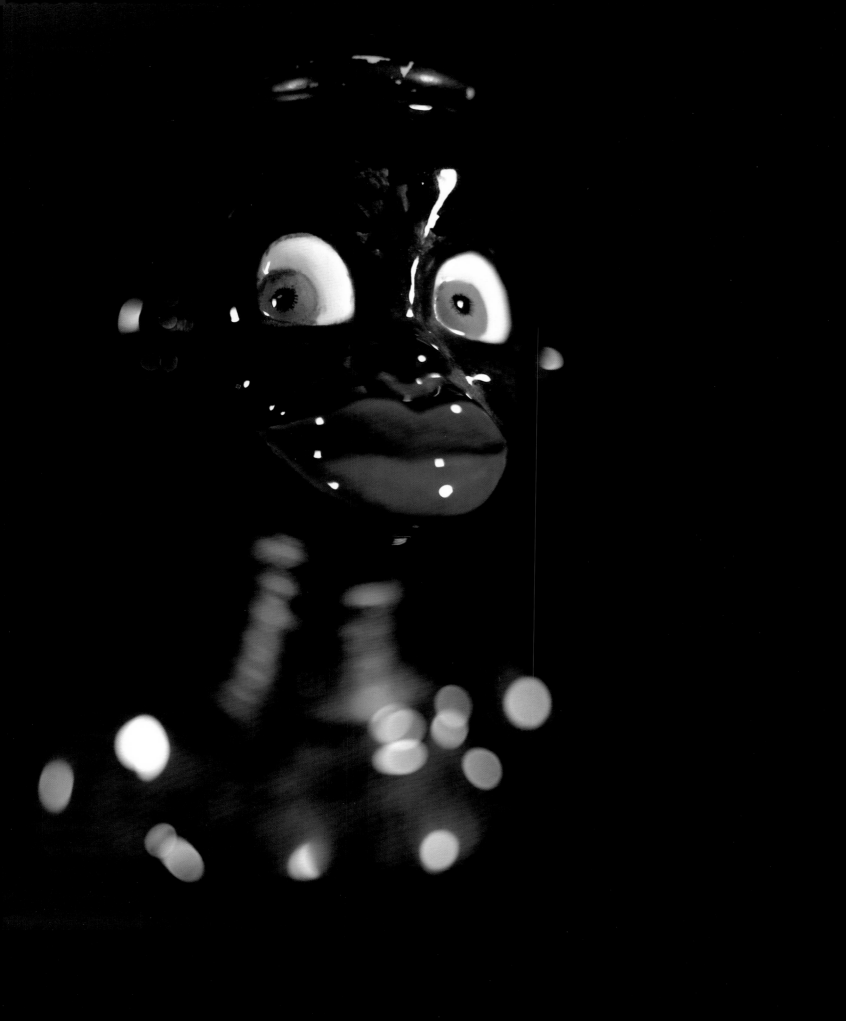

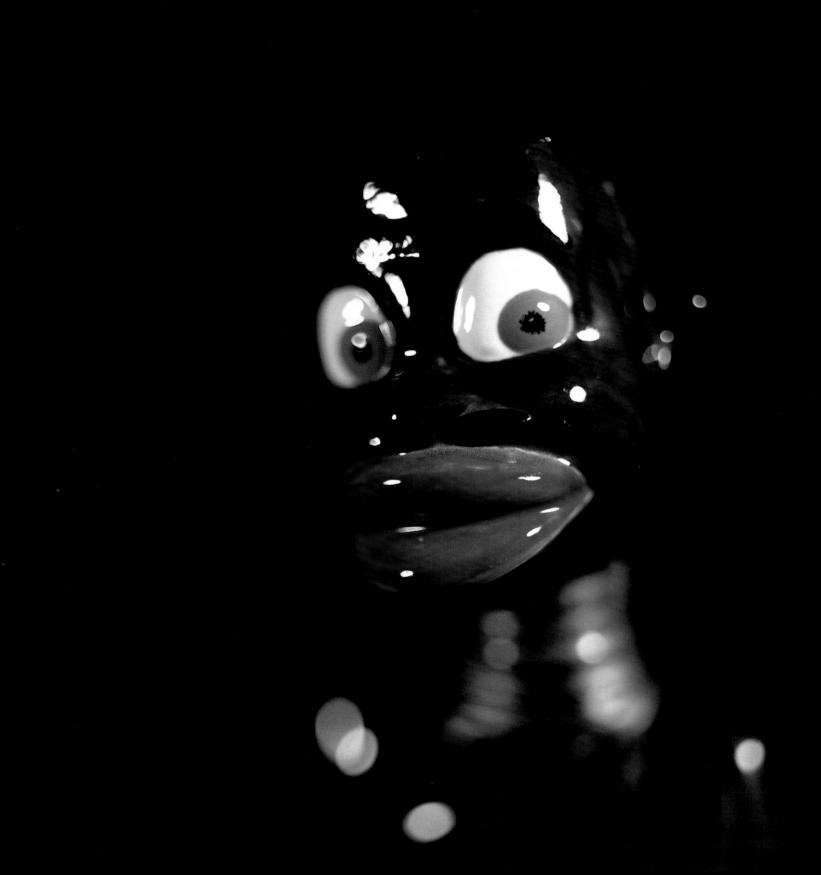

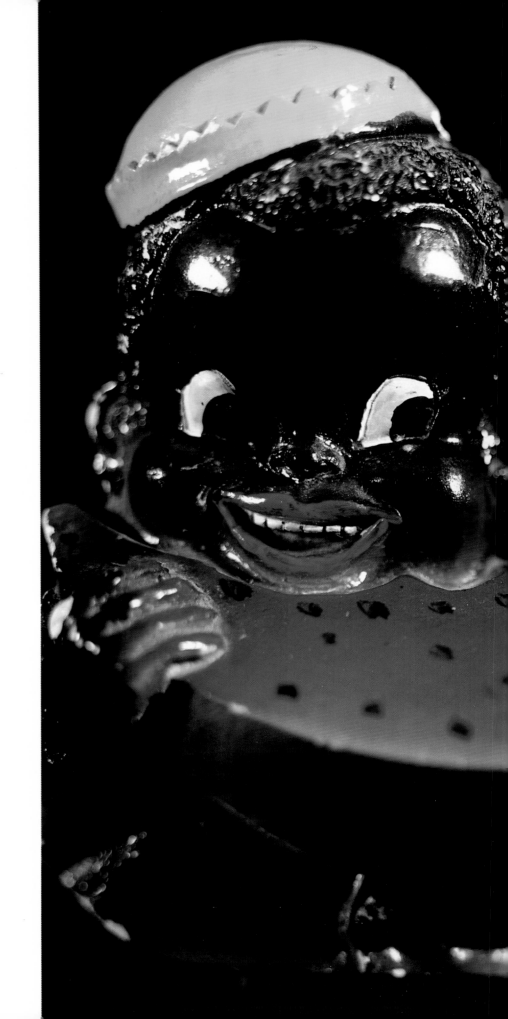

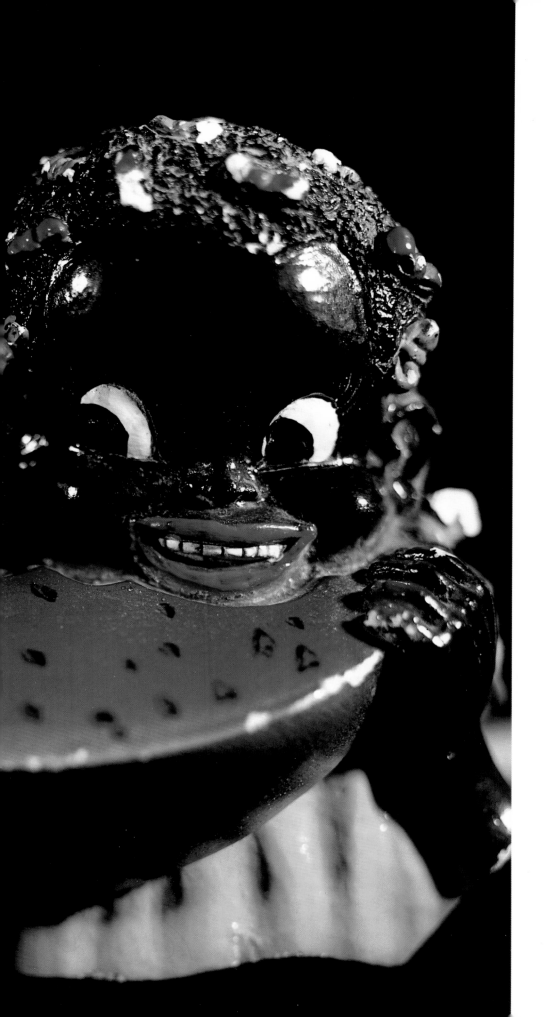

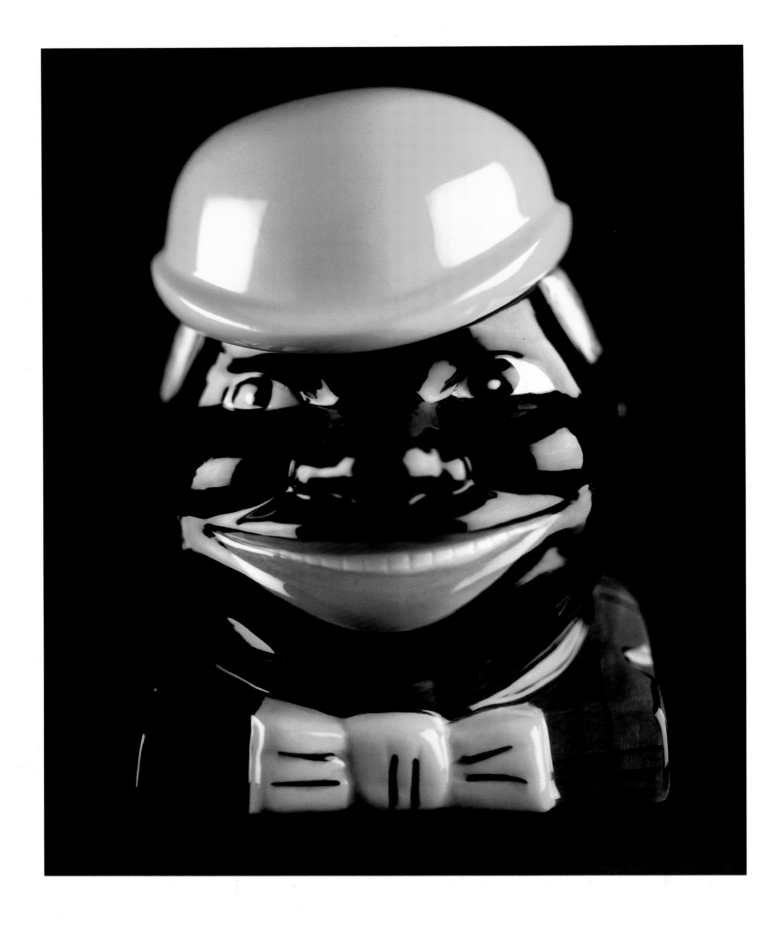

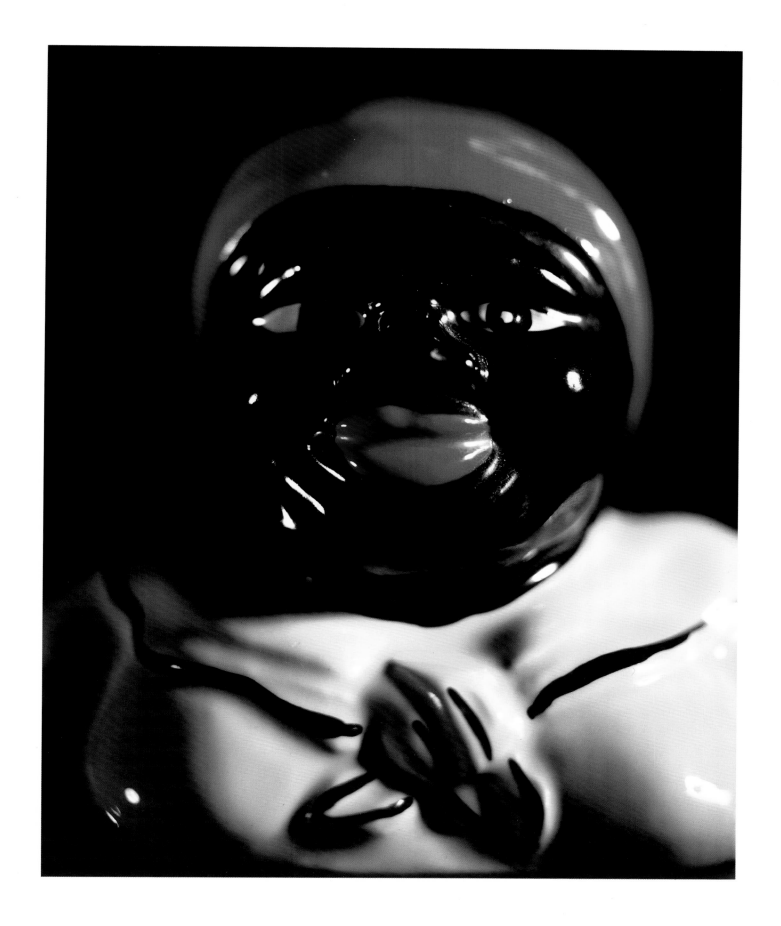

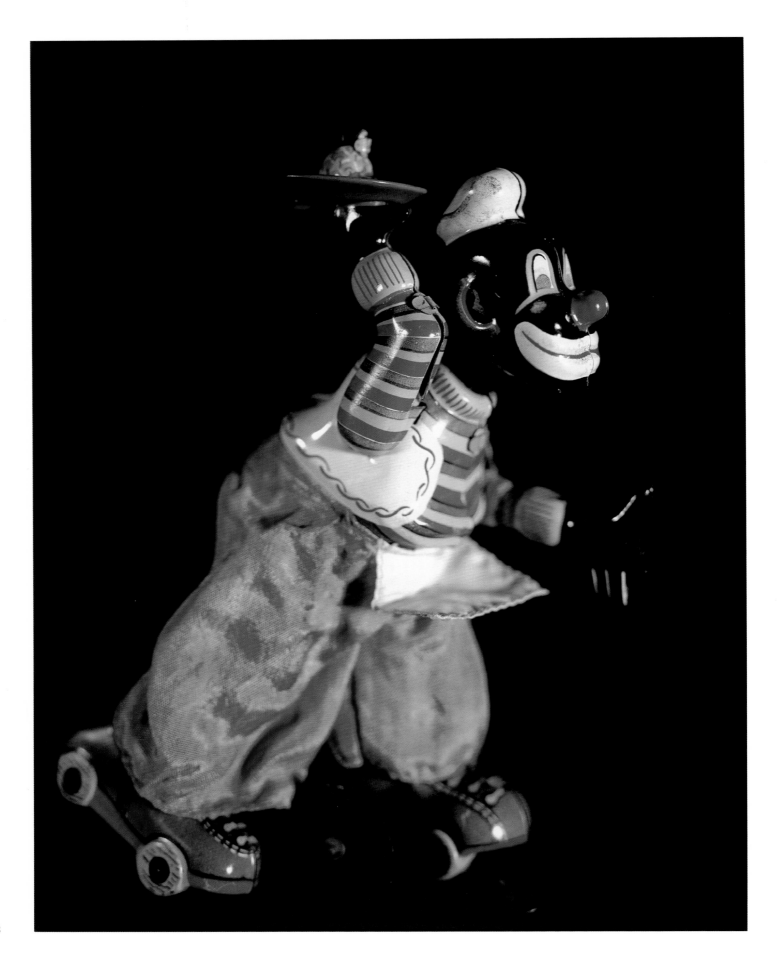

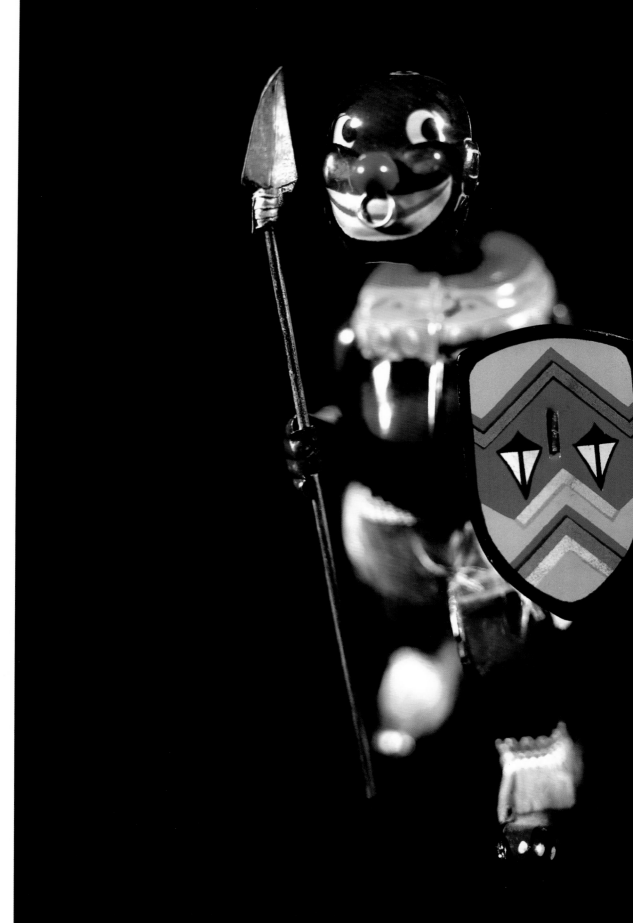

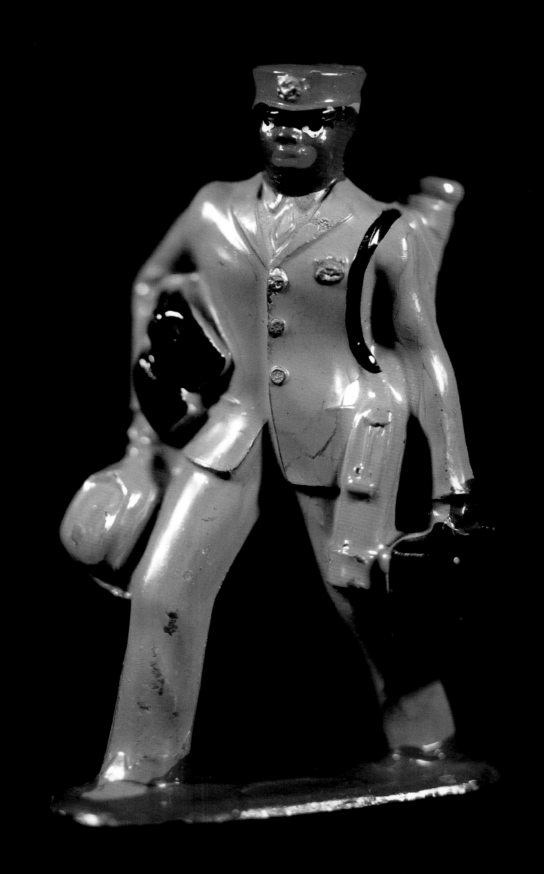

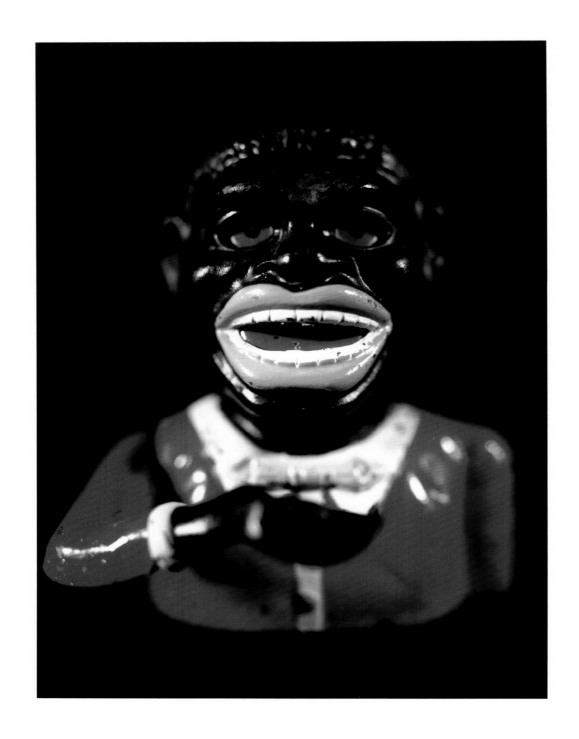

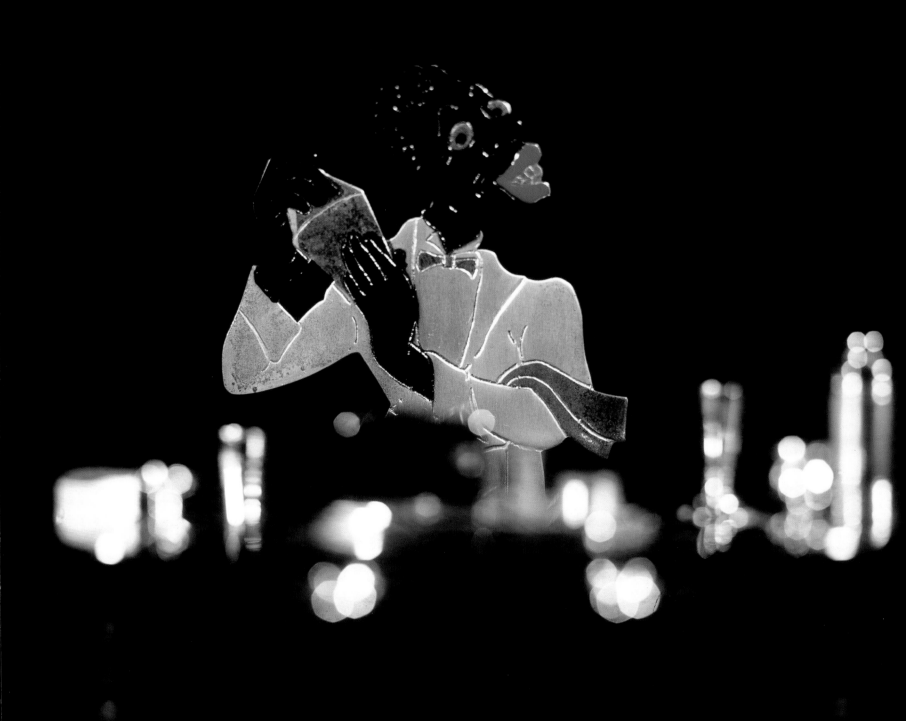

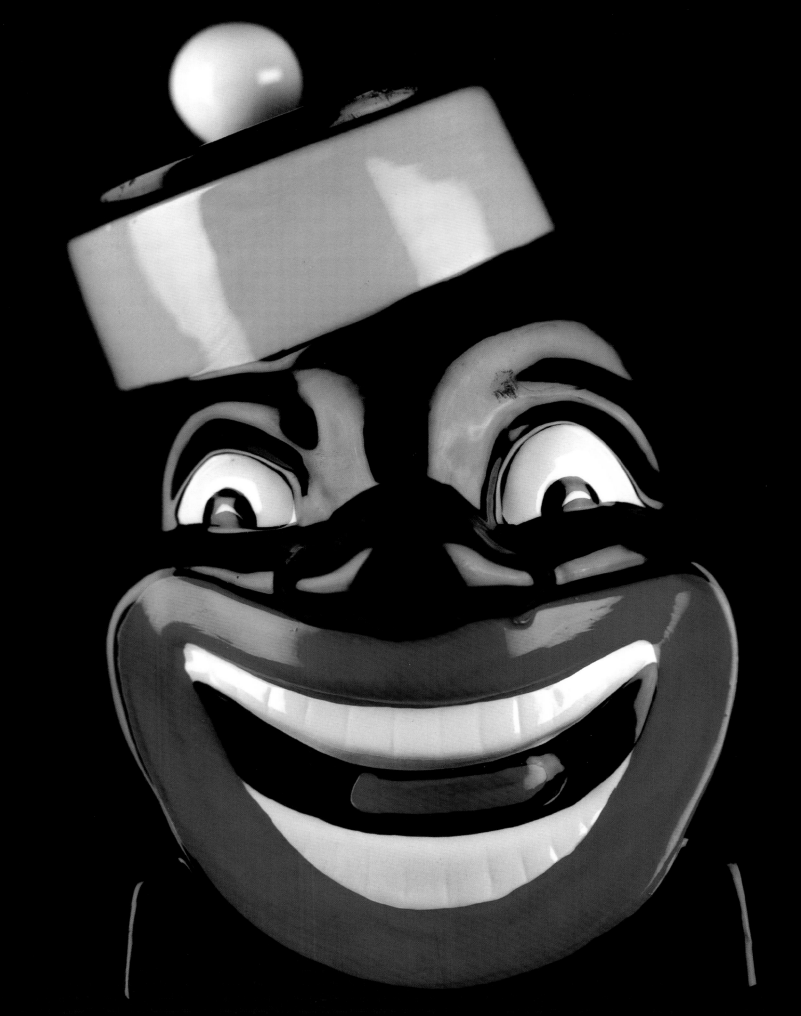

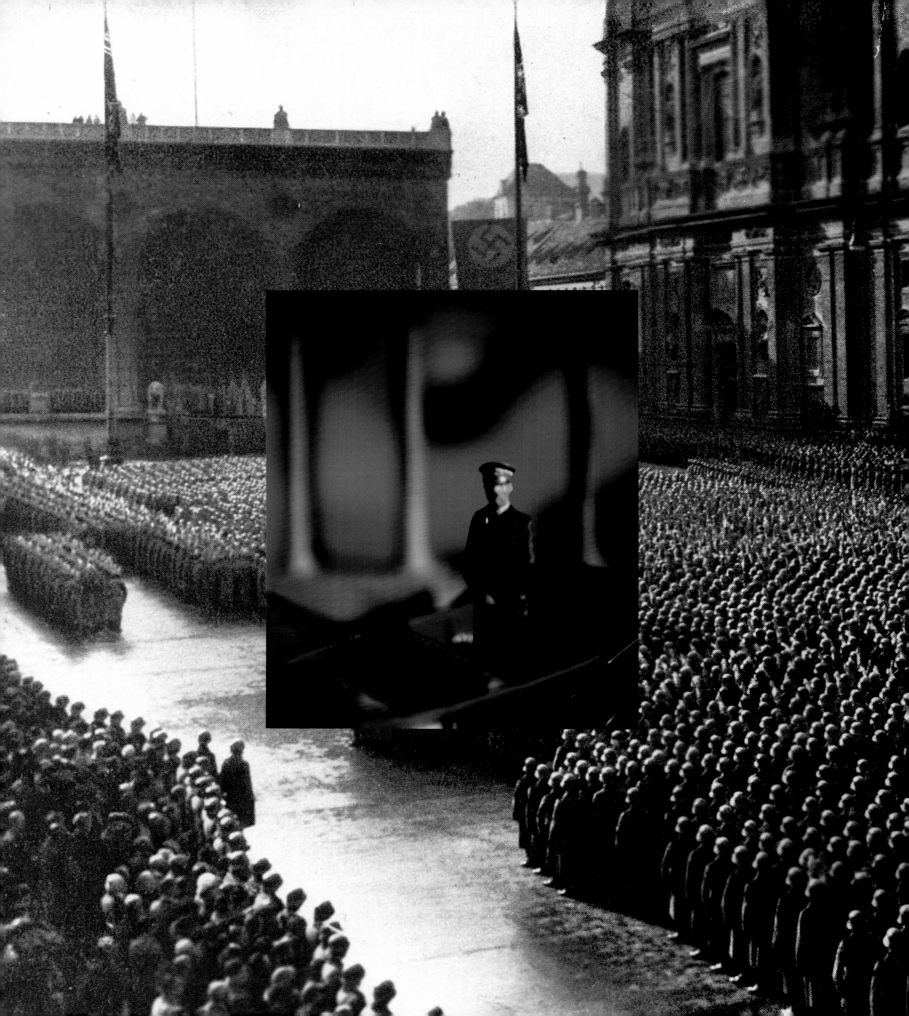

Born 1949, San Francisco
Resides New York

Education
1981 S.M. Management Science, M.I.T.
1973 M.F.A. Photography, Yale University
1970 A.B. Studio Art, Stanford University

Grants
John Simon Guggenheim Foundation
  Fellowship 1995
National Endowment for the Arts, Visual
  Artist's Fellowship 1990–91
Polaroid Corporation Artist Support Grants
  1987–89

Selected One-Person Exhibitions
1997 Craig Krull Gallery, Santa Monica, Calif.
  Janet Borden, Inc., New York
  Lisa Sette Gallery, Scottsdale, Ariz.
  Philadelphia Museum of Judaica
  "David Levinthal: 1975–1996,"
    International Center of
    Photography, New York
  Holocaust Museum Houston
1996 Judah L. Magnus Museum,
    Berkeley, Calif.
  Modernism Gallery, San Francisco

1995 University Art Gallery, University of
    New Mexico, Albuquerque
  Galerie H.S. Steinek, Vienna
  Craig Krull Gallery, Santa Monica, Calif.
  Megan Fox Gallery, Santa Fe, N.M.
1994 Modern Art Museum of Fort Worth,
    Fort Worth, Tex.
  Center for Creative Photography,
    Tucson, Ariz.
  Gilcrease Museum, Tulsa, Okla.
  Janet Borden Gallery, New York
  The Photographers' Gallery,
    London
  Bibliothèque Nationale, Paris
1993 The Friends of Photography, Ansel
    Adams Center, San Francisco
  Wiener Staatsoper, Vienna
  Galerie H.S. Steinek, Vienna
  Gene Autry Western Heritage Museum,
    Los Angeles
  Palm Springs Desert Museum,
    Palm Springs, Calif.
  Southeastern Center for Contemporary
    Art, Winston-Salem, N.C.
  Laurence Miller Gallery, New York
  Pastrays Gallery, Yokohama, Japan
1991 Janet Borden Gallery, New York
  Laurence Miller Gallery, New York
  Museum für Gestaltung, Zürich
  Forum Bottcherstrasse, Bremen,
    Germany

1990 Pence Gallery, Santa Monica, Calif.
  Laurence Miller Gallery, New York
1989 University Art Museum, California State
    University, Long Beach
  Jan Kesner Gallery, Los Angeles
1988 C.E.P.A. Gallery, Buffalo, N.Y.
  Laurence Miller Gallery, New York
  Clarence Kennedy Gallery, Polaroid
    Corporation, Cambridge, Mass.
  Allied Arts Gallery, Las Vegas
1987 303 Gallery, New York
  Philadelphia College of Art
1986 Visual Arts Gallery, University of
    Alabama, Birmingham
  Blatent Image Gallery, Pittsburgh
1985 Area X Gallery, New York
  Founders Gallery, University of
    San Diego, Calif.
1978 International Museum of Photography
    at George Eastman House,
    Rochester, N.Y.
  Quivera Gallery, Albuquerque, N.M.
1977 Carpenter Center of Visual Arts,
    Harvard University, Cambridge,
    Mass.
  California Institute for the Arts,
    Valencia

Selected Group Exhibitions
1997 "Devoir de Mémoire," Rencontres
    Internationales de la Photographie,
    Arles, France
  "Figured," Associated American Artists,
    New York
  "Making it Real," Independent Curators
    Incorporated, New York;
    The Aldrich Museum of
    Contemporary Art, Ridgefield,
    Conn.
  "The Mythic Image," David Adamson
    Gallery, Washington, D.C.
1996 "The Importance of Toys," Monique
    Knowlton Gallery, New York
  "Helman Gallery: Invitational," Joseph
    Helman Gallery, New York
  "Blind Spot Photography: The First
    Four Years," Paolo Baldacci Gallery,
    New York
  "The Secret Life of Toys," Art Museum
    of Western Virginia, Roanoke

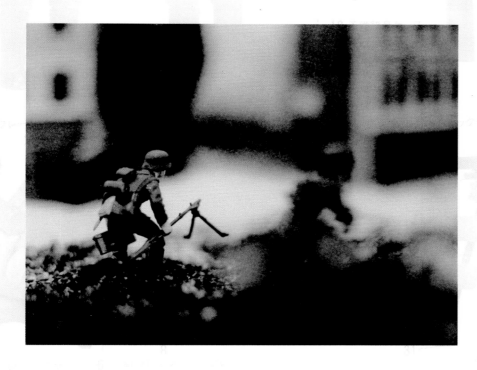

"The Painted Photograph: Hand-colored
Photography, 1839 to the Present,"
University of Wyoming Art
Museum, Laramie
"Prospect 96," Schirn Kunsthalle,
Frankfurt, Germany
"The Enduring Illusion," Stanford
University Museum of Art,
Stanford, Calif.
"Telling Stories: Narrative Tableau
Photography," Jacksonville
Museum of Contemporary Art,
Jacksonville, Fla.
1995 "Edward Hopper and the American
Imagination," Whitney Museum of
American Art, New York
"An American Century of Photography:
From Dry Plate to Digital," The
Hallmark Photographic Collection,
Kansas City, Mo.
"Representations of Auschwitz: 50 Years
of Photographs, Paintings and
Graphics," Auschwitz-Birkenau
State Museum, Auschwitz, Poland
1994 "After Art: Rethinking 150 Years of
Photography," Selections from the
Joseph and Elaine Monsen
Collection, Henry Art Gallery,
University of Washington,
Seattle
"Talking Pictures: People Speak about
the Photographs That Speak to
Them," International Center of
Photography, Midtown, New York.
Traveling to: 1995, The Friends
of Photography, San Francisco;
Washington Project for the Arts,
Washington, D.C.; High Museum
of Art, Atlanta, Ga.; Milwaukee Art
Museum, Milwaukee, Wis.; 1996,
Los Angeles County Museum of
Art; Delaware Art Museum,
Wilmington; Fine Arts Gallery,
Vanderbilt University, Nashville;
Center for Creative Photography,
Tucson, Ariz.; 1997, Louisiana Art
and Science Center, Baton Rouge
1993 "Memories, Facts & Lies," BlumHelman
Gallery, New York
"Dolls in Contemporary Art," Haggerty
Museum of Art, Marquette
University, Milwaukee, Wis.
"American Made: The New Still Life,"
Isetan Museum of Art, Tokyo

1992 "More Than One Photography,"
Museum of Modern Art,
New York
"Sofort-Bild-Geschichten, Instant-
Imaging-Stories," Museum
Moderner Kunst, Vienna
"Interpreting the American Dream"
(James Casebere, David Levinthal,
Richard Ross), Galerie Eugen
Lendl, Graz, Austria
"Illusions et Travestissements," A.B.
Galerie, Paris
1991 "Devil on the Stairs," Institute of
Contemporary Art, Philadelphia;
Newport Harbor Museum,
Newport Beach, Calif.
"Des Vessies et des Lanternes," La
Botanique, Brussels;
Palais de Tokyo, Paris
"Recent Acquisitions," Amon Carter
Museum, Fort Worth, Tex.
1990 "Odalisque," Jayne Baum Gallery,
New York
"Rethinking American Myths,"
Atrium Gallery, University of
Connecticut, Storrs
1989 "Surrogate Selves: David Levinthal,
Cindy Sherman, Laurie Simmons,"
The Corcoran Gallery of Art,
Washington, D.C.
"Photography of Invention," National
Museum of American Art,
Washington, D.C.
"The New Concept," Forum Stadtpark,
Graz, Austria
"The Mediated Imagination," State
University of New York, Purchase
"Abstraction in Contemporary
Photography," Hamilton College,
Clinton, N.Y.
"Constructed Realities," Kunstverein,
Munich
"Theatergarden Bestiarium,"
The Institute for Contemporary Art,
P.S.1 Museum, New York
1988 "The Return of the Hero," Burden
Gallery, New York
"The Constructed Image II," Jones
Troyer Gallery, Washington, D.C.
"Selections 4," Photokina 88, Cologne,
Germany
1987 "Avant-Garde in the Eighties," Los
Angeles County Museum of Art
"Photography and Art 1946–86,"
Los Angeles County Museum
of Art

1986 "Acceptable Entertainment," Bruno
Facchetti Gallery, New York
"Signs of the Real," White Columns,
New York
1985 BC Space, Laguna Beach, Calif.
1983 "In Plato's Cave," Marlborough Gallery,
New York

Selected Collections
Amon Carter Museum, Fort Worth, Tex.
Art Institute of Chicago
BankAmerica Corporation, San Francisco
Bibliothèque Nationale, Paris
Birmingham Museum of Art,
Birmingham, Ala.
The Brooklyn Museum, New York
Continental Insurance, New York
The Corcoran Gallery of Art,
Washington, D.C.
Eurostar, Graz, Austria
Gene Autry Western Heritage Museum,
Los Angeles
Georgia Museum of Art, Athens
Grand Rapids Art Museum,
Grand Rapids, Mich.
The Hallmark Photographic Collection,
Kansas City, Mo.
High Museum of Art, Atlanta, Ga.
International Center of Photography,
New York
International Museum of Photography at
George Eastman House, Rochester, N.Y.
Los Angeles County Museum of Art
Metropolitan Museum of Art, New York
Milwaukee Art Museum, Milwaukee, Wis.
The Minneapolis Institute of Arts,
Minneapolis, Minn.
Modern Art Museum of Fort Worth,
Fort Worth, Tex.
Museum of Contemporary Photography,
Columbia College, Chicago
Museum of Fine Arts, Houston
Museum of Modern Art, New York
National Gallery of New Zealand, Wellington
New York Public Library
Norton Gallery, West Palm Beach, Fla.
Polaroid Collection, Cambridge, Mass.
Progressive Art Collection,
Mayfield Heights, Ohio
San Jose Museum, San Jose, Calif.
Stanford University Museum of Art,
Stanford, Calif.
University Art Museum, California State
University, Long Beach
Whitney Museum of American Art,
New York

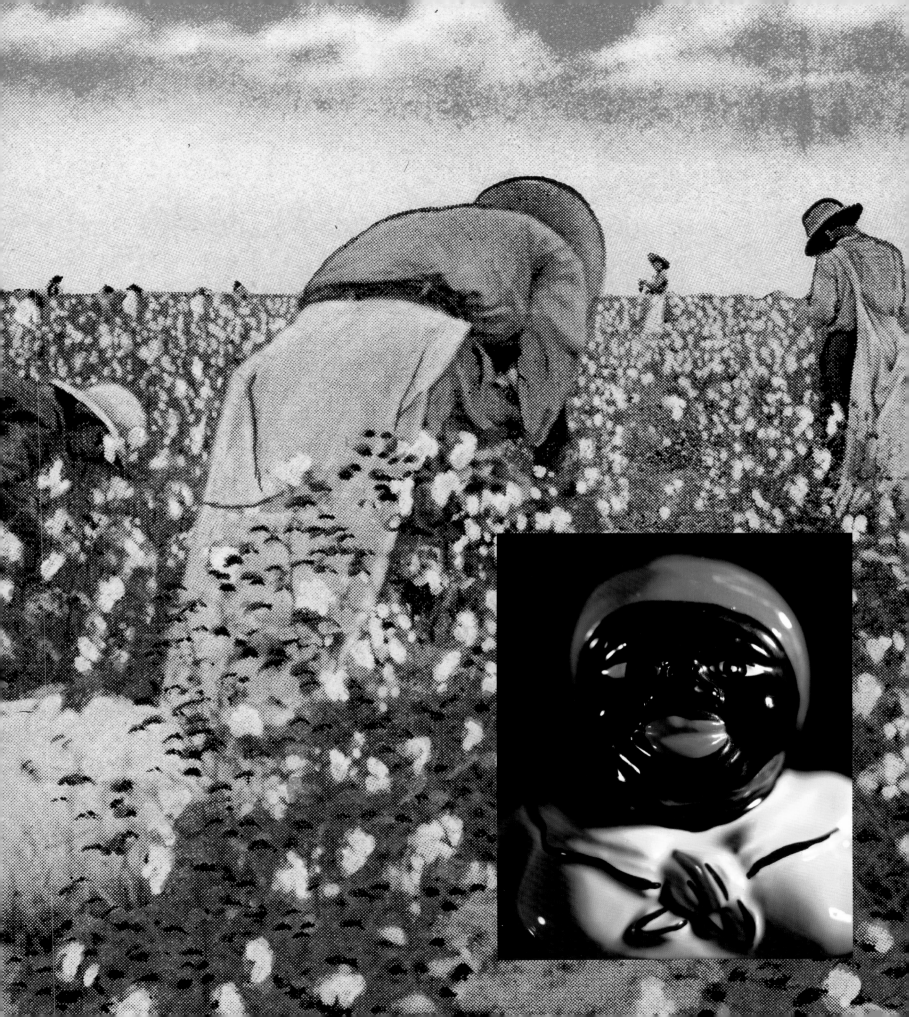

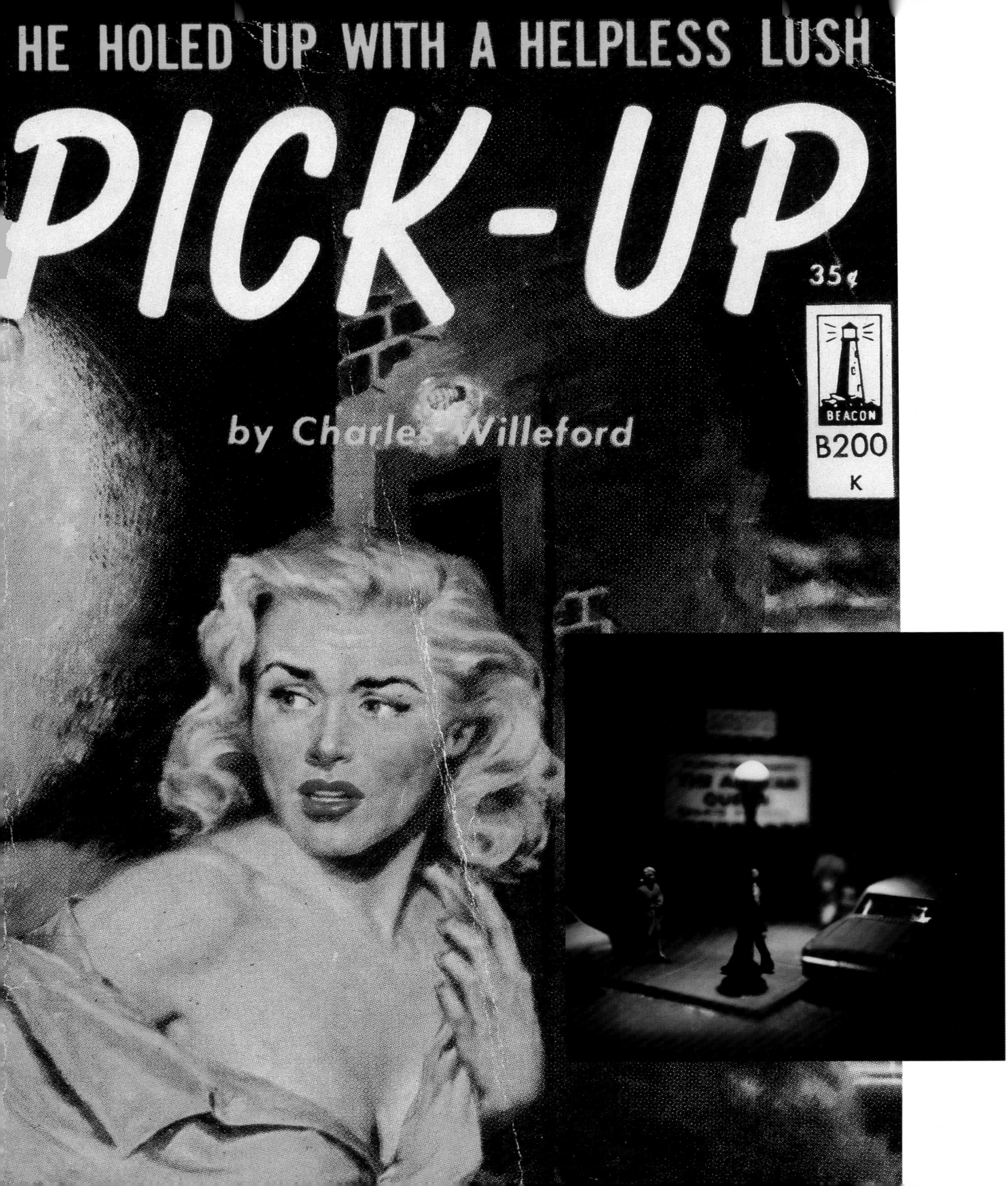
HE HOLED UP WITH A HELPLESS LUSH
PICK-UP
35¢
BEACON
B200
K
by Charles Willeford

Books and Exhibition Catalogues

Barnes, Lucinda. *Centric 35: David Levinthal.* Long Beach: California State University, 1989.

Davis, Keith F. *An American Century of Photography: From Dry-Plate to Digital, The Hallmark Photographic Collection.* Foreword by Donald J. Hall. Kansas City, Mo.: Hallmark Cards, Inc., in association with Harry N. Abrams, 1995.

Deville, Françoise, and Alain D'Hooghe. *Des Vessies et des Lanternes.* Brussels: Les Editions du Botanique, 1991.

Faber, Monika. *Sofort-Bild-Geschichten (Instant-Imaging-Stories).* Vienna: Museum Moderner Kunst, 1992.

Ferrer, Linda. *Eros.* New York: Stewart, Tabori & Chang, 1996.

Fox, Howard N. *Avant-Garde in the Eighties.* Los Angeles: Los Angeles County Museum of Art, 1987.

Grundberg, Andy, and Kathleen McCarthy Gauss. *Photography and Art: Interactions Since 1946.* New York: Abbeville Press, 1987.

Hirsch, Robert. *Exploring Color Photography.* Dubuque, Iowa: William C. Brown Publishers, 1988.

Hoy, Anne H. *Fabrications: Staged, Altered, and Appropriated Photographs.* New York: Abbeville Press, 1987.

Kolb, Gary. *Photographing in the Studio.* Madison, Wis.: William C. Brown Publishers, 1993.

Lang, Gerald, and Lee Marks. *The Horse: Photographic Images, 1839 to the Present.* New York: Harry N. Abrams, Inc., 1991.

Levinthal, David. *American Beauties.* Essay by Rosetta Brooks. Santa Monica, Calif.: Pence Gallery and New York: Laurence Miller Gallery, 1990.

——————. *Dark Light: David Levinthal Photographs 1984–1994.* Essay by David Allan Mellor. London: The Photographers' Gallery, 1994.

——————. *Desire.* Essay by Andy Grundberg. San Francisco: The Friends of Photography, Ansel Adams Center, 1993.

Levinthal, David. *Die Nibelungen.* Text by Julien Robson and Andrea Hurton. Vienna: Wiener Staatsoper, Galerie H.S. Steinek, 1993.

——————. *Mein Kampf.* Essay by James E. Young, Introduction by Roger Rosenblatt, Afterword by Garry Trudeau. Santa Fe, N.M.: Twin Palms Publishers, 1996.

——————. *Modern Romance: David Levinthal.* Essay by Barton D. Thurber. San Diego, Calif.: Aaron Press, in association with Founders Gallery, University of San Diego, 1985.

——————. *The Wild West: Photographs by David Levinthal.* Edited by Constance Sullivan. Essay by Richard B. Woodward. Washington, D.C.: Smithsonian Institution Press, 1993.

Levinthal, David. *Small Wonder: Worlds in a Box.* Essay by David Corey. Washington, D.C.: National Museum of American Art/D.A.P., 1997.

Levinthal, David, and Garry Trudeau. *Hitler Moves East: A Graphic Chronicle, 1941–43.* New York: Sheed, Andrews & McMeel, 1977.

Lord, M. G. *Forever Barbie: The Unauthorized Biography of a Real Doll.* New York: William Morrow and Company, Inc., 1994.

Muniz, Vik. *Making It Real.* Introduction by Luc Sante. New York: Independent Curators Incorporated, 1996.

Robson, Julien. *Interpreting the American Dream.* Graz, Austria: Galerie Eugen Lendl, 1992.

Solomon-Godeau, Abigail. *In Plato's Cave.* New York: Marlborough Gallery, 1983.

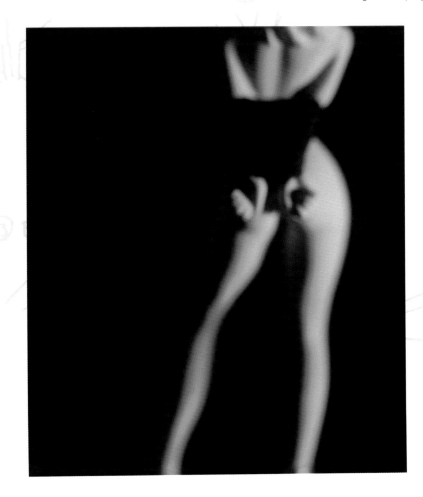

Solomon-Godeau, Abigail. "Photography at the Dock." In *The Art of Memory/The Loss of History*. New York: The New Museum of Contemporary Art, 1985.

Storr, Robert. *Devil on the Stairs*. Philadelphia: Institute of Contemporary Art, 1991.

Sultan, Terrie. *Surrogate Selves: David Levinthal, Cindy Sherman, Laurie Simmons*. Washington, D.C.: The Corcoran Gallery of Art, 1989.

Weiermair, Peter. *Prospect: Photography in Contemporary Art*. Frankfurt, Germany: Edition Stemmle, 1996.

Yoe, Craig. *The Art of Barbie: Artists Celebrate the World's Favorite Doll*. New York: Workman Publishing Co., 1994.

Articles and Reviews

Albig, Jörg-Uwe von. "Der Fotografie wird die Wirkchlichkeit Ausgetrieben." *Geo Extra* (Summer 1996): 150.

Aletti, Vince. "Valley of the Dolls." *The Village Voice*, May 21, 1991.

Aiger, Carl. "Mein Kampf/Hitler Moves East." *EIKON: Internationale Zeitschrift für Photographie & Medienkunst* (August 1995): 94–95.

Baker, Kenneth. "The Holocaust on a Whole New Scale." *San Francisco Chronicle*, May 14, 1996.

Benfey, Christopher. "Toys R Us: David Levinthal's Dollhouse History." *Slate*, February 19, 1997.

Berry, Wendell. "Property, Patriotism, and National Defense." *Aperture*, no. 110, "The Return of the Hero" (Spring 1988): 33–40.

Boxer, Sarah. "Hardly Child's Play: Shoving Toys into Darkest Corners." *New York Times*, January 24, 1997.

Brooks, Rosetta. "A Biennial of Our Own." *Seven Days*, May 3, 1989.

Carlson, Lance. "Enlarging the Photographic Impact." *Artweek*, April 29, 1989: 12.

Coleman, A. D. "Hitler Moves East Turns Fourteen." *Camera & Darkroom* (January 1992): 54–56.

_____. "Hitler Moves East." *European Photography* 12, no. 3: 47–49.

_____. "New York City as Subject and Inspiration." *New York Observer*, January 9, 1989.

_____. "The Image in Question." *Center Quarterly* 9, no. 4 (Summer 1988): 4–9.

Costello, Michael. "Tabletop History." *Afterimage* (April 1978): 18–19.

Eauclaire, Sally. "Hitler: A Chronicle of Horror." *Rochester Democrat & Chronicle*, February 19, 1978.

Ehrlich, Jane. "About Time, as Levinthal Photos Show in London." *The American*, April 22, 1994.

Foresta, Merry. "Toying with History: A Conversation with David Levinthal, William Christenberry, and Merry Foresta." *SEE: A Journal of Visual Culture* 1, no. 2 (1995): 25–31.

French, David. "Seeking Critical Dialog." *Artweek*, November 28, 1987: 6.

Goodman, Tim. "Absolutely Successful." *Palo Alto Weekly*, August 16, 1989.

Grundberg, Andy. "Where Blurred Focus Makes Sharp Statements." *New York Times*, December 20, 1987.

_____. "Image and Idea." *New York Times Magazine*, August 30, 1987.

_____. "David Levinthal: American Beauties." *New York Times*, May 25, 1990.

Hagen, Charles. "David Levinthal: Modern Romance." *New York Times*, September 13, 1991.

_____. "Treating Nazis in Art, Even Seriously, Is Risky." *New York Times*, November 25, 1994.

Heiferman, Marvin, and Carol Kismaric. "Getting Close to Gotham." *ARTnews* (September 1987): 106–111.

Hoffmann, Justin. "Das Neue Konzept." *Artis* (May 1990): 26–29.

Horn, Miriam. "Dark Stirrings in Toyland: David Levinthal's Disturbing Art Turns the Familiar into Strange." *US News & World Report*, February 3, 1997.

Illetschko, Peter. "Fabrik der Mythologien." *Der Standard*, May 8, 1992.

"Imaged Documents." *C.E.P.A. Quarterly* (Winter/Spring 1988): 15–17.

Kent, Sarah. "Macho Pink." *Time Out*, June 8, 1994.

Kessler, Pamela. "The Created Event." *Washington Post*, March 26, 1988.

Knight, Christopher. "Photographer Levinthal Goes West." *Los Angeles Herald Examiner*, April 14, 1989.

Kozloff, Max. "Hapless Figures in an Artificial Storm." *Artforum* (November 1989): 132.

Levinthal, David. "Captain Gallant." *American Art* (Winter/Spring 1991): 60–67.

Levinthal, David. "'Hitler Moves East.'" *Camera Austria* 33/34 (1989): 49–56.

Loke, Margarette. "Up Now, David Levinthal: International Center of Photography." *ARTnews* (March 1997): 108.

Matis, Gretchen. "Photos Display Myths, Romanticism Shaping Our Perspective of the West." *Atlanta Journal/Atlanta Constitution*, April 6, 1993.

Mendelsohn, John. "Toy Story." *Jewish Week*, March 7, 1997.

Murray, Joan. "Memorable Books." *Artweek*, January 7, 1978: 13–14.

Newhall, Edith. "Photography : The World's a Stage." *New York Magazine*, January 20, 1997.

Pagel, David. "David Levinthal." *Art Issues* (September/October 1989): 28.

_____. "Toys in Bondage." *Los Angeles Times*, August 8, 1991.

Richards, Jane. "Mein Kampf, the Polaroids." *The Independent*, May 25, 1994.

Rowe, James. "Hitler Moves East." *Review* (November/December 1989): 6.

Schjeldahl, Peter. "Down in Flames." *The Village Voice*, February 4, 1997.

Singer, Mark. "Toy Stories." *The New Yorker*, January 20, 1997.

Starenko, Michael. "Modern Romance." *Afterimage* (January 1986): 21.

Strasser, Teresa. "Controversial Photographer Toys with Holocaust." *Jewish Bulletin of Northern California*, May 17, 1996.

Thorson, Alice. "Camera Records Invented Worlds." *Washington Times*, April 21, 1988.

Walker, Ian. "David Levinthal: Photographer's Gallery." *Untitled* (Summer 1994).

Welzenbach, Michael. "Static, Photographic 'Surrogate.'" *Washington Post*, January 25, 1989.

Weiley, Susan. "The Darling of the Decade." *ARTnews* (April 1989): 143–150.

Wise, Kelly. "Photos Miniature the Old West." *Boston Globe*, February 13, 1988.

Woodward, Richard B. "David Levinthal." *ARTnews* (March 1989): 108.

_____. "Taking Toys Seriously: Mini-Movement or Sideshow." *New York Times*, February 26, 1989.

_____. "Color Blind: White Artist + Black Memorabilia = No Show." *The Village Voice*, June 25, 1996.

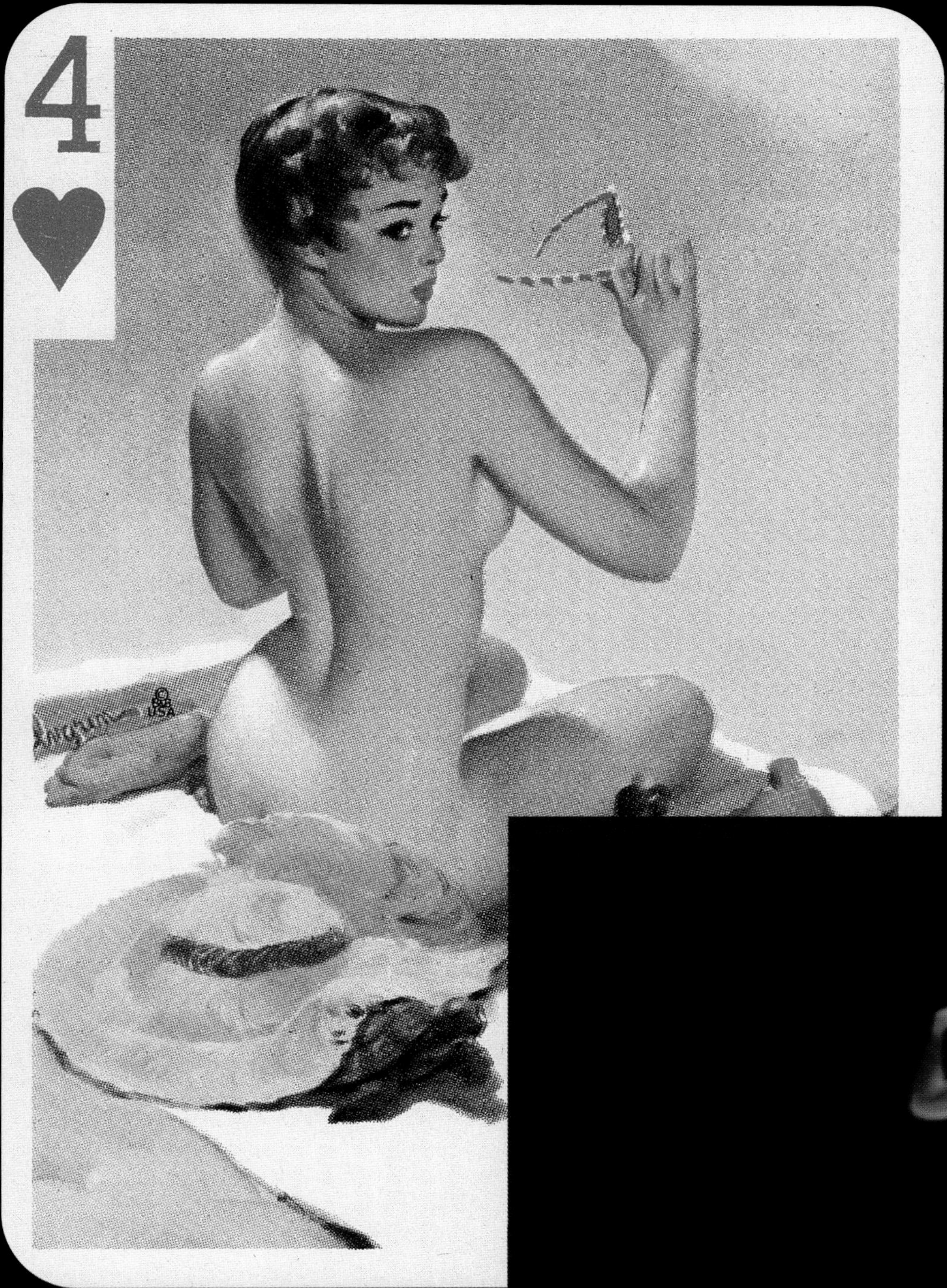
4

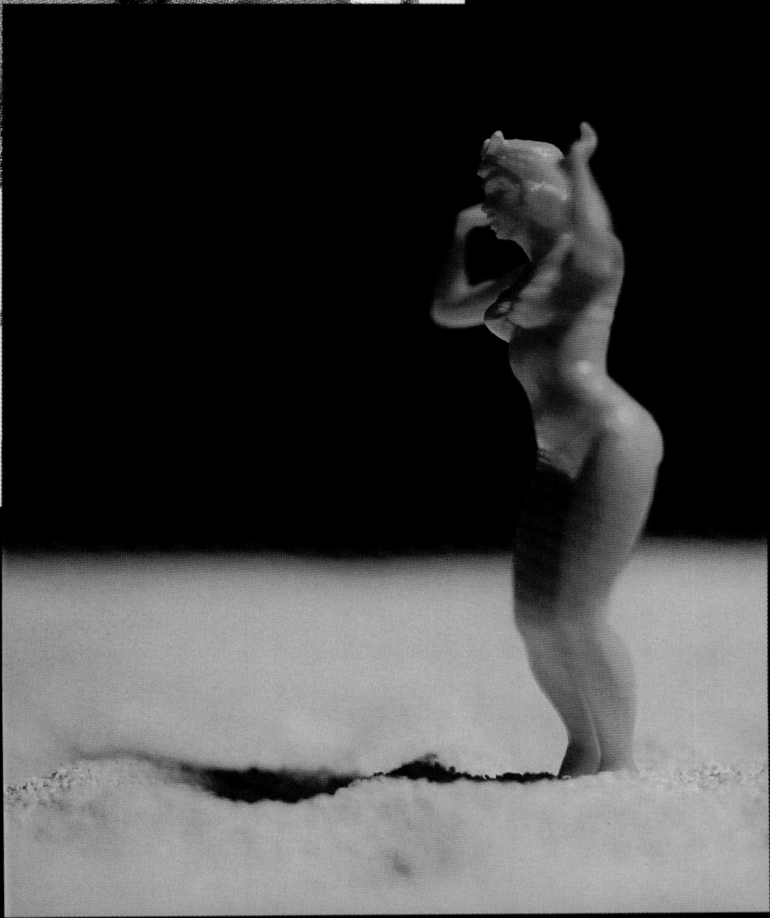

ACKNOWLEDGMENTS

This publication essentially began after I viewed an exhibition of Levinthal's *Hitler Moves East* photographs at the George Eastman House in Rochester, New York over twenty years ago. This first encounter with Levinthal's work utterly confused me; yet I never forgot it. Over the years I saw a Levinthal photograph here, an exhibition there, shifting my initial response of slight unease when viewing photographs of toys playing adult games to one of sheer delight. Three years ago, after seeing a small selection of images from the *Mein Kampf* series at the artist's studio, I finally understood my initial reservations. These seemingly simple pictures of toys trigger our shared cultural memories and the complexities therein.

The provocative nature of this work, often veiled by the striking presence and beauty of the images, is intensified by the realization that the images are small-scale fictions about big issues. Levinthal's images, which have been exhibited extensively and have been collected by many museums and individuals, have never had a comprehensive showing at an American museum. This publication, planned in conjunction with the exhibition at the International Center of Photography (ICP) in early 1997, serves two important purposes. Firstly, it functions as an introduction for countless individuals previously unaware of the breadth and originality of David Levinthal's twenty-five odd years in photography to date. It also provides a focused look at seven of his most important photographic series and the concerns which have remained constant throughout his career.

The organization of *David Levinthal: Work from 1975–1996* at ICP and this publication were massive undertakings. Both would have been unthinkable without the assistance of numerous individuals, in capacities both small and large, that truly made these projects a success. First and foremost, I must extend my sincere appreciation to David Levinthal for making this entire project a truly enjoyable experience. His attention to countless details, endless amounts of good humor, and his appreciation for the notion of collaboration have been essential to this undertaking. His rare combination of modesty, patience, and unpretentiousness have made our many hours together in conversation and resolution of the seemingly neverending details of the project a delight.

Without the assistance and commitment of my colleagues and friends at ICP, the exhibition and book would have been impossible. Many people deserve a special note of thanks, but I must first extend my sincere gratitude to two individuals: Willis Hartshorn, Director of ICP and my longtime friend, for his support, encouragement, and insight through every stage of this project; and Cornell Capa, Founding Director Emeritus of ICP, who for many years has given me the opportunity to explore photographic possibilities outside of his own concerns and

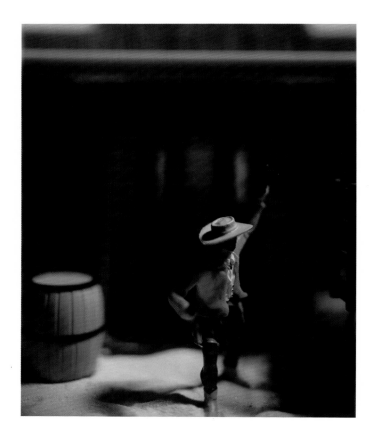

appreciation. Additionally, but no less importantly, the staff of ICP's Exhibitions Department—Samantha Hoover, David Howland, Robert Hubany, Suzie Ruether, Marc Roman, Jennifer Katell, Marion Kocot, and particularly Ellen Handy—have been extremely helpful, working well beyond the call of duty. I must also acknowledge the enthusiastic assistance of Lisa Martin throughout the project. Working closely with David Levinthal in preparing, organizing, and tracking material for this exhibition, she was tireless and totally irreplaceable. I would also like to extend a special note of thanks to John Reuter, Director of the Polaroid Studio in New York. David has often noted that without John's expertise he would not have been able to so readily translate his ideas and his vision into stunning large-scale prints.

Early discussions I had with David led to the agreement that essays alone in this publication would not suffice; rather, a dialogue about his various series of works would provide the best forum to understand the far-reaching context of his photographs. Richard Woodward added an extremely important voice to this publication. His contributions, particularly his illuminating and thoughtful essay, were essential.

The book itself benefited tremendously from Amie Cooper and the Actualizers' crew, who oversaw the lengthy and complex production process. Special thanks must also go to Arni Sigurdsson and everyone at Oddi Printing, Reykjavik, Iceland. Philomena Mariani deserves a very special note of appreciation for her judicious attention to the seemingly endless details of editing all of the texts in this publication, especially my essay. This book is the result of countless hours of effort by many people but the ultimate success, the look, is the result of the extraordinary efforts, intelligence, and patience of Bethany Johns. Her sensitive design, which so accurately reflects the complex nature and historical context of David Levinthal's work, enabled the various elements of the book—photographs, essays, interview—to work together seamlessly.

On behalf of David Levinthal and ICP, I also want to acknowledge Robert Guenther, Charles McCrea, and Barbara Hitchcock of Polaroid, and Anne and Joel Ehrenkranz. Their continual support and encouragement has been important not only to this project, but more importantly, to contemporary art and photography. Additionally, Megan Fox of Megan Fox Gallery in Santa Fe, New Mexico, provided tremendous support throughout the project, as did Janet Borden of Janet Borden Inc., New York; Julien Robson and Silvia Steinek of Galerie H.S. Steinek, Vienna; Lisa Sette of Lisa Sette Gallery, Scottsdale, Arizona; Craig Krull of Craig Krull Gallery, Santa Monica, California; Sharon Gallagher and Avery Lozada of D.A.P./Distributed Art Publishers, New York; Michael Bzdak of Johnson & Johnson, New Brunswick, New Jersey; Jason Burch; Merry Foresta; Rick Hock; Diane DeGrazia; David Lubarsky; Charles Melcher; Marilyn Zeitlin; and especially Joanne Ross, Max Stainback, and Elizabeth Glassman.

Lastly, on behalf of the International Center of Photography and David Levinthal, I want to extend our gratitude and appreciation to Polaroid Corporation, and to the Harriett Ames Charitable Trust, Rob Beyer, Arthur Fleischer, Johnson & Johnson, Bicky and George Kellner, Rhoda and Elliott Levinthal, Barbara Foshay-Miller and Chuck Miller, Meryl and Robert Meltzer, Alan V. Tishman, and Thomas Walther for their support of the *David Levinthal: Work from 1975–1996* exhibition and publication.

Charles Stainback
Director of Exhibitions
International Center of Photography

COLOPHON

David Levinthal: Work from 1975–1996 was designed by Bethany Johns Design, New York, produced by Amie Cooper at The Actualizers, New York, and printed and bound by Oddi Printing, Reykjavik, Iceland on 170 gram Gloss Media Print paper. The typefaces used in this project are Alternate Gothic, Allison, Amazone, Ariston, Courier, Engravers Gothic, FalseNegative, Scala, Fraktur, Frutiger, Memphis, and Mesquite.

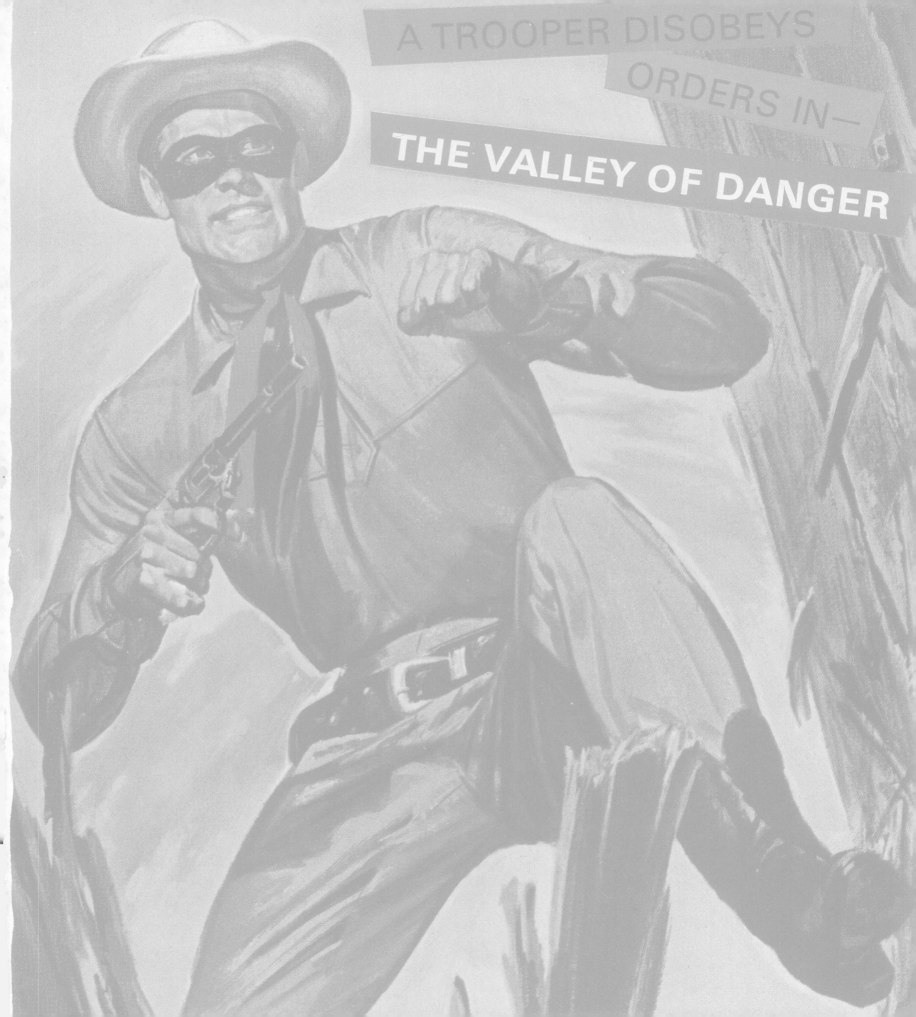

A TROOPER DISOBEYS ORDERS IN—

THE VALLEY OF DANGER

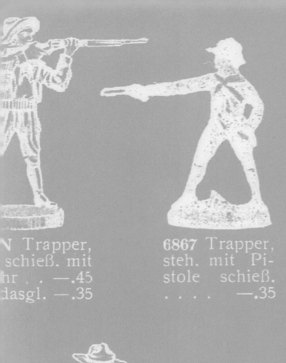
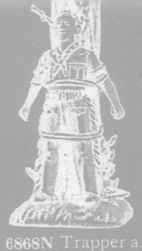
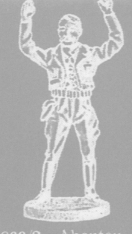
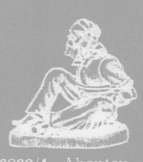
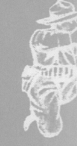

N Trapper,
schieß. mit
hr . . . —.45
dasgl. —.35

6867 Trapper,
steh. mit Pi-
stole schieß.
. . . . —.35

6868N Trapper a.
Marterpfahl —.80
6868 einfach. Aus-
tührung . . —.55

6869/2 Abenteu-
rer Hände hoch
. . . . . . —.45

6869/4 Abenteu-
rer sitz. gefesselt
. . . . . . —.45

6864 N
kniend

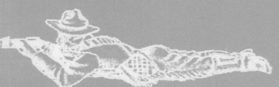
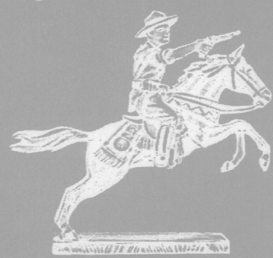
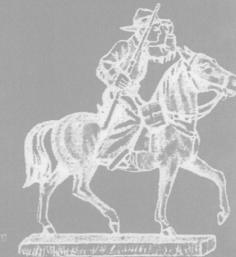

N Trapper liegend schießend . —.45
einfache Ausführung . . . . —.35

6902 N Trapper zu Pferd,
mit Pistole schießend 1.—

6904N Trapp. z. Pferd, späh, -.80
6904¹/₂ N Trapp. m. Standpferd,
spähend . . . . —.90

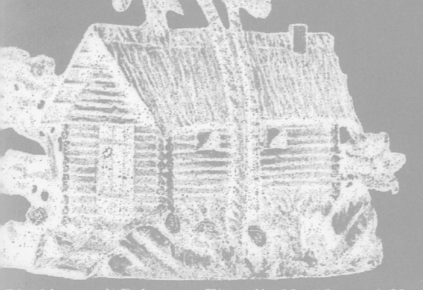
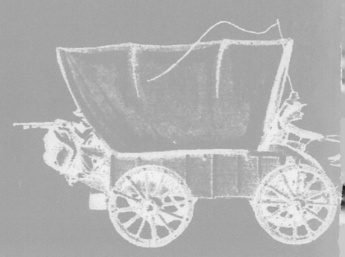

Blockhaus mit Palme aus Elastolin 20×19 cm 1.25

6994/2 Präriewag. m. Plane u. Pferdegesp. i. Galo
6994/4 dasgleiche, jedoch mit Doppelgespan